COUNSELLING IN HEALTH CARE SETTINGS

Counselling in Health Care Settings

A Handbook for Practitioners

Robert Bor, Sheila Gill, Riva Miller
and Amanda Evans

First published 2009 by
PALGRAVE MACMILLAN

Palgrave Macmillan in the UK is an imprint of Macmillan Publishers Limited, registered in England, company number 785998, of Houndmills, Basingstoke, Hampshire RG21 6XS.

Palgrave Macmillan in the US is a division of St Martin's Press LLC, 175 Fifth Avenue, New York, NY 10010.

Palgrave Macmillan is the global academic imprint of the above companies and has companies and representatives throughout the world.

Palgrave® and Macmillan® are registered trademarks in the United States, the United Kingdom, Europe and other countries.

ISBN-13: 978–0–230–54942–5
ISBN-10: 0–230–54942–X

This book is printed on paper suitable for recycling and made from fully managed and sustained forest sources. Logging, pulping and manufacturing processes are expected to conform to the environmental regulations of the country of origin.

A catalogue record for this book is available from the British Library.

A catalog record for this book is available from the Library of Congress.

10   9   8   7   6   5   4   3   2   1
18 17 16 15 14 13 12 11 10 09

Printed and bound in China

This book is dedicated to our patients and their families, as well as to our own families

Contents

Part D: Themes and Issues Relating to Counselling Practice

List of Figures

About the Authors

Professor Robert Bor is Lead Consultant Clinical Psychologist in the Medical Specialities Directorate at the Royal Free Hospital, London. He is a Chartered Clinical, Counselling and Health Psychologist, as well as a Fellow of the British Psychological Society. He is a Chartered Scientist and a UKCP Registered Family Therapist, having completed his specialist training at the Tavistock Clinic, London; and a clinical member of the Institute of Family Therapy, London. He is a member of the American Psychological Association and the American Association for Marital and Family Therapy. He works in hospital, community and primary care settings, with both acute and chronically ill patients and their families. He has a special interest in developing evidence-based and time-limited therapeutic practice in health care and other high-risk settings. He acts as a consultant to medical and nursing colleagues regarding the psychological care of their patients, and teaches communication skills to medical students. He has published widely on the impact of illness on families, and serves on the editorial board of numerous international journals. He is consulting psychologist to several clinics and medical centres in London: the London Clinic and the London Oncology Clinic, both in Harley Street; the Hampstead Group Practice; the Fleet Street Clinic and the Brondesbury Medical Centre. He is also a child and adolescent therapist and is the Consulting Psychologist to St Paul's School, the Royal Ballet School and JFS. He is also in private practice. In addition, he is an aviation clinical psychologist with expertise in passenger and crew behaviour, and provides a specialist consultation and assessment service to leading airlines for aircrew who suffer emotional problems. He is a Churchill Fellow.

Sheila Gill is a UKCP Registered Psychotherapeutic Counsellor, an Accredited Member and Supervisor of CPC, a Senior Accredited Member of BACP and a Registered Independent Counsellor. She has worked in primary care settings and in student counselling for many years. She currently manages the Counselling Service at the Keats Group Practice in North London, and works as a counsellor at the London School of Economics and Political Science (LSE). She has contributed to the training of counsellors and psychologists at City University, London and London Metropolitan University. At LSE, she has contributed to the creation and implementation of in-service training programmes for both managerial and support staff, and helped to devise the successful student mentoring scheme at LSE. Her postgraduate training has included studying cognitive behavioural therapy (CBT) at the Cognitive Behavioural Therapy Unit of the Department of Psychiatry and Behavioural Science at University College London; also, Primary Care Counselling at City University, London, and she studied systemic therapy at Kensington Consultation Centre. Her particular interests and areas of expertise are the implementation and refinement of time-sensitive, evidence-based models of therapy to promote competence and coping in patients in both primary care and student counselling contexts. She is co-author of a number of books on the theory and practice of counselling in health care settings.

Riva Miller has a background in medical social work. She trained as a family therapist at the Tavistock Clinic, at the Institute of Family Therapy and with the Milan Associates in Italy, going on to work in a medical setting with people who were chronically ill. She currently works privately as a Systemic Psychotherapist and as a Family Therapist in the Haemophilia Centre, London. She started and ran the HIV counselling service at the Royal Free Hampstead NHS Trust, London, until 2000. She is Honorary Senior Lecturer in the Royal Free Hospital School of Medicine. Since 1985, she has held a consultancy at the National Blood and Tissue Service, helping colleagues to consider ethical issues, instigate counselling policies and offering staff support. She has acted as an adviser for the World Health Organization, running many workshops on their behalf on HIV infection. Her particular interests and expertise are in integrating systemic approaches to treatment and care in busy medical settings. She is a UKCP Registered Systemic Therapist.

Amanda Evans is a Chartered Psychologist and has worked in a hospital setting for the past twenty years, specializing in working with people affected by HIV infection: patients, partners, families and children. She is based at the Royal Free Hospital, London, and works with patients from widely diverse backgrounds, using a blend of cognitive and systemic techniques. She takes a lead in the training and supervision of counselling staff in a busy HIV testing clinic, and is involved in the supervision of trainee psychologists specializing in this field. She also works in private practice in London. Her contributions to publications have included evidence-based practice issues, and the discussion of topics such as ethical dilemmas in health care settings and psychological interventions in HIV prevention.

Acknowledgements

We dedicate this book to all the patients and their families with whom we have been privileged to work over the years. They have both challenged us professionally and enriched our personal experience.

We are especially grateful to our partners and families for their support in our work with patients, and in the writing of this book.

We are fortunate in having supportive and inspiring colleagues in the many different contexts in which we each have worked: our medical and nursing colleagues at the Royal Free Hospital, the Hampstead Group Practice, the Brondesbury Medical Centre, the London Oncology Clinic, the Keats Group Practice, the London Clinic, the Fleet Street Clinic, Chase Lodge Health Centre and Golders Hill Health Centre, all of whom have been immensely supportive throughout. We are grateful to them for providing such rich contexts in which to develop many of the ideas contained in this book.

A book of this kind is always the product of wider collaboration and our psychologist and therapist colleagues, Susan McDaniel, Heather Salt, Chistine Parrott, Kate Stevenson, Debbie Levitt, Claire Singer, Brett Kahr, Linda Papadopoulos, Peter Scragg, Peter du Plessis, Carina Eriksen, Joan Kingsley, Janet Reibstein, Teresa Schaefer and Martha Latz, have all over the years generously offered their time and wisdom to help us to refine some of the ideas and skills described in this book.

We are very appreciative of our mentors and supervisors, all of whom have nourished and supported us and have inspired us with their unfailing dedication to the alleviation of human distress.

We would also like to thank our many non-medical colleagues, among whom are: Katie Porror, Chris Connelly, Gethin Roberts, Shanna Hyder, Sam Kung, Liz Barnett, Adam Sandelson and team, Jean Jameson and

Jane Sedgwick and all at the LSE who have always worked so positively with us and in the spirit of active collaboration. Our numerous administrative colleagues also deserve our gratitude for supporting all our interactions with patients with quiet and determined dedication. Collaborative practice continues to make possible the work we do with patients.

We are indebted to Dr Noel Gill, Debbie Lissowski, Keith Povey and Brandon Storey for their editorial assistance and advice.

We are grateful to Palgrave Macmillan Publishers for kindly giving permission to reproduce parts of one chapter entitled 'How Have You Managed to Cope so Well?', from Bor *et al.*, *Doing Therapy Briefly* (2004).

Finally, our editor at Palgrave Macmillan, Catherine Gray, has offered unstinting support, guidance and encouragement throughout the project, and we are most grateful to her for helping us bring the project to fruition.

ROBERT BOR
SHEILA GILL
RIVA MILLER
AMANDA EVANS

Notes about Terms and Clinical Cases Used

Language and terminology are important in therapy, as they are a signal of how people relate. We explain briefly here about the words and terms used in this book. Instead of listing counsellors, therapists, psychologists and social workers each time we refer to the primary readership of the book, we have abbreviated these to 'counsellors', and what they do as 'counselling'. At all times, we recognize the diverse range of trained professionals who practise therapeutically – doctors and nurses, as well as psychotherapists – but have chosen to simplify our references to each of them. In addition, we refer to 'patients' rather than 'clients' or 'counsellees', because we work in hospitals and clinical settings. This should not be taken to mean that the person is necessarily physically ill, or that we only work within a medical model of practice or context. However, using this term also enables us to work more collaboratively in any context with our medical colleagues, and this important point is discussed in the book.

In order to strike a gender balance in the book, we have decided to make our counsellors female and our patients male in odd-numbered chapters, starting with Chapter 1 – and conversely male counsellors and female patients in even numbered chapters, starting with Chapter 2, excepting specific case studies.

CLINICAL CASES

Throughout the book, clinical cases have been used to illustrate the theory and practice of counselling. To respect the confidential nature of the patient–counsellor relationship, all names and facts, identifying features and much of what happened during therapy have been altered, and so bear little similarity to actual clinical cases we have encountered. Any perceived similarity is therefore entirely coincidental and in no way intentional.

Part A

Introduction and Clinical Concepts

Introduction

Health care settings are different from the traditional counselling setting. There is a different pace to the work and different views about confidentiality, working practices, length of sessions and duration of counselling. It is essential to be adaptable and creative, to respect the demands and constraints of health care settings, and to utilize the potential inherent in working in health care contexts, especially by drawing on the skills mix of the multi-disciplinary team.

This book has been written mainly for counsellors, therapists, psychologists and those using or needing to use psychotherapeutic skills while working within a health care setting. Trainees at an advanced phase of their professional development may also find that the ideas and skills presented have direct relevance to their clinical practice, and be further stimulated to explore their theoretical knowledge about the application of therapy to different problems and contexts.

Our main focus is on developing an understanding of:

- How physical illness affects individuals, couples and their family relationships.
- How to work positively and effectively in a setting where there are limited resources.
- How to work with two main groups of patients: those suffering from a definable medical illness and those who present within health care settings with emotional distress and common psychological problems such as depression and anxiety.
- How the counsellor can practise effectively and creatively using evidence-based approaches, even in complicated and emotionally intense clinical situations.

■ How the health care context affects the counsellor's role and shapes the therapeutic process.

■ How the dynamics of interprofessional consultation work with an emphasis on working collaboratively with other health care professionals.

Our experience of working in different health care contexts and with people being forced to cope with a myriad of health problems, both physical and psychological, brought to our attention the limitations of training and the lack of practical guidelines for counsellors. This was especially evident when focusing on how counsellors can face the challenge of working within multi-disciplinary teams as much as with patients, families and relatives. We felt it would be helpful to describe our ideas about counselling after many years of clinical practice, close collaboration and carrying out and publishing research. In this book, we have attempted to address the following questions:

■ What does a trained counsellor need to know about practising in a health care setting?

■ How can we describe a framework of practice, congruent with recommended evidence-based models, that is likely to complement the reader's area of clinical practice and preferred approach to therapy, rather than being at variance with it?

Almost all health care professionals provide counselling in the course of their work. Patients increasingly expect health care providers not only to be experts in their chosen field, such as medicine or nursing, but also to have the sensitivity and skills to discuss complex treatment and care issues, as well as to help them to manage associated psychological distress. These health care professionals constantly interact with patients, giving information, clarifying treatment options and helping people to adjust to new and sometimes unwelcome circumstances. Therapists, on the other hand, are expected to have advanced training and qualifications in their field. The special problems that arise in health care settings and when working with people affected by health problems, coupled with time and resource constraints in some clinical situations and the powerful feelings evoked by this work, may challenge even experienced practitioners. This book conveys an approach to counselling, both in hospital settings and in primary care, that has been applied to a wide range of social and clinical problems, taking into account the unique culture and atmosphere that exists in these settings (Bor and McCann, 1999).

In spite of a recent trend towards standardizing mental health care through evidence-based practice and the promotion of national guidelines for treatment (for example, the National Institute for Health and Clinical Excellence (NICE) in the UK), no counselling approach described in published literature teaches one 'what to say when'. The ideas in this book aim to offer a framework for practice, and extend the repertoire of ideas and skills available to counsellors by highlighting some of the unique and specific challenges of working as a counsellor in a health care setting. The book also considers in detail the impact and influence of the health care context on therapeutic engagement.

The challenge for counsellors in modern health care settings is to be an efficient and effective practitioner. Like all practitioners, the authors of this book have all been schooled in discrete models of therapy (for example, systemic, client-centred and so on); no particular model of therapy has been espoused over another in this book. What is privileged are ideas about therapy and ways of working with patients in the health care context that are evidence-based and have proved to be helpful. Systemic theory and cognitive behavioural therapy are the main theoretical frameworks that underpin the skills described. The book aims to describe, scrutinize and make as transparent as possible what happens in the interaction between counsellor and patient that makes it beneficial for patients to have that encounter.

There can sometimes exist an unhelpful preoccupation on the part of counsellors with their specific model of working. No evidence exists, however, supporting the view that any single approach to therapy can at all times be more efficacious than another. Such a preoccupation can serve to divert attention from focusing on and understanding what it is that makes therapy successful. The emphasis in the approach described in this book is on the patients' responses to any therapeutic intervention. These responses are scrutinized and considered in at least equal measure to the therapeutic intervention itself. One of the most useful and simplest ways of knowing if counselling is helping, that it is 'on track' and relevant, is to ask patients directly. Such an apparently simple principle can challenge the 'expert' basis of many models of therapy and help to redress embedded attitudes towards patients as passive recipients of treatment.

The language adopted by the authors of this book is simple, direct and jargon-free. However, simplicity should not be confused with being simplistic. Clinical experience has taught us that using simple and direct language is most helpful when people are in distress. High levels of psychological distress can give rise to confusion, produce anxiety and obstruct normal resourcefulness. People do not necessarily need or want complex psychological processes explained to them when they are upset, disturbed or in pain. Distress is, however, always complex. This book attempts to tease out, explain and make transparent such complexity. The challenge for the counsellor is to be able to engage in a simple way with such complexity.

Therapy is a highly professional activity that is accountable to the patient, the work context and to colleagues. Counselling is not a process of 'doing something to someone', but can better be described as an interactive process. In this way, it differs from the medical model, which is diagnostic and prescriptive of treatment protocols. There are many definitions of counselling and psychotherapy, and it is therefore important to clarify our definition:

> Counselling is an interaction in a therapeutic setting, focusing primarily on a conversation about relationships, beliefs and behaviour (including feelings), through which the patient's perceived problem is elucidated and framed or reframed in a fitting or useful way, so that the problem takes on a new meaning and new solutions are generated for the patient.

We fully acknowledge the huge diversity in the client groups we serve. Indeed, one of the most interesting challenges we all face as therapists is to ensure that therapy is centred on the needs of each unique person with whom we work. A fundamental principle underlying this approach is that one should never assume that a shared cultural background between counsellor and patient means that there is a natural affinity between them that might affect the course, nature and duration of psychological treatment. Patients increasingly come from diverse backgrounds. This is now a topical and pressing issue, as global migration creates new challenges. Both genders are represented. Patients come from across the age and developmental spectrum, reflect a myriad of national, racial, religious or cultural groups and may be challenged by certain visible or hidden disabilities. They also self-identify with different sexualities. Such is the diversity of the patients with whom counsellors work that it is unhelpful to approach specific cases with greater 'cultural sensitivity'; rather, counsellors should regard *every* clinical encounter as being culturally different. After all, personal differences are not merely an issue of race, social class or gender, however important these may be. They are reflective of different core ideas and personal beliefs about coping, and the only way to learn about these is through a client-centred approach that actively seeks to elicit patients' stories and to understand as far as possible the unique circumstances of each person. The ideas and cases presented in this book illustrate, in a small way, the diversity that counsellors encounter in their work.

The process of counselling can help people to cope with and adjust to new and unwelcome circumstances. People bring complex and varied feelings to health care settings, some of which may be triggered as a result of the patient's encounter with a health professional and the information that is shared in this encounter. These feelings may also be projected onto staff, including counsellors, as well as on to the patient's own support system. Counselling can also help family members to adapt to the changes brought about by a physical or psychological illness, or the illness of a loved one, whether it is an acute episode or a chronic condition, a life-long (inherited) or a life-threatening disease. The notion of 'needing counselling', however, can sometimes inadvertently undermine an individual's ability to cope and adapt, because of the associations between mental health and illness. For example, it is easier for most people to consult their doctor for a physical ailment, such as a sore shoulder, than for a low mood. Some unique and specific issues arise in health care settings that have an effect on how counsellors work and how they approach their work. These include:

- How does a counsellor work with patients in the health care context who are affected by illness?
- How can counsellors in the health care setting help patients who present with emotional distress to cope with their difficulties?
- Where does a counsellor fit into a multi-disciplinary health care team?
- How can counsellors contribute to helping patients cope and live with enduring, or even terminal, medical conditions?
- Does a counsellor need to have detailed knowledge of a medical condition in order to counsel someone about it?
- Should counsellors give information to patients about medical conditions and treatment; and, if so, under what conditions?

■ How do confidentiality rules apply in health care settings?
■ How can counsellors work in a setting where privacy may be lacking and where time constraints exist?
■ How does a counsellor work with a person who has been referred for counselling but does not want it?
■ How do counsellors work with family members?
■ How should a counsellor approach a patient who has just been given bad news by a doctor?

This book aims to address some of these questions, by providing the reader with sufficient theory and skills to give effective counsel to patients and families affected by illness in a range of health care settings.

Irrespective of the health setting in which patients are counselled, the issues and approaches are broadly similar and these are described in this book. However, it is important to note that no two counselling services are the same. Each has its own micro-culture and for this reason the nature of the service, methods used and outcomes may differ. While the medical approach of diagnosis and treatment differs in many ways from modern psychotherapeutic models of care that emphasize client autonomy and expertise, a natural fit can still exist between counselling and health problems. The relationship between psychotherapy and medicine has not, however, been without tensions and complications. The mind–body debate and the entry of non-medically-trained counsellors and psychotherapists into the medical arena have presented a series of challenges, some of which continue to be debated by practitioners. Recently, there has been tremendous growth in the amount of published professional literature examining the role of psychological processes in the prevention, onset and treatment of physical illness.

Collaboration with medical colleagues will become increasingly important, as indicated by the growth in the number of psychotherapists and counsellors working in clinics, hospitals, wards, primary health care, nursing and medical schools, specialist health charities, patient support organizations and even in health care management. This is an era of increasing specialization in health care. Guidelines are needed, however, for focused and contextually appropriate counselling that can be used across specialities and be effective in new situations with a range of problems. Increasing complexity in health care (standardized guidelines for clinical practice, a requirement for measuring outcomes, new technology, medico-legal concerns, changing resources and so on) and the promotion of patient choice, necessitate effective communication between health care providers and patients and their relatives.

Patients may live longer with chronic illness these days and this in turn may have an impact not only on the relationship between the patient and his family, but also between the patient and health care providers. All health care providers are expected to be effective communicators, able to counsel their patients about their problems, investigations and treatment, and to consider how illness can be reduced or prevented. Furthermore, in an era in which medico-legal issues are becoming prominent in health care, with litigation a more common outcome, counselling and psychotherapeutic skills, especially skills that promote the participation of patients, could be central in reducing the risk of adverse outcomes and, if possible, avoiding litigation. While counselling and communication skills have always been central to the provision of medical care, it is clear that they are now assuming a new level of importance (Lloyd and Bor, 2009). Counsellors and psychotherapists, whose specialist understanding of the complex dynamics associated with communication and relationship problems is well recognized, are now sought increasingly to work in health care settings with medically ill patients and their families.

Progress in counselling in health care settings can be jeopardized by (a) a lack of skill or an insufficient understanding of psychotherapeutic theory and practice; (b) persistence with an idea or intervention in spite of feedback from patients (and/or their social network or family) that it is not helping; or (c) inattentiveness to the difficulties or tensions inherent in the counsellor's role in relation to doctors, nurses, health service managers and other professionals. These topics are considered in more detail in some of the following chapters.

Traditionally, counselling and psychotherapy can imply weekly or more frequent sessions with a trained counsellor over many years. While this may be necessary or helpful for some patients, there is also a place and increasing demand for focused, problem-solving counselling in health care settings. Indeed, effective counselling can at times be conducted in a single session or through consultations with other professionals caring for the patient, which may obviate the need for a face-to-face contact between the patient and the counsellor. Furthermore, the traditional fifty-minute counselling session may not always be appropriate. The number of sessions may also be fewer than with a conventional open-ended contract (Bor *et al.*, 2004). Creativity with regard to the use of time and the location and timing of sessions is a topic considered in several chapters of this book.

Physical and mental illness are both, on one level, a private and individual matter, but on another level they have implications for both family and social relationships. In spite of many significant advances in the diagnosis and treatment of medical conditions, a degree of ill health inevitably affects most people in their lifetime; and some may have to endure lifelong and chronic ill health. Illness not only evokes fears and anxieties – be they about pain, suffering, loss of functioning, or death – but it also has a direct effect on relationships. Partners may become carers; children may be called on to provide care and support; and hospitalization may lead to periods of separation from the family and dependence on professional carers. The emotional ripple effect of illness does not only run through the patient's family system, but it may also affect professional care-givers. For this reason, it can be difficult at times for counsellors to distance themselves from all aspects of their clinical work. After all, everyone has at some point in their life been touched by illness or have been affected by the illness of someone close to them. For this reason, one cannot emphasize too strongly the importance of adequate supervision and training for this specialist work. It is vital that counsellors do not let their own personal issues impede their professional work, and there may be times when the counsellor needs to seek help to deal with the emotional toll of their work – for example, through their own therapy, supervision, training or even a period of absence from work if this is necessary. The importance of staff support is given more detailed consideration in the last chapter of the book.

Chapters 1 to 4 (Part A) in this introductory section describe the theoretical ideas underpinning the skills outlined in the rest of the book, and how the unique context of the health care setting impacts the therapeutic process. Chapters 5 to 7 (comprising Part B) are more practical in their orientation and illustrate the essential skills necessary for structuring and conducting counselling sessions in health care settings. In Chapters 8 to 11 (Part C), we focus on the application of more specialist psychotherapeutic skills as applied to health care settings and for dealing with health problems. The final part of the book, Chapters 12 to 18 (Part D), covers a range of themes, including managing confidentiality issues; giving information and bad news to patients; counselling for loss, terminal care and bereavement; and counselling those with health anxieties. We also examine some concerns that may challenge all counsellors, such as how to deal with an impasse in the therapeutic relationship, as well as counsellor stress and burnout.

We stress that, in counselling, one can never convey an approach that teaches 'what to say when' to patients. By definition, effective counselling is interactive, pragmatic and, above all, empathic towards patients' needs. As authors, we have set out to describe a 'map' of practice that we hope will be relevant to the reader's particular context and be an aid to improving both confidence and competence.

Chapter 1

Theoretical Concepts

INTRODUCTION

Specific beliefs underpin each approach to counselling practice. These beliefs come from one's training, clinical experience and ongoing professional development. The core beliefs that underpin the approach described in this book can be summarized as follows:

1   The starting point in counselling is with the patient's experience and story.
2   Health-related problems have implications for relationships and attachments between the patient, family members and health care providers. We focus as much on the patient's external world as on his internal world.
3   The counsellor's task is to help patients to identify what meaning this particular illness has for them and to discuss the consequences of this. One must avoid situations in which patients may feel pushed to see things in the way counsellors see them, or where counsellors inadvertently disqualify their ideas or feelings. To this end, the counsellor assumes nothing about the patient, his experience and how he should cope.
4   Patients are encouraged to collaborate in the process of counselling. This is a major departure from the traditional hierarchical configuration in counselling, in which the counsellor is seen to have the expertise, power and control. The counsellor elicits the patient's active participation in the session and in his own well-being. The patient is

regarded as an expert on his situation and the patient's own resources should be elicited in managing the problem.

5   The 'family' is the patient's most important social system. Modern definitions of family incorporate not only blood relatives but also close social relationships. Counselling addresses the patient's experience of illness as well as the impact this has on family relationships.

6   Problems can arise at different points in the course of illness, or preexisting psychological problems may be exacerbated by current distress associated with either physical or mental illness. It is imperative to use all the skills available to the counsellor, from the full range of available psychological interventions, to address and solve problems, and to help alleviate the patient's suffering.

7   It is important to be mindful of both the social context of the patient and the context in which counselling is provided. Context gives meaning to the psychological problem and, to a large extent, determines the range of possible solutions to it.

8   Health care settings operate according to a different set of rules and demands compared with 'normal' counselling, and these rules have a direct influence on counselling practice. These affect which models of practice are acceptable, expectations surrounding confidentiality, length of sessions, where the counselling takes place and how professional colleagues relate in the multi-disciplinary team.

9   There are many approaches and skills within counselling that can be used to equal effect. Whichever approach is used, a 'map' helps to conceptualize problems and their possible resolution. Counsellors should strive to practise in an accountable and time-sensitive manner.

Some conceptual ideas about practising as a counsellor in a health care setting are described in this chapter. An ability to approach each new case and problem with a receptive openness and to recognize that each patient may require a different therapeutic approach, is an ever-present challenge. This attitude needs to be balanced by a level of competence in tried and tested counselling approaches and interventions.

WHAT CONSTITUTES THE THERAPEUTIC SYSTEM?

An important distinction needs to be made between professional work with a patient (counselling) and work with other professionals who are caring for that patient (consultation and collaboration). Counselling in a health care setting should always involve both. This is a basic tenet of a bio-psychosocial perspective (Engel, 1977; McDaniel *et al.*, 1992) that stresses the interaction and interrelatedness between disease, the affected individual, the patient's family, health care providers and other systems. A minimum of three systems are usually

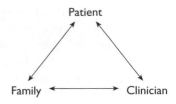

Figure 1.1 Minimum fundamental unit of health

involved in dealing with a medical problem: patient, family and clinician (see Figure 1.1). Of course, some patients may not have families, or they may be separated from them. None the less, it is still important to address family and social support, as it is through 'family' that we all come to acquire and develop ideas about coping with illness and about psychological resilience, which may need to be explored in the course of counselling. Doherty and Baird (1983) referred to this triangle as the minimal fundamental unit of health.

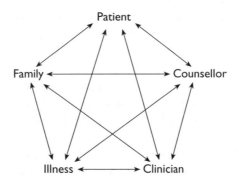

Figure 1.2 Pentagon depicting transactions that include a counsellor in the system

The participation of a counsellor and the inclusion of the illness as a part of the interactional system results in a more comprehensive depiction of transactions, as illustrated in Figure 1.2.

As the counsellor has to attend to issues involving himself, the patient, family, clinician and illness, within a given yet ever-evolving context, it is more accurate to illustrate the complex interactions within the counselling context as shown in Figure 1.3:

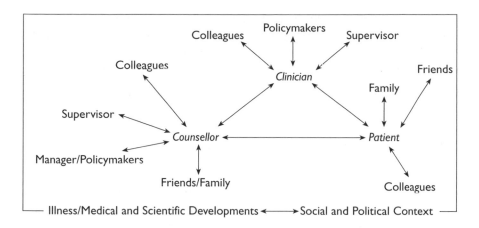

Figure 1.3   The system within which the counsellor works

Using this framework helps to avoid the notion that a human problem is discrete, either physical or psychosocial. Instead, all problems are viewed as having bio-psychosocial consequences (integrating biological, psychological and social features). Psychosocial problems have physical components or features, and physical problems have psychosocial ramifications. Interprofessional liaison is needed to ensure that problems (and solutions) are managed collaboratively. Providers of care, including counsellors, are viewed as part of, rather than being apart from, the treatment system. This challenges directly the view that counsellors can remain neutral observers of their patients, detached from the psychological process. When working with people coping with health problems, counsellors may be confronted with complex interactions between different elements of the system, such as family members or hands-on carers (for example, nurses) that develop into an intense emotional climate, especially in the face of pending or actual loss. This framework also helps to highlight the many different people who might be affected, directly or indirectly, by the patient's illness and who may therefore need to be considered in counselling sessions, as their actions or beliefs may influence how the patient (and his family) copes.

The application of a bio-psychosocial approach to counselling has been illustrated extensively by McDaniel et al. (1992). There is a need for the counsellor to work collaboratively and without undue emphasis on either biological or psychological processes (to the detriment of the other).

Social, medical and psychological events and processes are viewed as being interconnected, and all require the ongoing attention of the counsellor. There is sometimes a tendency to over-emphasize psychological and social processes, whereas biomedical events may be equally relevant and give rise themselves to psychological problems.

CONSIDERATIONS FOR COUNSELLORS WORKING IN HEALTH CARE SETTINGS

We have identified nine main considerations for the counsellor that reflect the unique and specific features of therapeutic work with patients in health care contexts. These are derived from different theories of counselling and psychotherapy as well as from clinical experience. The considerations are as follows:

Context

It is important to understand the effect of the context in which problems are identified or treated. The setting or context may be an in-patient or out-patient clinic, a GP's surgery, a ward or a private practice setting. Each will influence or constrain the amount of time available for the patient, the degree of privacy during counselling sessions, and sometimes also the psychotherapeutic approach used. The context determines how problems are viewed, what can be done about them and who should be involved in the treatment and care (Selvini Palazzoli *et al.*, 1980a). For example, patients in primary care settings may only have access to time-limited counselling in a GP's surgery, whereas more extended counselling may be offered in more specialist settings, such as in certain cancer treatment centres.

Beliefs

Beliefs about health, illness and traumatic life events are central to an understanding of how people are affected by such occurrences, and are core to counselling practice in health care settings. We have devoted a whole chapter to this topic (see Chapter 2).

Attachment

The connection between attachment anxieties later in life and secure or inse-cure attachments to parents in infancy and childhood (Bowlby, 1975) helps us to understand how people relate to one another. The advent of either physical or mental illness can intensify, challenge or alter these patterns of attachment. Not only does ill health have the potential to threaten existing attachments (especially where there is the possibility of death), but ill health can also give rise to new attachments, such as in the patient–health care provider relationship. Exploring with the patient such changes in patterns of attachment is central to the work of counsellors in health care settings. Actual or anticipatory loss can threaten bonds between people, sometimes triggering intense feelings of anxiety or depression. Some people may with-draw from key relationships where attachments are threatened through illness or a fear of loss through death, giving rise to intense psychological distress in family members. These feelings and patterns in relationships may be replicated in or transferred to the patient's relationships with health care providers, including doctors, nurses and counsellors. Attachment problems may also arise when nursing shifts change in a hospital, or where the patient's care is transferred to another doctor. Disrupted or changing patterns of attachment are core concepts and a primary point of focus for the counsellor working in health care settings. John Byng-Hall (1995) has provided a clinically useful model for understanding attachment in human relationships, especially in the context of changing family relationships.

Typology of ill health

An understanding of the main characteristics of an illness is important in order to determine how a person may be affected. Rolland (1994a) distin-guished between four dimensions: onset, course, outcome and degree of incapacitation. It is not always necessary to have an extensive under-standing of a particular physical illness in order to offer counselling to an affected person, but it is important to appreciate the time phase (especially if it is a chronic illness) and practical consequences of the condition. Experienced counsellors are likely to at least have a good understanding of the possible causes and maintaining factors of mental health problems. This knowledge can help to determine the possible ramifications for the patient's relationships.

Development and life cycle

Illness does not have the same effects on everyone and there are many different factors that influence if, whether and how people cope and adjust. Developmental and life-cycle issues determine how an individual, couple or family are affected by ill health, either physical or psychological. For an individual, this will depend on whether the person is a newly-born infant, a child, an adolescent, an adult and so on. Couples and families also progress through a series of developmental phases and each may imply or lead to changes in relationships between people. A newly-wed couple, reconstituted family, or couple facing the 'empty nest' may each be affected differently in response to illness, or adverse or traumatic events in the family. The loss by a family of an elderly relative who had been suffering from poor health for several years might have a different impact from the loss of a young child from leukaemia, for example. Furthermore, some young people have been found to exhibit poor control of diabetes during their adolescence as a way of not letting an illness control them, or even as a rebellious act against parents and others 'in authority', such as doctors and nurses. Carter and McGoldrick (1981) and Edwards and Davis (1998) have written extensively about the psychological impact of health problems at different stages of individual, couple and family development.

Curiosity and questions

Counselling proceeds in many different ways. Reflection and interpretation are probably associated most commonly with the process of counselling. However, the clinical interview, using carefully thought out questions, provides an important source of information for the counsellor (Tomm, 1987a, 1987b). In addition to reflection, questions are a main catalyst for patient change and healing. Different types of questions can be used to link comments on behaviour, beliefs, feelings and ideas about the future. As we shall see later, questions embody the counsellor's sense of curiosity (Cecchin, 1987), helping to avoid the counsellor becoming judgemental of, or having a fixed view of, the patient and the problem. Circular, reflexive and hypothetical or future-orientated questions provide the patient and his family with the opportunity to view themselves in the context of relationships and to recognize different perspectives of the problem. Socratic questioning, as applied in cognitive behavioural therapy, can help to reveal and challenge underlying assumptions and in the construction of new possibilities in therapy (Padesky, 1994; Mooney and Padesky, 2000).

Language, narratives and meanings

An effective health care experience should provide patients and their families with the assurance that their concerns and experiences are legitimate. Counselling draws on the language and stories of the patient and his family, helping to reveal meanings in problems, and how problems come to be viewed as such. Patient stories or narratives are elicited when working with the full range of somatic and psychological symptoms (Anderson and Goolishian, 1988). Their use avoids stigmatizing or blaming the patient, as they are entirely patient-centred. Language, of course, helps to resolve or alleviate problems associated with health-related issues, as much as it can itself also give rise to problems (Griffith and Griffith, 1994). Different groups of professionals, for example, are taught to think about psychological problems in different and seemingly incompatible ways. Ailments of the mind and body are often conceptualized differently by counsellors, psychotherapists and family therapists from the way that they are by doctors, nurses and other health care providers. Some counsellors may not think to explore 'medical' meanings associated with psychological problems, assuming that their medical colleagues have already done so. The problem becomes more complex when treating patients whose symptoms appear to lie at the intersection of the psychological and physical, such as those suffering from 'psychosomatic' disorders, including non-electrical seizures or persistent headaches.

Cognition and behaviour

The direct (and circular) relationship between cognition (thought) and behaviour (action) is central to an understanding of how problems are experienced, maintained and can be resolved. Many psychological problems or symptoms associated with health-related problems can be treated effectively with cognitive behavioural therapy (Roth and Fonagy, 2004). Cognitive behavioural therapy is especially useful when treating patients suffering from anxiety, depression, insomnia and other problems typically seen in both mental health care settings and primary care, as well as for pain management and chronic fatigue syndrome. As we shall see in Chapter 11, identifying early experiences, dysfunctional assumptions, negative automatic thoughts and other factors that may maintain the problem are first steps towards its resolution. Thinking errors or cognitive distortions are often implicated in mood-related problems. For patients referred for counselling because of a fear of physical pain or separation from the family, behavioural methods (such as desensitization) can be used to ameliorate some symptoms (Leahy, 2003).

Time and timing

Physical or terminal illness brings into sharp focus issues about time and longevity. The prospect of a shortened life-span, or one in which quality of life is drastically curtailed, is often a source of psychological distress. Long-term counselling approaches may not be feasible in a context in which there is high demand for psychological care, where there are constraints on the provision of services or where patients cannot regularly attend counselling sessions because of their illness. Counsellors may be required to be flexible and improvise in order to remain responsive to the patient's needs. Decisions have to be made about which problems can be treated and the duration of counselling. Modern, focused counselling approaches have developed in the health care context that have proved successful in addressing common psychological problems.

The need to focus more on issues of timing in counselling is becoming increasingly necessary in the health care context. Some patients may not require a lengthy lead-in to counselling; they may be willing and able to work at a deep level from the outset. Others – whether because of their views about counselling, or the problem itself, or how they view themselves as coping – may never benefit from the range of psychotherapeutic interventions that are available. The challenge in these settings is for the counsellor to work more quickly and intensively. It is important to keep in mind how others view progress and outcome in counselling, as this will influence whether the patient continues in treatment and whether the counsellor continues to receive referrals from the medical team. Some constraints may also exist in relation to the physical setting, such as a lack of privacy or nowhere to sit comfortably with the patient while he receives medical treatment (for example, medication via a drip), and these may affect when sessions can be arranged and how long they last.

LEVELS OF COUNSELLING

Different levels of counselling illustrate the range of activities carried out by counsellors, and the 'mode' the counsellor may be engaged in at a particular time. Each level suggests a different relationship with the patient. The different levels of counselling should be viewed as a continuum rather than as discrete and unrelated activities:

- *Information-giving*: the provision of factual information and advice about medical conditions, laboratory tests, treatments, drug trials, disease prevention and health promotion, among others. This may also include the use of self-help materials such as books and computer-based aids, which are used increasingly in counselling for the treatment of common psychological problems such as depression and anxiety. Contrary to some beliefs about counselling, it is sometimes necessary for the counsellor to give information about treatment and care. This is usually in highly specialized fields where dedicated counsellors are part of a multi-disciplinary team such as oncology, endocrinology, HIV, infertility, organ transplant specialties, neurology, haemophilia and paediatrics.
- *Implications counselling*: a discussion with the patient and/or others that addresses the implications of the information for the individual or the family, and the patient's personal circumstances.
- *Supportive counselling*: in which the emotional consequences of the information and its implications can be identified and addressed in a supportive and caring environment.
- *Psychotherapeutic counselling*: focuses on healing, psychological adjustment, coping and problem resolution.

The titles of 'counsellor' and 'psychotherapist' are largely interchangeable. Professional training, the preferences of other colleagues and the tasks undertaken may influence which professional title or 'hat' is chosen. It is a reasonable assumption that, in health care settings, all counselling work involves psychotherapy, and vice versa. However, those trained only to undertake information-giving and implications counselling must undergo further training and supervision before treating patients by the use of psychotherapeutic approaches and techniques. Untrained and unsupervised counsellors may be ineffective or even damaging to the patient.

STAGES OF COUNSELLING IN HEALTH CARE SETTINGS

Most counsellors feel comfortable about exploring issues and concerns with patients without too much reliance on a structure or agenda. There is a wide variation in the way that sessions are conducted and managed, usually in response to the needs and concerns of the patient; for example, where the patient is seen, the context in which the counsellor works and the counsellor's professional training. In health care settings where patients are physically unwell, counsellors must be able to respond to and cope with what can be a high level of unpredictability and emotional intensity. Ideally, a range of issues needs to be covered with patients in the initial session, in a reasonably logical manner, progressing from one issue to the next.

The special circumstances and features of counselling in health care contexts may mean that, in some cases, an initial consultation is the only direct patient contact. Consequently, the counsellor needs to be adept at forming a therapeutic relationship, making an assessment and intervening all in the same session. Unlike the case in some other settings, patients may not benefit from follow-up, because they may not want or need further sessions. They may opt to be treated elsewhere and receive psychological support in another setting; they may recover and be discharged; or they may become more unwell and even die. Flexibility is required to ensure that the patient's needs are highlighted and met. This is also achieved by promoting multi-disciplinary practice, as described below.

PRACTICAL HINTS FOR IMPROVING MULTI-DISCIPLINARY PRACTICE

All counsellors have to be mindful of the dynamics that exist within any health care setting. For example, not every professional in a given health care setting, such as a GP's surgery or ward in a hospital, may share a similar level of enthusiasm for having a counsellor as a part of the team. This may stem from a belief that some of the counselling is already being provided in their role of nurse or doctor, and they may feel displaced by the counsellor's presence. It is helpful always to work collaboratively and positively with other professionals in health care settings, both to be valued as a team member and to be effective in one's work with patients. Some ideas that have helped to achieve this in many different health care settings are listed below.

■ *Be humble*, but communicate directly. Learn from others and be tentative if you are unsure. Do not overstate the importance of counselling – patients rarely live or die by what happens in counselling, and medical and nursing interventions may take precedence regarding the treatment of physical illness. Refer patients to other colleagues where appropriate, but be prepared to offer suggestions if you think these would be helpful.

■ *Learn about health care issues* by attending case meetings and lectures, sitting in with doctors when they meet patients, learning the language of the health care staff and acquiring and developing an interest in anthropology and sociology so as to learn more about the health care setting.

■ *Be curious*: adopt a stance of receptive openness and ask questions. Avoid making assumptions and becoming prescriptive.

■ *Be flexible* about where you see patients, when you see them, your working hours and approaches used in counselling for which there may be a special demand in a health care setting (cognitive behavioural therapy in particular). Work at the patient's pace and determine whether the problem is best solved by open-ended, exploratory counselling, or by problem-focused counselling.

■ *Be time conscious*: aim to achieve the best result within the time constraints. Learn how to counsel in a time-conscious way (Bor *et al.*, 2004). When feeding back to other colleagues, either verbally or in a letter, be brief and keep to the point; avoid wordy and lengthy reports and unfocused discussions about patients.

■ *Be proactive* in eliciting problems so that they can be identified and addressed as early as possible and the patient becomes an active agent in creating desired changes in his life.

■ *Where appropriate, give information*: counselling should always be a dialogue more than a monologue. Do not be afraid to give information or to suggest to whom the patient may talk if he requires more specialist information (however, doctors and nurses must be consulted if the information required is about medical concerns).

■ *Practise defensively*: patients are increasingly conscious of their rights and what they can expect from health care professionals and during the course of their treatment. In some cases this can lead to litigation or a complaint to hospital/clinic managers or the counsellor's professional body. The likelihood of this happening is reduced if counsellors (a) work to ensure that patients are actively engaged in the therapeutic process, so that responsibility for problem resolution is shared; (b) refrain from making unrealistic claims; (c) collaborate with doctors or nurses when in doubt about how to deal with the medical aspects of a problem; (d) keep factual notes of what happens in sessions, but limit opinions to what has been deduced from observations of behaviour (that is, have evidence); and (e) be curious and only offer ideas and opinions tentatively. Be accountable to your profession, colleagues and managers of the institution or setting in which you practise, by giving feedback about your work and related problems without breaching patient confidentiality.

■ *Be practical*: as counsellors we are sometimes long-winded and over-cerebral in response to patients' problems. Learn to make rapid decisions, take small risks and think imaginatively, but practically, about possible solutions.

■ *Evaluate your practice*: it is good practice to audit and evaluate your work. This can also help in the maintenance and development of your counselling service. Decisions about health care delivery are made increasingly on evidence-based practice. Evaluation and audit of counselling practice should be part of everyday practice for counsellors, as much as it is for others in the health care team.

■ *Dress according to the context*: unlike doctors and nurses, counsellors do not have a uniform or any props (stethoscopes or white coats) to identify them. Even so, most hospitals and clinics are rather conservative establishments and expect dress to be conservative and formal. Expectations may be different for counsellors working in community and outreach settings.

■ *Teach and consult with others*: the accusation that some counsellors do not help other health care professionals to understand more about the psychological process and counselling is not without foundation. Offer to give seminars, invite colleagues to case discussions, collaborate in research and offer to see patients jointly with another professional colleague. Foster a climate of openness about your work; this may help others to understand better what you do with patients, and may lead them to be more supportive of your service.

Even the best-trained and most highly experienced counsellors will either have limited success or fail completely in their practice if they assume that the practice of counselling in health care settings is the same as in other settings, such as in private practice. Counsellors will find that other professionals in health care settings already counsel in the course of their work and consequently there may not be a clear boundary between those who counsel and those with counselling skills. Counsellors may also experience indifference or hostility from their colleagues if they 'hide' behind a veil of secrecy about their work, derived from extreme ideas about how confidentiality operates in these settings. This will merely set them apart from their colleagues, which is unlikely to further their practice.

CONCLUSION

Counselling in health care settings takes into account not only the patient and how he copes with illness but also the family and interactions with other health care professionals. Counsellors can help to reduce stress by providing patients, their families and professionals with a treatment model that uses many perspectives. Counsellors can re-frame stress or tension as being positive by pointing out, for example, that in health care relationships it is common for patients, and sometimes doctors and nurses, to experience stress, and that some tension is useful because it increases both personal and professional vigilance. Attentive counsellors can interrupt emotionally damaging cycles of reactions between patients, families and health care professionals at the beginning of health care. However, counselling is often offered in health care treatments only as a last resort after the traditional methods for treating patients' emotional cycles have been exhausted. Medication, expensive investigations, surgery, rehabilitation, diet, behaviour modification and so on are commonly prescribed first. Counselling, as relief for emotional stress and tension, is hardly ever offered, which is unfortunate, because any illness affects not only patients and their family members but also the health care professionals involved.

An individual's understanding of what is meant by illness, health care experiences and health is situated within family, cultural, societal and universal meaning systems. These are held publicly and privately by patients, families, social groups and health care professionals. Meaning systems impact on each other through values and beliefs about illness, diagnosis, symptom recognition, treatment and the recovery process.

Health care relationships are unique because they are formed at a specific time, for a specific purpose and require degrees of intensity and involvement from all the participants (for example, the patients, their families, social agencies and health care professionals). The following two chapters examine the importance of adapting psychotherapeutic practice to the health care setting and the central place that beliefs and meaning systems have to counselling in health care settings.

Chapter 2

Beliefs about Ill Health and Counselling

INTRODUCTION

Human systems such as families, health care teams and cultural groups may hold common values; for example, specific beliefs about appropriate and inappropriate behaviour by individuals and family members. The term 'meaning system' can be understood as a collection of verbal and non-verbal communications that explain, give meaning to and provide an understanding of personal, family and social experiences. The specific meaning system explored in this chapter is the illness meaning system and its impact on patients, family members and health care professionals in relation to medical experiences. The chapter provides a brief overview of the meanings around ill health and their relevance to counselling.

THEORETICAL BACKGROUND

Each convention for making sense of illness encompasses a specific social or cultural group sense of illness. This can involve rituals, special foods, or religious beliefs held by other members of a patient's group. The beliefs of patients about their bodies can connect them to, or disconnect them from, medical experiences in many ways. The perceived relationship between body and mind varies from culture to culture. Western culture, for example, often views patients' bodies as being separate from their thoughts or emotions; while non-Western societies often view patients' bodies as being linked with, and connected to, other members within their cultural group.

Subtle forms of idiosyncratic illness communication are present in all families and may emerge in interactions with health care professionals when patients present with illness. These communications may become so pronounced that they interfere with information-gathering in a health care setting. When this occurs, the direct attention of a counsellor can be helpful to avoid potentially detrimental or emotionally damaging effects for patients and their family members. The following is an illustration of how a family's and health care professional's local, universal and idiosyncratic illness communications affected a health care situation.

> An infant was rushed to hospital by her mother and grandmother. The little girl's father followed in another car. The health care team had difficulty in gathering information essential for treating the infant because the mother and grandmother were exchanging heated words over who should provide the answers. Both women were trying to answer the nurse's questions.
>
> The Asian nurse was aware that the younger woman was the baby's mother, but her cultural and social background inclined her to ignore the mother in favour of the grandmother. The mother, father and grandmother stayed with the baby and they continued to fight among themselves. The doctor noted that the baby showed additional signs of distress each time the mother's voice was raised in response to the grandmother's claim that it was because of the father's questionable heritage that her granddaughter was prone to ill health.

In this situation, each participant had his or her own ideas about illness as well as appropriate behaviour and all were unaware of how each other's system had a subtle impact on the health care situation. In other words, the parents, grandmother, nurse and doctor each made their own interpretation of what was happening during the medical emergency.

The parents and grandmother came to the hospital already deeply involved in a pattern of beliefs and communications about their medical history, current health concerns, and past and present coping skills. The health care professionals were unaware of how this family interacted on a daily basis with each other, or how their world-views affected what they did. The health care professionals were also unaware of how their own meaning systems, as well as cultural, societal and professional values, could affect this family in a less than helpful manner.

However, this family and the health care professionals shared enough universally held meanings and verbal and non-verbal communications to impart information about illness as well as behaviour. The new relationship and communications were a blending, first, of the patient–family–nurse; and second, of the patient–family–nurse–physician. Note that:

- Each member's level of skill in making verbal or non-verbal communications clearly influenced the behaviour of other participants and the degree of support received and created unnecessary distance by conveying emotions such as anger.
- Each member was affected by the other participants' meaning systems in this health care situation.
- A more self-reflective and referential meaning system might have been useful for this young couple and their daughter, to help them to cope with their medical experience.

A counsellor, by being self-reflective and referential, can join a relationship with patients and their families through their meaning system and world-view. This is where an understanding perspective begins. The well-informed and astute counsellor can offer other health care professionals different interpretations and alternative considerations about patients, their families' interactions and illness meaning systems, to reduce emotional stress for all involved.

Trained counsellors who are able to intervene with such families can alert colleagues, such as doctors and nurses, to the different illness meaning systems that influence patient and family communications about illness, and can promote awareness that no one way of communicating is better than another. Acknowledging differences makes it easier to separate patients' psychological reactions to biomedical symptoms from psychopathological displays that warrant intervention in themselves. This can bring about a great improvement to the health care experiences shared by patients, their families and medical professionals.

STIGMA AND DISCRIMINATION

Some diseases may carry a moral illness stigma arising from specific cultural or moral values. This may foster a lower biomedical priority for certain illnesses, particularly when there is a belief that the disease is 'self-inflicted' – such as lung cancer from cigarette smoking, coronary heart disease from diet or lifestyle, and HIV disease from unprotected inter-course or the sharing of contaminated intravenous needles by drug users. Some psychological problems, such as anxiety or depression, may at times elicit censure of the individual. When illnesses are imputed to be self-inflicted, confined to a specific gender, or have a stigma attached, the stresses of the health care experience may increase.

Counsellors and health care professionals can form different relation-ships with patients and their families by exploring and helping to develop unique illness meaning systems that include all participants in health care settings. These newly formed health care relationship illness meaning systems can be a blending of each participant's individual meaning system. This blended meaning system can help the patient, family and health professionals to clarify perceptions about one another's reactions to the health problems involved. Often, these unrecognized perceptions result in additional stress for the health care professional, which in turn raises the level of emotional stress for patients and their families. This in turn affects subsequent patients who are diagnosed, treated and living with illnesses that carry stigmas, which in turn increases *their* stress level and pain.

The following example of a patient and a health care team working with a counsellor shows how meaning systems can be coordinated to provide satisfactory health care for patients. In this case, the patient sought coun-selling as she felt very angry with her doctor for not discussing the impli-cations of her treatment with her. This left her feeling out of control, and this seemed an important area to explore with this distressed patient.

Patient: *I had no idea this was going to happen to me. This was a big shock and that's why – I was . . . I feel so angry. I didn't even have a chance to do anything to investigate it or to prepare myself or to say no, I want this doctor, I want that doctor. I went in for tests and woke up with tubes and stuff . . . wh-where was I? That's my anger. Everyone made choices for me.*

Counsellor: *So you think that if you had been able to talk right after the surgery, that it would have been different for you?*

Patient: *It would've – yes, because every time I wanted to say some-thing about it [referring to her surgery], I would get shut up. You've got to be glad you're alive. Look at it, you could*

Patient: *have been dead, you could've been in a box, you could've been this – I know I could have been all these things, but that doesn't mean that I don't have feelings, as to the way it* [her surgery] *occurred and I recovered.*

Counsellor: Umm hmm.

Patient: *That's why I'm upset. You know what I'm saying? I'm not saying that the end result was not beneficial to me. Of course it is. I'd have to be a moron to say that it was not beneficial as far as I'm concerned. Okay, that I understand. . . . I have to say things . . . that gotta come out. And if they don't come out, they choke me. And pills aren't the answer. I'll come away from you with hope back here* [she points to her heart]. *And then the rest is up to me. I had to make the time, I had to make the effort, it's my job – it's my life and my body and my mind. You can't be with me seven days a week and certainly not for ever. But this is a temporary thing, I think, just to get me on my feet, which I appreciate. Don't get me wrong. But I have to still do the work.*

Counsellor: *Mm hmm. I must say you have really been doing the work by going through it and sharing your experience.*

Patient: *I try very hard.* [cries]

Counsellor: *You've been going through it.*

This patient needed to process the meaning of her medical experience, which was very important to her, because these unexpressed feelings were impeding her recovery. She was left with feelings of loss of control and dissatisfaction until the presence of the counsellor allowed her to express her feelings. During the interview the counsellor discovered that this patient had a legitimate reason for being dissatisfied. In the following extract, the patient refers to her scar and her reactions to it.

Patient: *Now, I don't like him. I don't like me. I don't like the way I look. I hate this scar. The doctors tell me, 'You're lucky to be alive.' I say, yes . . . but I feel unlucky. You know, I have a useless left arm which I learnt to live with. But at least I had a nice bust-line. Now, I have this ugly scar down my chest and scars across my breasts. I don't like to look at me and I don't like my husband to look at me. I'd like to punch whoever sewed me up. I'd like to punch him out. Didn't he know he was working on a woman? I can say it and feel it and I don't care who the fuck hears me. Because he did not consider me as a woman, because I have been in that hospital – I can't tell you how many times I've seen his other patients. I haven't seen one patient that has scars like mine or with staples on their chests except this schmuk sitting here. And why didn't I question it before? Where was my brain?*

Counsellor: *You were just saying to me how quickly everything was done, how quickly the surgery came about, how quickly you were feeling anger and you were in for tests and boom, you're on the operating table, just about. Um, I think maybe you're feeling shock and I think . . .*

Patient: *[Interrupts] Maybe. I – I remember telling him – I remember even saying to Dr Sloane when he first told me about it. He said there was no way to avoid it. I'm so mad at myself. How stupid, so stupid I am.*

Counsellor: *So what could you do now not to be so mad?*

Patient: *I think this is it. I am able to say it. I'm able to get it out and say it. I don't have to think about it and swallow it. And doing something about it. [She was also going to a plastic surgeon.] The surgeon said that he was very glad I came in when I did. He said if I had waited for a year, that he doesn't know if anything could have been done for me unless it was surgical. Now he is treating my scar and now I have hope. Uh, let me tell you. I undid a little last night. And looked for the first time and it's uh, it's flat like this [points to the table top] and it's not quite a week. It's already disappearing. But the lumps – and the discoloration will fade eventually. It will become flat and that's what I want. I don't care if it's a flat scar. I'm only concerned that it doesn't stick up. I'm not complaining that I have a scar here. What I complained about is that it's so ugly and raised. He injected it with silicone. And over it placed a rubber strip that I have to wear all day. He said it'll probably take about two to three months. It will be better.*

Counsellor: *Does it go all the way down from the neck?*

Patient: *Yes. I really – I really get excited about this part – and over*

	here or somewhere, about this much is flat [takes finger to illustrate the measurement]. *I have to go back a week from Friday and he'll look at how it's doing, he may have to inject it again but we'll go from there. Okay, he said, the chances of it working by itself were maybe 10 per cent. If I had waited a year like people say, wait a year and it will fade. So whereas now it's about 90 per cent that it will work because the incision is still new. I dread telling my cardiologist about the plastic surgeon but I have to handle it when the time comes.*
Counsellor:	*Why would you dread telling the cardiologist?*
Patient:	*Because he likes to be the one* [laughs] *who says do this or do that. And he's – I tell you he brushed it off* [the scar] *and I should be happy to be alive. Like it was all over my head. About needing this surgery. Even the plastic surgeon said that it was an ugly scar.*

This example illustrates that patients and health care professionals can each have a different understanding of which issues are important to focus on or act on for the patient's successful treatment and recovery from surgery.

EXPLORING BELIEFS IN COUNSELLING SESSIONS

The emphasis so far in this chapter has been on the dynamics of illness meaning systems and their relevance to counselling. We now look at the ten most relevant beliefs about health, illness and treatment that are likely to arise in the course of counselling and how to set about exploring these in sessions.

Beliefs may either be constraining or facilitative (Wright *et al.*, 1996), and are at the heart of understanding how patients and their families cope with and adapt to illness. A counsellor can gain an understanding of these beliefs by asking the patient or family directly about them. For example: 'What is your view about how this new treatment will help with these symptoms?' and 'I see your doctor has written down a diagnosis of depression; what is *your* understanding of depression?' Meanings are important because they can further or inhibit understanding. A lack of consensus about meaning can cause or exacerbate psychological problems, or even prove hazardous. A patient may, for example, believe that her illness has been caused by some 'wrongdoing' earlier in her life and consequently seek out a traditional healer rather than a medically qualified doctor for assessment and treatment. Another patient may not be fully informed about recent advances in the treatment of a condition and erroneously believe that she is about to die. Disagreement over the diagnosis and views about the efficacy of treatment may lead to the patient not complying with the prescribed treatment regime.

I Ideas about what counselling can offer

The majority of patients seen by counsellors in health care settings are unlikely to have had previous experience of therapy and counselling. Some may be bewildered or frightened by a referral, expressing concern that others may feel they are not coping well, or that it implies that they are psychologically disturbed. Others may welcome the contact and an opportunity to talk with a receptive professional who is not the caring doctor or nurse, but may have little understanding about how counselling could help. Previous experience of counselling that was perceived to be unhelpful or harmful may result in the patient feeling resistant or behaving in an unco-operative manner. It is always advisable to ask directly about the patient's beliefs or past experiences of counselling. Open discussion with patients about the referral, their expectations and their needs can help to avoid misunderstandings that might otherwise affect the therapeutic process adversely.

> 'Have you previously talked to a counsellor or therapist?'
>
> 'What first went through your mind when it was mentioned that it might be a good idea for us to meet?'
>
> 'Do you have any ideas about how this meeting could be of help, or how you would like it to be of help?'

2 Information from the medical system about the problem

It is important to understand what the patient has been told by doctors and nurses about her illness, its cause and possible outcome. The counsellor may wish to explore what the patient understands about the diagnosis and what the patient feels about what she has heard, and whether she has alternative views. Some examples of questions that may help to open up these issues are:

> 'What have you been told by the doctors?'
>
> 'What do you think they see as the problem?'
>
> 'What is your understanding of the diagnosis given to you?'
>
> 'Do you have any ideas as to what might have caused this problem?'
>
> 'Have you been able to discuss these with the doctor? If not, what has prevented this from happening?'
>
> 'Is there anything you want to know more about that has not been discussed with you?'
>
> 'Are there aspects of your condition that you would prefer not to be told about?'

3 Information from the patient and family about the problem

In the same way, the views and beliefs of other family members should also be discussed with the intention of exploring whether there is agreement or some difference of opinion between the patient, the family and health care professionals, as this may be the source of relationship and personal problems.

> 'What do family members think about the problem?'
>
> 'Do they all agree with one another or are there differences of view within the family?'
>
> 'Whose ideas do you agree with the most?'
>
> 'Have any family members discussed your condition with the doctor?
>
> 'What came of that?'
>
> 'How might you deal with disagreements that may arise between yourself, the family and the doctor?'

4 Ideas about the source or cause of illness

Knowledge about how the patient believes she might have contracted the illness may help in understanding the patient's views about and attitude towards treatment, especially if an alternative (and possibly conflicting) view has been raised by others, such as a relative or another professional. Some ideas about the cause of illness are socially created; for example, the view that infertility automatically results from a past sexually transmitted disease and is therefore just punishment for premarital sexual intercourse. In stress-related illness, the individual may be 'blamed' for incompetence or an inability to cope.

> 'How do you think you contracted this condition?'
>
> 'What do you think caused your illness?'
>
> 'Do you have any ideas about why this has happened now?'

5 Previous history and experience of health-related problems, and meaning of illness or disability

How a person reacts and subsequently adjusts to their illness can be influenced by previous personal experience, either of illness or of helping others to cope with illness. Patients often fear that they will suffer in the same way as a relative who, for example, had cancer, depression or another debilitating condition. Similarly, a person who has enjoyed several months free of symptoms while their illness was in remission might find it especially difficult to face up to the prospect of re-hospitalization for further treatment and may deny the fact that they have relapsed. It is therefore important to explore previous experience of illness and treatment.

> 'Have you previously had a serious illness? Have you felt this low before?'
>
> 'What helped you to cope?'
>
> 'Has anyone else in your family or any close friend suffered from depression?'
>
> 'What effect did this have on you?'
>
> 'How does this affect how you see things now for yourself?'

6 Ideas about what medical investigations and treatment can offer

Although similar to the first point, this addresses directly the issues of prognosis and the likely endpoint of certain medical treatments and their consequences. Patients suffering from a chronic or life-threatening condition are likely to reflect on the limits of modern Western medical treatment and to consider either alternatives (for example, complementary therapies), or the cessation of the active treatment. Sometimes it may be difficult to discuss issues of this nature openly with the patient, particularly if the doctors continue to treat the patient when palliative or respite care may be more applicable. Patients, families and health care staff may each hold different views as to the limits of active treatment and these may also change during the course of the illness – and from patient to patient. Open discussion about these views can help to avoid unnecessary suffering and conflicting opinions about treatment.

> 'What are your views about how the treatment is helping?'
>
> 'Who would be inclined to agree with you?'
>
> 'What have been/might be their views?'
>
> 'What might need to happen for your ideas to change?'

7 Ideas about information and its dissemination

Patients may present with problems that are medical but have psychological and social implications. Foremost among these are issues pertaining to confidentiality and secrecy. In an attempt to 'protect' others, patients may choose not to tell anyone else about the illness, thus denying themselves the benefit of social support. The effect of keeping a secret is seldom completely positive or completely negative. Confidentiality between members of a health care team can also give rise to problems, as some colleagues may feel excluded by virtue of not having being told about a patient's condition. It is important to recognize that the patient's views about who should be told may change over time, not only because of the obvious signs of advancing disease or disability, but also in response to counselling or discussion with others.

'Is there anyone you would like to tell about the diagnosis you were given today?'

'How do you think this may affect him or her, and his or her relationship with you?'

'At what point, if at all, do you think your views about this may change?'

'How do you think you might feel if the disease progresses and you have not told your children that you are unwell?'

8   The person's position or role within the family

Life-cycle and developmental issues affect how people view the impact of illness. Views may be different depending on whether, for example, it is a child or a young parent dying, or an elderly relative who has been unwell for several years. Similarly, the loss may have different implications if the person is a mother, a child, a breadwinner, a childbearer and childrearer, or a single parent. Exploring the actual or anticipated loss associated with a person's position or role within the family can help them to address the meaning and implications of different losses and how they might cope and adapt.

'What position or role do you hold in the family?'

'If you were unable to fulfil this role, who else might be able to do so, do you think?'

'Who could provide additional help and support so that you could continue to fulfil this role?'

9   Ideas about the psychological resilience of the patient or family members

Perceptions of, or assumptions about, how people may cope (whether it is the patient or family) determine how people relate to one another and what is said between them. If, for example, the health care professional or family members believe that a person would not cope well with bad news, this will influence whether, how, what and when this news is conveyed. Some views may be derived from family myths about coping, or actual events in the past when severe psychological problems were linked directly to news of illness or death in the family.

> 'How do you imagine your husband will cope with the news?'
>
> 'What makes you think that he would not cope well?'
>
> 'How would you know that he is or is not coping?'
>
> 'Do you think coping and being distressed at the same time is possible?'

10 Ideas about the future

This is similar to views about treatment and prognosis (see above), but addresses directly the outcome at a psychological level and can help to open up discussion about the most feared outcome or fantasy (an approach for doing this in counselling is discussed in Chapters 6 and 13). It is important to explore whether the future is feared or welcomed by different family members and not to make assumptions about how people might adapt and cope. Problems may arise if hopes or fears are unrealistic in the face of medical evidence, possibly creating an impasse in treatment or leading to potentially hazardous outcomes, such as the patient not attending regularly for follow-up.

> 'As things stand now, how do you see the future?'
>
> 'Does it look any different from when we last spoke?'
>
> 'How do you think others see the future for you?'
>
> 'What do you most look forward to?'
>
> 'What, if anything, do you most fear?'

CONCLUSION

Exploring illness beliefs and meanings is core to counselling in health care settings. The counsellor is not required to assert one belief over another, or to guide the patient to see things from the counsellor's perspective. Instead, the counsellor should first seek to understand the different illness meanings that may either facilitate or hinder open communication, effective care and patient coping. If this exploration is carried out sensitively and with an appreciation that different views and beliefs exist, the counsellor will open up a powerful opportunity to empathize and connect with the patient and those around her. This understanding may cement the relationship between the patient and the counsellor, as well as others. This therapeutic connection may be especially important where more complex and potentially more challenging and distressing issues and news emerge, for which the patient seeks further counselling.

Chapter 3

Adapting Psychotherapeutic Practice to the Health Care Context

INTRODUCTION

The individual's response to a medical diagnosis is diverse, unique and unpredictable in its nature and intensity. It is common, however, for many people to experience some degree of anxiety, fear or sense of loss in the presence of a serious medical condition. Distress is also commonly presented in the health care context in the guise of physical symptomatology, even though the individual may not be ill. Distress is not the same as illness. Evidence suggests that a third of clinical presentations in the primary care context are psychological in nature (Layard Report, 2006). Clinical depression contributes 12 per cent of total non-fatal global illness (Utsün *et al.*, 2004). Furthermore, a high percentage of people present to their doctor with mental health problems. In order to gain access to support, distress may be 'medicalized' in the form of physical symptoms by the patient and by the medical practitioner, to 'legitimize' the provision of services (Middleton *et al.*, 2005). The misery associated with clinical depression and chronic anxiety is the biggest contributory factor to psychological distress experienced in Britain at the time of writing (Layard Report, 2006). It is essential for health care professionals (and particularly those in the primary care team) to develop and enhance their psychotherapeutic skills as well as their medico-scientific knowledge to respond effectively and efficiently to all their patients' needs. Research suggests that, when the psychological needs of patients are catered for, utilization of medical services is reduced and patient satisfaction improves (Hoyt, 1995). The medical setting in which distress is increasingly recognized, addressed and treated is also undergoing change.

A wide array of socio-economic and cultural issues affect and shape the medical setting. It is a context 'in flux'. Medical settings such as GP practices and hospitals are constantly being called upon to change, in order to respond to increasing demand. Yet there are resource constraints and fluctuations in ideology that may hamper such change. In the work-driven modern Western urban society, the individual too is being challenged to change in a variety of ways. In a world dominated by market forces, consumerism and e-communication, individuals may either feel stimulated, energized and invigorated or over-extended, overwhelmed and at times overlooked. The individual's worth and identity may even be perceived to be coterminous with his or her ability to keep pace and be productive. The incumbent precariousness, seeming dispensability and pressure to succeed may contribute to the individual being prey to stress-related illness. There may also exist a parallel dearth of meaningful human communication and sense of connectedness, particularly in the modern urban setting. Social life and relationships may be sacrificed. This may contribute to the individual feeling alone, isolated and depleted of personal resources.

The connection between psychological stress associated with lack of emotional support and societal change is now well documented (Utsün et al., 2004). As a consequence, there is an increasing trend for people to offload their personal distress and feelings of vulnerability in the health care context, especially in primary care. Personal issues, work stress, traumatic life events and the consequences of fractured relationships, that do not come directly within the traditional remit of the health care professional, now inform more frequently the content of medical consultations. Coupled with this is the huge increase in migration that is having a significant impact on services in many countries.

To ignore the psychological care of the patient is no longer an option in the modern, accountable health care setting. Medical professionals have, of course, always attempted to respond to the emotional and psychological needs of their patients, in addition to caring for their physical needs. Clinical experience, interpersonal skills and preferences, however, vary considerably from one practitioner to another, making such responses episodic, intermittent and, at times, even negligible when seen from the patient's perspective. Counsellors may find themselves engaged increasingly with distressed patients as their medical and nursing colleagues attempt to meet their own targets and cope with ever-increasing workloads.

Doctors are trained in the diagnosis, treatment and prevention of illness. Indeed, mental and emotional well-being is often defined simply as the absence of disease or illness. The emotional and psychological care of the patient may at times therefore be assigned to second place in terms of priority and/or contracted out to professionals with specific skills and training, such as psychologists, psychotherapists and counsellors. It is, however, frequently the generic health care professional who is left to identify, acknowledge and respond to the psychological and emotional needs of the patient.

ADAPTING PSYCHOTHERAPEUTIC PRACTICE TO THE HEALTH CARE SETTING

As we have already seen, health care settings are very different from traditional psychotherapeutic settings – challenging traditional working practices; how the patient is viewed; how the counselling process itself is understood; ideas about confidentiality, number and frequency of patient contacts; the ever-increasing demand to be transparent about working practices; and financial accountability. All this has required the world of psychotherapeutic care to reconsider its conceptual basis and to re-invent itself in terms of practice. Counselling, while retaining its ethical base, has had to become commercially aware and accommodate advances in evidence-based practice. The challenge to counselling to adapt to health care settings has been both positive and painful. Certain concepts, principles and practices arise that can serve as a guide to underpin and inform the adaptation and development of counselling skills in the health care practitioner, and in health care settings generally.

BENEFITS OF COUNSELLING IN THE HEALTH CARE SETTING

In a world where there is no consensus about fundamental human values and beliefs, the health care context, virtually uniquely, still retains a position of almost universal trust and respect. Demands for accountability work largely to benefit the patient. What is delivered by health care professionals is under constant scrutiny. The privacy, intimacy and confidentiality traditionally associated with the medical context contributes powerfully towards allowing for profound and relevant human communication between professional and patient. Counselling practice in health care settings is growing more robust despite inherent theoretical tensions between medical and psychotherapeutic approaches to the amelioration of distress. Significantly, when there is both an agreed consensus and a collaborative approach forged between medical practitioners and therapeutically focused colleagues about the nature and priority of the psychotherapeutic care of the patient, the potential inherent in the therapy process is greatly enhanced (Hoyt, 1995).

PITFALLS OF COUNSELLING PRACTICE IN THE HEALTH CARE SETTING

Traditionally, the medical model is hierarchical and expert-orientated. The patient's role is to be 'compliant' with treatment. Competence and responsibility for problem resolution are assigned to the professional. The view of the professional as the expert is deeply embedded in Western culture. The practice of psychotherapy in the health care context is a complex art. Psychological care is increasingly being 'medicalized'. It is often 'prescribed' alongside other medicalized treatment options and regimes (for example, National Institute for Clinical Excellence Guidelines for the Management of Depression (NICE, 2004). A common understanding of the role and function of the counsellor may be equated with the ability to make specific diagnoses that fit those in the psychiatric classification systems, exemplified in DSM IV (APA, 1994), and to develop appropriate treatment protocols. While such clinical expertise on the part of the counsellor is indeed a valuable commodity, psychotherapeutic care is much more than the diagnosis and treatment of identifiable mental disorders.

The essence of psychotherapeutic care is about a process of engagement between professional and patient. The medium of change is the therapeutic relationship more than a treatment protocol (Foster and Murphy, 2005). The objective of therapeutic engagement is to forge a profound, meaningful, boundaried and purposeful connection with the patient, directed towards the exploration, reduction and resolution of problems and the alleviation of distress. The significance of a process of engagement in terms of the patient–professional relationship is that *both* parties, professional *and* patient, are active participants in that relationship. The patient is seen and engaged with as a person. Illness, problems or disability are not the only focus. Responsibility for problem resolution is shared and the patient's competence, strengths and resilience are actively elicited.

It is important to identify and understand what contributes to a process of engagement between professional and patient. Psychological research suggests that a successful psychotherapeutic outcome is related to the quality of the patient's participation in the process of communication (Miller *et al.*, 1997). Eliciting the patient's participation in the therapeutic process as well as diagnosing what is wrong with him therefore become primary and simultaneous objectives. The following four factors contribute to an understanding of an 'engaged' relationship between patient and counsellor.

I Understanding the nature of distress

The nature of distress remains the same whether it is related to the diagnosis of a medical condition, is the result of living with a medical condition, or arises out of an adverse or traumatic life event. In our experience, there are two components to psychological distress that the counsellor needs to be aware of and address selectively and appropriately. The first is the normal reactive process a patient may experience that results from a medical diagnosis or a traumatic or adverse life event. This may involve 'normal' feelings of pain, sadness or loss. It may also, as we shall see in the next chapter, include beliefs about a person's ability to cope in the future. The second is the patient's own view of, or the significance he assigns to his own reactive process. In cognitive behavioural terms, this may sometimes be referred to as the 'worry' about the worry. In systemic terms, it can be referred to as the 'meta' position to the problem. For example, if a patient is diagnosed with obsessive compulsive disorder (OCD), he may experience the 'normal' distress associated with repetitive hand washing. In addition, he may also experience a number of negative emotions such as feelings of shame, personal weakness, incompetency or inadequacy for having the problem in the first place. The counsellor should always be aware of these two components and target both if necessary. If the therapeutic intervention is to be successful, therefore, for any particular individual, his reaction cannot be assumed. Indeed, the reaction needs to be recognized as being particular to the individual, actively elicited and addressed by the therapist. In some cases, it is possible to help patients significantly by targeting directly the patient's own meaning of the problem.

It is not surprising that one of the defining characteristics of distress is an acute sense of isolation. Every individual's experience of distress is unique. Commonly, too, there can be an accompanying 'paralysis', so that the patient no longer functions optimally. He is less able to access his normal coping mechanisms when distressed. In this regard, the importance of understanding the psychotherapeutic process as one of engagement cannot be overstated. The essence of the counselling process is that it is interactional in nature. The counsellor cannot 'prescribe' a cure, as a doctor may at times be able to, without the patient's active involvement. The patient's involvement is an essential part of the process of therapy as understood in this book. When a sense of connection is forged between professional and patient, the sense of isolation that the patient has hitherto suffered may be pierced. This is a pivotal moment in the therapeutic interaction. Once the patient experiences a sense of connection, he may begin to regain some sense of autonomy and control in the situation and begin to re-access his own expertise.

2 Eliciting the patient's point of view

Patients participate in counselling when they feel listened to, respected and taken seriously. Once patients begin to participate and engage actively in the counselling relationship, they are likely to feel more at ease, allowing them to access, discover and express their anxieties. When these are expressed and their distress validated and addressed, it becomes more likely that patients' motivation will be elicited and they will become more active and cooperative participants in treatment. The process of engagement itself can cut through the patients' experience of distress and herald the beginning of recovery of psychological well-being. The approach to therapy described in this book seeks to make every therapeutic encounter an individually tailored one. Working positively and creatively with individual difference is at its core.

3 Seeing the patient as being competent

The imparting of expert knowledge by the health care professional to the patient has traditionally characterized the professional relationship in the health care context and informs and shapes a major part of the communication between patient and professional. To view patients differently – as people who are experts on their own life – challenges both the medical professional and the patients themselves. For the medical professional, this might mean developing the capacity, temporarily, to suspend the inclination to impart expert skill, knowledge or information. This process may initially feel de-skilling and unfamiliar. For patients to see themselves as competent and able challenges them to be both active and *responsible* within the context of the professional relationship.

Shared responsibility for therapeutic process and outcome is no longer an optional issue. With heightened awareness of patients' rights and access to information on the internet, patients find they are compelled to be more informed and active in the promotion, maintenance and choice of treatment options in terms of their own health care. The recently introduced IT package 'Choose and Book' in the National Health Service (NHS) in the UK, for example, actively promotes patient choice, but to be able to choose, one needs to be informed. Patients are also challenged to re-think their role in the patient–professional relationship, which may run counter to feelings of helplessness and vulnerability. Patients are increasingly directly involved participants in complex treatment options. Indeed, hardly a week goes by where there is not some national debate or controversy over a treatment method and access to it, which may add further impetus to the need for patients to be optimally informed and engaged with the decision-making process.

In more common and routine situations, it is never a time-wasting effort on the part of the professional to elicit patients' feelings and beliefs about different medical options. A patient faced with substantial and systemically invasive chemotherapy options, for example, should feel sufficiently supported to be able to make an informed personal choice about embarking on such a regime. This freedom can only arise in the context of an engaged, collaborative, adult-to-adult relationship between professional and patient. 'Informed' consent in the medical context has no meaning outside such a relationship. Counsellors are inherently a part of this collaborative arrangement with patients, and are core to helping people feel informed and encouraging them to be both responsible and competent rather than helpless and vulnerable.

4 Working positively within time constraints

Health professionals have always had to 'school' themselves in the economics of time and in this regard have provided inspiration, stimulus and challenge to counsellors to re-think some of their most basic assumptions about working within time constraints. People expect doctors and nurses to be busy! From the professional's point of view, it contributes to informing an attitude that is purposeful and focused. Issues are prioritized and addressed accordingly. The intensity that is then generated can contribute to fostering a sense of engagement between the patient and the health professional. For many counsellors, this has necessitated a radical re-think of working with open-ended time contracts. Many of the interventions described in this book have evolved from working in a context where significant constraints on time constantly operate.

The use of time in counselling, in terms of optimal time, length and frequency of sessions, has become the focus of intense debate (see Kadera *et al.*, 1996) – a debate that has contributed much to the re-shaping and re-configuration of a modern psychotherapeutic response, tailor-made and appropriate for the health care setting. The link between therapeutic intervention, outcome, cost and the duration of treatment have had to be considered carefully. As a consequence, new attitudes have been forged in terms of working positively, differently and efficiently.

ADOPTING A QUESTIONING APPROACH

An attitude of interest and positive enquiry is characteristic of the approach described here. This is embodied by the professional adopting a questioning approach or 'technique' in addressing the patient. The objective of asking a question is to invite active participation and not simply to elicit factual information. Utilizing the phrase: 'Help me to understand . . .' as a preface to almost every statement summarizes the components of an attitude in the professional towards the patient that has proved to be most helpful. It conveys an attitude of respect for the patient. It takes the patient seriously. It contributes to problem definition and the prioritization of concerns. It denotes an attitude of attentiveness and it is invitational in nature. The patient's viewpoint is essential to the process. Neither is it without 'muscle', as it challenges the patient to participate and to work. The subject of adopting a questioning technique, illustrated by using different kinds of questions, is considered in detail in Chapters 6 and 8.

UNDERSTANDING THE CONNECTION BETWEEN THOUGHTS AND FEELINGS

Many evidence-based psychotherapies are brief, interactive and forward-looking, such as cognitive behavioural therapy, which has demonstrated its effectiveness in treating a number of psychological conditions (Roth and Fonagy, 2004). The breakthrough in modern cognitive models of therapy that currently underpin and inform much of psychotherapeutic care in the medical context, based on empirical evidence (NICE, 2004), is that human feelings are intrinsically linked to and are a consequence of their thought processes. Low mood, or clinical depression, is not, although many people describe it as such, 'a black cloud' that descends from nowhere. It is less the issue or the adverse event that is significant, but how the individual thinks about and understands it – and the meaning and significance assigned to it by that individual – that is most important and relevant in counselling. Optimally, it should be possible to work with the treatment protocols as recommended in the guidelines (NICE, 2004) without having to compromise therapeutic engagement.

Case Study

The following case vignette has been selected to illustrate some of the principles and processes already identified and that underlie the counselling approaches in this book. The case described here attempts to provide a snapshot of the ebb and flow of the psychotherapeutic interaction between patient and professional while adhering to the cognitive principles as recommended by the guidelines (NICE, 2004). The health professional in this case study is a counsellor, but the interventions, questions and responses chosen have been specially selected to be utilized readily and easily by the generic health care professional.

Guy, a 60-year-old man, following an episode of transitory but significant impairment of function in both legs, was given a neurological diagnosis that would lead eventually to 'multiple system atrophy'. For three days he had been unable to walk without assistance. Guy's reaction to this diagnosis was one of calmness and equanimity, contrary to the expectation of his GP, who admitted later that she had found this 'rather global' diagnosis to be 'mind blowing'.

Guy had been in a warm and supportive relationship with 'the love of his life' for twenty-five years. He was also socially well supported and was very active in his community. Guy continued to live his life over the next few months as he had always done, without manifesting or experiencing undue anxiety.

A few months later, Guy experienced an unrelated medical problem that warranted investigation. In the course of this investigation, Guy's original diagnosis was revised. He was told instead that he was suffering from Parkinson's disease. He

▰▰▶

was also told that he was 'on the mild end of the spectrum' for this condition. Guy was prescribed appropriate medication, which led to a complete remission of his minor neurological symptoms. Guy's psychological well-being did not, however, keep pace with his physical state, and his emotional condition deteriorated severely. Some weeks later he presented himself to the GP with substantial and debilitating anxiety and panic symptoms. He was in a highly agitated state, with a number of significant biological symptoms. He was constantly tearful. He was unable to rest, sleep or eat. He was no longer able to concentrate on his academic work as a scientific researcher. His wife described his behaviour as having a sudden onset and 'was out of character'. Guy had withdrawn himself from his community. He was unable to perform simple domestic chores. Guy was well known to his GP, who at that point prescribed Guy appropriate anxiolitic medication.

Over the next few months, Guy's psychological condition continued to deteriorate, despite his use of the prescribed medication. He could no longer work. The GP admitted to 'being completely puzzled'. She said she could not understand how Guy's reaction to his second 'substantially less serious' diagnosis, could be so severe and acute as it currently was. Guy was free from all neurological symptoms. It was at this time that the GP asked the practice counsellor to see Guy. In doing so, the GP was working within the 'remit' of a collaborative relationship with the counsellor. She was looking 'beyond' the merely physical aspects of Guy's medical diagnosis and took his emotional distress seriously. The counsellor, mindful of the positive and supportive relationship between Guy and the GP, agreed to see Guy. Given the medical complexities of the case and the nature of Guy's diagnosis, the counsellor thought it might be of benefit to Guy if the GP was also present, at least at the beginning of the first meeting. Both the GP and Guy readily agreed to this proposal.

The meeting between the three participants was held in the GP's practice, with its attendant professional, confidential and boundaried context. Given that the therapist was aware that Guy and the GP knew each other well, she began directly by asking,

'Guy, your GP tells me that she is "completely puzzled" by how you currently feel, given your revised diagnosis, which to her mind is much less serious than your first diagnosis. Can you help us to understand how that is so?'

In the time-limited context of the medical setting, the prime concern needs to be addressed directly. A questioning format was utilized by the therapist, based on the belief that Guy was the expert in this situation. Only he could 'unlock' the mystery of his severe symptoms. A question that utilizes the format: 'Help me to understand . . .' is respectful to the patient. It also conveys the idea to the patient that his help will be needed to formulate the answer. It thus contributed to eliciting his participation in the process, thereby fostering engagement. He was being challenged to work. The ultimate objective of utilizing a questioning technique is to help the patient to think afresh about the old problem and to elicit his engagement in the relationship with the professional. ⅠⅠⅠ➡

Guy responded to the counsellor's questions by recounting the fact that ever since he had been given the diagnosis of Parkinson's disease, he had had flashbacks to a specific episode that had occurred during a time in his youth that he had worked as a hospital orderly. Guy described a scene in which he had been asked to assist the medical team in getting a very distraught patient into a straitjacket. Guy was tearful throughout this account. The therapist then asked Guy what he remembered about the patient that was significant.

'He had Parkinson's disease!' Guy replied. 'I had forgotten that detail 'til you questioned me.'

There followed a technical discussion between Guy and the GP about the absence of any evidence directly linking Parkinson's disease with psychotic features. Guy was later to recount that this brief discussion with his GP had contributed to severing the powerful cognitive association he had made in his mind between Parkinson's disease and psychosis. Guy had never previously mentioned these 'flashbacks' to the GP. At this point, the counsellor asked Guy,

'Given all that you are going through, Guy, what is bothering you the most?'

This apparently simple question: 'What is bothering you the most?' is a useful one. As a counsellor or health practitioner it can be easy to feel overwhelmed by the amount of information a patient can reveal in the process of any meeting, especially when working within time constraints. The above question – simply by being in question form – is respectful of the patient's story, but it also challenges the patient to think, organize and prioritize his main concern thereby bringing a focus to the therapeutic conversation. To acknowledge and to prioritize the patient's main concern is a primary objective of the psychotherapeutic discourse in a time-limited context. Guy's response came in the form of asking another question:

'Do you think that I am mad? I cannot eat, sleep, sit still. I am unable even to sit at the table and eat a meal'.

When a patient suffers substantial biological symptoms, as Guy had done, with such acute anxiety that he was unable to sleep, eat, concentrate or function, it is not uncommon for that person to begin to question his or her sanity. The counsellor responded:

'I'm not a psychiatrist, Guy, but I now understand very much better the feelings of panic and anxiety you have experienced since you were given the diagnosis of Parkinson's disease. They are entirely consistent with your thought processes. You believed that you were going to go mad. The severity of your physiological symptoms make sense. I think I'm going to have to disappoint you though, as I do not think that you are mad. Indeed, you make perfect sense!'

Here, the counsellor was doing two things. First, she was spelling out the most fundamental principle that underlies cognitive behavioural therapy – the inherent link between thoughts and feelings. In addition, she was targeting the 'meta' level or the 'worry' that Guy had experienced, which was the belief that he might be losing his sanity because he had Parkinson's disease. The disease itself appeared to trouble him minimally. The therapist continued the intervention by asking the question: 'By the way, do you know anyone who, believing he was going mad, would not be anxious and fearful?'

Appropriate use of humour in the psychotherapeutic process can 'rescue' the discourse from being overly serious and can instil some sense of hopefulness into the situation. The look of relief on Guy's face was patent. His body posture relaxed. He released his grip on the chair handles that he had clutched and smiled for the first time. He replied simply,

'No!'

This simple response from Guy was an endorsement of his realization that his behaviour was within the 'normal' range and did not herald 'madness'. The GP's smiling assent after the counsellor's response to Guy's question added a further significant and powerful confirmation of Guy's 'normality'. The puzzle for Guy was being solved. In making the link between his thought processes, as embodied by the intrusive 'flashbacks' and his acute panic and anxiety symptoms, Guy began to experience some sense of both release and relief, as demonstrated by his more relaxed body posture. When the patient begins to experience this release, he is better able to access his own coping skills and a sense of mastery in the situation.

The GP intervened here, adding,

'I'd like to remind you, Guy, that your current absence of neurological symptoms is extremely encouraging. It probably places you at the mildest end of the spectrum with regard to Parkinson's disease. There is an excellent chance that this may well be how things will remain for you.'

Guy was clearly strongly engaged in the process, as reflected in his newfound sense of ease. He responded:

'It's really helpful for me to be reminded of this. I feel like I'm emerging from a tunnel. There is light at the end of it.'

By his positive response and active engagement, Guy was demonstrating his receptivity to the information the GP was imparting. He had previously been unable to acknowledge this informed opinion.

This encounter is illustrative of the potential for a complementary relationship to exist between a medical team member and a counsellor in a medical setting. The GP in this case understood and took seriously the need for counselling. Medical intervention alone was not productive. The joint meeting between the patient,

IIII➤

counsellor and GP illustrates the potential benefit to the patient when the medical and psychotherapeutic processes mutually enhance one another.

Subsequent to this meeting, Guy was more easily able to mobilize his own resources and competence. In the following weeks, he created a number of manageable and practical goals. In the first week, he set himself the task of recommencing some minimal domestic and gardening chores that he enjoyed doing. By the end of the second week following this first meeting, Guy could sit at the table at mealtimes and had again begun to enjoy sharing a meal with his wife. These behavioural goals were Guy's own accomplishment, which he recounted to the therapist when they met for a second time. Guy began the second session by exclaiming:

'You're meeting the real Guy today. I am who I used to be!'

Guy recounted how his psychological and physiological symptoms had greatly subsided, and continued,

'I hadn't understood the connection between the flashbacks I was having and the way I was feeling. When we talked together last time it all became clear. It was like a light bulb going on in my head.'

The counsellor asked Guy to identify the most helpful aspect of the first meeting. He replied unhesitatingly:

'You telling me that I wasn't mad. You took my worry seriously.'

'You took my worry seriously' is a statement worthy of consideration. In the course of the first meeting, Guy had felt safe enough to articulate his most profound belief, without fear of dismissal, criticism or ridicule. Indeed, his 'worry' had been validated and taken seriously by the counsellor, and most importantly it was 'normalized'. Having made the link between thoughts and feelings, the patient needs to be helped to challenge the content of the thought process that is causing distress. In Guy's case, this was done by both the counsellor and the GP talking him through his fears about losing his sanity. In cognitive behavioural terms, the 'meta cognitions' were targeted successfully (see Chapter 11).

Guy's belief that he was 'going to go mad' or was currently 'mad', supported a whole array of disturbing and unfamiliar emotions that had rendered him almost non-functional. Evidence emerged that the meeting with the GP and counsellor had been successful in identifying the link between thoughts and feelings, and the belief that he 'was going mad' had been elicited successfully, listened to and challenged, which contributed to his being able to 'shed' his dysfunctional behaviour with remarkable ease. It took Guy some weeks to regain his confidence and enjoyment in daily events and activities, but his improvement continued. His desire to cease taking the medication for anxiety was honoured and monitored by the GP. He returned to work a few weeks after the first meeting with the GP and the counsellor.

CONCLUSION

In terms of professional time investment, a fifty-minute session – the length of time of the first meeting between Guy, the GP and the counsellor – might be a period of time that could be difficult to set aside in a busy health care setting. Overall, however, it was an investment that was cost-saving in terms of the use of medication, further assessment and medical time in terms of the ongoing monitoring of Guy's enduring severe symptoms. Possible referral to secondary care had also been an option contemplated by the GP. This, too, had been avoided. Drawing incapacity benefit had also been averted.

This case study has been included to illustrate an active and positive approach to engaging a distressed patient. The possibilities inherent in an engaged and positive relationship between patient and health care professional extend the understanding of the traditional patient–professional relationship. The process of engagement is best facilitated when the professional detaches him/herself from the patient deficit model and moves to a competency model in the way the patient is viewed. This case study highlights how the patient's competence and confidence may be elicited and enhanced at a time when these may be most depleted, by an understanding of the psychological process attendant on distress.

Chapter 4

Models of Consultation and Collaboration

INTRODUCTION

The hospital, GP practice or other health care setting is an organization. It is sometimes helpful to think about how problems arise within organizations by drawing a parallel with problems in families. Most health care settings comprise several departments and disciplines. This inevitably leads to people having different views within departments, and between the health care setting and other institutions. These differences may stem from competing models of care, different resources, conflict over hierarchies and relationships, or different generations of workers who may not share similar values and approaches to the delivery of health care.

This chapter describes how different approaches to professional collaboration and consultation in health care settings can help in identifying and addressing the psychological needs of patients. The ideas can also be applied to facilitate a wider range of interesting and creative ways of working with both colleagues and patients, enabling counsellors to have a secure place in the health care team. Clarification with referrers and other colleagues about the role and position of the counsellor in the multidisciplinary team is an important first step. Failure to attend to relationships with the referrer or other health care professionals throughout the duration of counselling could undermine the service and even lead to its termination.

DEFINING CONSULTATION AND COLLABORATION

It is helpful for counsellors to start out with an assumption that a counselling service is usually not viewed as a primary resource in most health care settings. This can help to anticipate scepticism or a lack of confidence in such services, especially where financial considerations may place limits on the provision of such a service. Irrespective of the level of enthusiasm shown, however, some counsellors might encounter conflicting messages about the value of counselling (for example, 'Yes, we want a counsellor, but we don't really have much faith in what you can do').

Counsellors can work directly with doctors, nurses and other health care specialists, as well as with patients, to help them deal with the complex psychological processes that arise in the context of clinical care. It is important to differentiate between the role of the counsellor when working with patients and when working with professional colleagues. It is helpful to think in terms of discrete activities:

- *Consultation.* A consultation in a health care setting can be (a) *with a large system* (for example, team, ward, unit or professional group) about how they are managing a particular task or activity; (b) *with an individual or team* about their treatment and care of a particular patient; or (c) *directly with a patient* or her family who have asked to see or been referred to the counsellor. Consultation may not involve direct patient contact.
- *Collaboration* is working with colleagues towards an agreed objective and is advanced through direct consultations with patients and colleagues.

Consultation and collaboration are closely connected. One of the aims of consultation is to improve interprofessional collaboration (Seaburn *et al.*, 1996). Collaboration through open discussion and a willingness to consult can help to establish the position and credibility of the counsellor in a multi-disciplinary environment. The addition of a counsellor to a team is potentially complex and may be demanding of professionals' time. The need for a counselling service may arise for a number of reasons, one being that, in some medical specialities, there is published evidence that supports the value of counselling as having a direct or indirect effect on clinical outcomes and/or improves quality of life. Another stems from the recent increase in patient claims against health providers and clinicians as a result of negligence, errors and poor communication, which has brought heightened awareness that behavioural scientists and psychologists can help to reduce error and improve communication within medical teams and between clinical staff and patients.

How a counselling service is introduced and developed within a broader health care setting may also depend on whether there are existing protocols for psychosocial care. The counsellor should always adopt a non-oppositional stance, irrespective of whether the environment is receptive or more cautious. This stance can help the counsellor to integrate with the team and gain acceptance from colleagues. This entails having small goals; starting by learning about the unit and gradually 'building up credit' with colleagues. Attitudes towards one's professional colleagues may stem from myths or stereotypes about each professional group, either from past experience or from 'folklore'. They may also be a defence against the introduction of something different or new, such as counselling. Counsellors and health care professionals sometimes have stereotypical views of one another (McDaniel and Campbell, 1986), such as:

Doctors' and nurses' myths about counsellors

- They are 'do-gooders' who cheer people up.
- What they do with patients is plain common sense.
- They are glorified agony aunts offering a listening service.
- A last resort with difficult patients.
- They are time wasters who sit and talk.
- Useful only for dealing with hypochondriacs, panic attacks and troublesome patients.
- Outcome or effectiveness cannot be measured.
- They analyse too much.

Counsellors' myths about doctors and nurses

- They are preoccupied with boundaries and limits of competence.
- They do not share easily.
- Their bedside manner is superficial.
- They are territorial and do not work easily with new colleagues.
- The medical model of practice is vastly different from the counselling model.
- They assume power and act in a patronizing manner.
- They are stressed and some could do with counselling.

Some of these ideas may, at first, seem amusing or even ludicrous. But the fact remains that, however amicably members of some multi-professional health care teams get on with one another, they may approach and deliver patient care differently and hold constraining, and sometimes erroneous, beliefs about one another. An awareness of these unhelpful stereotypes may help counsellors to avoid acting on them. This will go a long way towards building up collaborative working relationships with colleagues.

The context or setting in which the counsellor works also affects the range of possible collaborative relationships that can be fostered. Different models of practice are described and illustrated below.

MODELS OF PRACTICE

For historical, practical and conceptual reasons, counselling services may develop differently in different health care settings. What may begin as a counselling service for children undergoing renal dialysis may be extended to all children in the renal unit, and later to all paediatric patients in the hospital. Similarly, a smoking cessation group, or a stress management and relaxation clinic for patients attending a GP's surgery may in time become the basis for a primary care counselling service. Others may have a range of different roles within the health care setting, leading to close collaborative relationships with a limited number of departments or units. Within each of these settings, the counsellor can organize his or her practice in a number of different ways, depending on the needs of the service and his or her level of competence and experience. This involves direct or indirect patient or colleague consultations, or any combination of these. Counsellor practice can include:

- Consultations with patients only.
- Consultations with professional staff only about their care of patients.
- Consultations with professional staff about staff relationships.
- Consultations with both staff and patients.
- Ad hoc consultations with either staff or patients (that is, consultation–liaison practice).

An understanding of the context in which treatment and care are provided is a vital first step. Having a framework for consultation with other health care professionals in health care settings can help to achieve these aims.

CONSULTATION WITH PROFESSIONAL COLLEAGUES IN HEALTH CARE SETTINGS

Consultation with colleagues working in the same organization is a special professional situation that is common in health care settings. The unique feature of internal consultation is the relationship between the counsellor and the consultee, which adds another dimension to the consultation process. Many factors may lead to requests for consultation. The request also implies a focus on what is happening, not only to a patient, but also to the dynamics of the caring team, as well as other organizational matters.

Requests for a consultation might stem from a dilemma or a need for specialist discussion about a problem. It may be that a lack of consensus over how to manage a problem has itself created further difficulties. Consultation begins when someone affected by a problem discusses their difficulty with someone else, be it in a formal consultation meeting, over the telephone after working on a difficult case, in a ward meeting, or in any other setting. It is the activity of discussing the problem, rather than where this takes place and for how long, that defines consultation. There is a tradition in medical care that complex problems are discussed with colleagues (who may be more knowledgeable or senior), or referred to them. So, consultations with counsellors about psychological problems are commonplace in these settings. The relationship between the counsellor and consultee may be challenged when the consultation takes place with someone within the same organization, as illustrated in the case below.

Case Study

A counsellor in a general hospital was asked by a doctor to offer ongoing consultation to an oncology team because the team worked in a stressful field, and a consultation could help to raise staff morale. One of the dilemmas faced by members of the oncology team was that, should morale improve, they would be expected to provide more psychological support to patients in the unit and this would require additional time and skills. The counsellor, on the other hand, had already been offering a support service to some patients. For this reason, the counsellor already had some views about staff relationships in the oncology unit, and was aware that not all of the nurses and doctors wanted to become involved in patient support and psychological counselling. The dilemma for the counsellor was that she had been asked by the head of the oncology unit to consult with the group. A reluctance to become involved in the management of problems between members of professional staff might ultimately result in fewer referrals being made: and this might also impede the research project in the oncology unit that the counsellor was hoping to pursue.

What prompts a request for consultation?

When consultation is requested, it is likely that the doctor or health care team requesting the consultation will have the view that they need to improve their sense of competence in relation to a clinical or management situation. Cost and practical concerns (for example, highly confidential patient information) might preclude engaging a consultant or counsellor from outside the organization to help solve a problem or improve competence. Other possible reasons for requesting a consultation are:

■ The experience and expertise of the counsellor is valued.
■ The counsellor may be more flexible about time than an external consultant, if he is from the same organization.
■ The consultee wants to relinquish responsibility for a case or problem and intends to pass it on to the consulting counsellor.
■ The problem is apparently 'highly confidential' and there may be a fear that 'dirty washing' will be openly displayed. There may be a belief that there will be greater loyalty and support if the consultant is from within the same organization.
■ The consultee may experience feelings of isolation in the hospital or clinic and the counsellor may create a new connection or relationship.
■ It may be more helpful to have someone in greater authority in the organization to confirm or reinforce a view or idea, or offer a different view.

Consultation is requested and occurs not only when there is a problem but also when people in a 'healthy' team are ready for more growth. Problems or events that typically prompt a request for consultation in health care settings stem from one of four possibilities, even though they may be linked. These are listed below, with each definition of a problem or issue followed by an example:

■ *Problem with patients.* A medical specialist asks for advice from a counsellor about how to help a patient who will not comply with treatment.
■ *With managers.* The director of a medical disaster team is asked to redraft their operational plan and pay greater attention to the care and support of victims and their relatives. A counsellor is invited to comment on this aspect of the draft document and make suggestions for its improvement.

- *With colleagues*. High staff turnover in a nursing team prompts senior nursing staff to consult with a counsellor to see whether this problem might be caused by staff relationship problems, morale or by how the service is organized and managed.
- *Within a team*. A new staff member joins a team in order to develop a new clinical and research project. A counsellor is invited to facilitate a team-building event.

There are many other examples of consultation work and it is important to stress that many of these are only concerned indirectly with patient problems.

How does a counsellor become a consultant?

Most counsellors who act as consultants to other staff undertake consultation in addition to, or as a part of, their clinical work. The following are five attributes of consultants which, individually or collectively, may have led to their achieving this position:

- *Seniority* within the setting.
- *Authority* or seniority within one's profession.
- *Experience* in dealing successfully with similar problems.
- *Position* of impartiality by not being attached to any one unit.
- *Respect* for one's ability to think clearly and to solve problems.

The choice of consultant may be determined by the nature of the problem. If the problem is concerned with the patient's behaviour or relationships, it is more likely that a counsellor will be approached for a consultation. Consultation skills are rarely taught formally in universities or health settings. Initiation into consultancy work in health settings is usually through experience of problem-solving with colleagues, and as a result of close, collaborative working relationships. A typical opening scenario from a colleague seeking consultation may be: 'Can I discuss a clinical problem with you?' or 'I'm having some difficulty writing up my proposal for more nurses in the community care programme. Would you have a look at my draft proposal?' Two central points underpin consultation: the definition of relationships between colleagues and the view of the health care setting as an organization.

Defining relationships through consultation

Consultation in the form of discussion or case review provides an opportunity for new views to emerge and for some relationships to be redefined. This is not to suggest that every piece of clinical work should be preceded by extensive consultation in relation to the task and outcome. This may be neither warranted nor practical. It is important, however, for the consultant in the health care setting to be clear about the nature of his relationship with the consultee; that is, whoever is clinically responsible for the case. There is a difference between a referral and a request for consultation over a clinical case and the counsellor may move between these positions in relation to a case. The counsellor's consultant position must be mutually defined: the consultee requests a consultation and the counsellor agrees to consult. A colleague may, for example, refer a case and the counsellor may choose to consult another colleague about how he can develop his work with the patient rather than personally taking on the case.

There must be agreement between the professionals that consultation will take place. As the counsellor may move between different positions, he needs to be flexible, adaptive and able to 'observe' himself in different interactive positions. Some different consultation positions are listed below:

- *Between colleagues.* A doctor asks a counsellor working in the same team for some advice about how to break bad news to a patient.
- *Between units/departments.* Members of staff on the Intensive Care Unit (ICU) request consultation from a counsellor based in a GP practice for help with bereavement issues.
- *Between hospitals.* Senior members of staff in an infertility counselling unit are engaged in consultation with colleagues in another district hospital who are in the process of setting up an infertility unit in their own hospital.

While the consultation task remains the same in each, the counsellor will have different relationships with a range of people, depending where they are in the hospital hierarchy. There is a tendency to be more formalized and thorough about setting up and conducting the consultation the further one is socially, hierarchically or physically (in terms of localization) from the consultee.

The aim of consultation is to elicit and address different views of problems and generate a climate in which new ideas, beliefs, alternatives, meanings and behaviours can emerge. In the same way as it is essential to have a structure or approach for counselling sessions with patients, it is desirable to have guidelines for conducting consultations with colleagues.

STEPS IN CONSULTATION

Planning the consultation

There are several stages in planning any consultation. The initial stage, already described above, amounts to a 'map' conveying a procedure for setting up and organizing a consultation session. The structure offers some guidance in the consultation procedure. All the stages are listed below, with the later ones being described in detail after the list:

- Understanding the request for consultation and defining the problem.
- Developing ideas about the consultant–consultee relationship.
- Discussing a consultation contract.
- Conversations about the problem.
- Feedback and re-evaluating the contract.
- Case closure.

Understanding the consultant–consultee relationship

A list of questions to help consultants clarify and define the consultant–consultee relationship includes:

- Who has requested the consultation? What is that person's level of seniority in the hierarchy? Is there consensus in the consultee's department that the consultation should be requested?
- Is there an expectation that the consultation will uphold a particular view (that is, he will not feel that he can introduce new or potentially controversial ideas)? Does the counsellor have some autonomy and flexibility in relation to the consultee?

A further step is to understand as much as possible about the effect it might have on established relationships if the consultation goes ahead.

This includes clarity about whether the consultee is trying to create an alliance with the counsellor, or hand over work or a task (redefining it as a liaison relationship). Posing the following questions to oneself is a useful way of speculating about these processes:

- To whom am I ultimately accountable; and does this consultee have the authority to enter into consultation and institute any changes? What relationship do I already have with the consultee that might affect the nature, course and outcome of consultation?
- What other parts of the organization might be affected by my participation; and how might they view my involvement in this problem?
- What levels of the health care system (for example, senior management) might need to be involved; and how might this affect my position in the institution if I had to engage them in our consultation?
- How will I deal with confidential information relating to the case that might be important for both the process and the outcome of the consultation?

Three different situations can be covered in moving from liaison to consultation, illustrated in Figure 4.1. In situation (A), the counsellor accepts the referral and sees the patient; in situation (B), a link is made with the referring person and together they see the patient; and in situation (C), the referrer keeps the case, undertakes the counselling and consults the counsellor over difficult aspects.

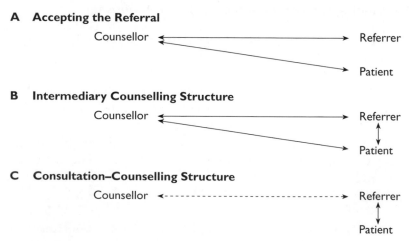

A   Accepting the Referral

Counsellor   Referrer

Patient

B   Intermediary Counselling Structure

Counsellor   Referrer

Patient

C   Consultation–Counselling Structure

Counsellor   Referrer

Patient

Figure 4.1   Moving from liaison to consultation

Before the session it is agreed that one person will interview the patient and the other will observe and consult. If there are points that have not been addressed, the consultant will be free to point these out to his colleagues during the session. In this way, the clinician retains control over both the questioning and the session. This method of a joint consultative session has proved to be helpful in general medical problem-solving, in case management and in developing and enhancing relationships with colleagues.

Discussion with the consultee

Once some ideas have been developed about the relationship with the consultee, a meeting can be arranged to discuss any of the points listed above that might impede the consultation process. A meeting is arranged with the person who requested the consultation in the first instance. Some meaning has to be given to the meeting and for this reason the purpose of the meeting might be defined as follows:

Counsellor: *Dr Smith, thank you for coming to my office this morning. I think we agreed to meet for fifteen minutes and then to arrange for another meeting if we need some more time. As you may recall, I said to you over the phone that before I could undertake consultation meetings with you and members of your department, I would first like to think over some ideas about my working with you over this problem. The reason for this is that, in my experience, the success of consultation depends on several things, and these include being clear about my role and my task. I believe it is especially important to think about these because we need to consider whether I am the most suitable person to work with you on this. First, do you have any thoughts on the matter?*

Consultee: *Well, actually, I'm very pleased you've brought this up. It was not an easy decision for me to approach you, particularly because I know that you're very busy and also because, frankly, Dr Jones (the co-director) had some thoughts that perhaps we should be approaching someone outside the hospital.*

Consultant: *Thank you for sharing that with me. How did you come to make the decision to ask me?*

Consultee: *Dr Jones and I had heard about your work in the Rheumatology Unit, and in fact it was he who first suggested we get in touch with you. I think he got cold feet, though, when he thought that if things 'went wrong', so to speak, it would make it difficult to refer patients to your counselling team in the future. I suppose he was trying to protect our good working relationship.*

Consultant: *If there were any disagreements or problems in our relationship, how might you handle the situation?*

Consultee: *I know that I could always talk to you. Perhaps Dr Jones would be more inclined to blame me and also to remind me that we might have been better off with someone outside.*

Consultant: *What made him choose not to come to this meeting? (And so on . . .)*

Discussing a contract

Making a contract is the basis of an agreement between the consultee and the counsellor as to what will be discussed in the course of the consultation, how long it might take, and to clarify professional boundaries. It is also important to establish whether the consultee has the authority to enter into a contract. The consultee might be asked, for example:

> To whom are you accountable? Is this person aware of our meetings? Do you need this person's permission in order to be discussing these problems with us?

Some provision must be made for flexibility within this. For this reason, the contract does not set out conditions or fixed endpoints but, rather, guides the consultant–consultee in the relationship until the contract is renegotiated by virtue of new and evolving problems or ideas. The contract might take some of the following points into account:

- There is an agreement to meet for consultation.
- The consultant may work with a team of colleagues.
- What is said in the context of consultation is confidential to the consultation context.

■ Consultation is to be distinguished from any other collaborative clinical work between the teams or any members of the teams.

■ Meetings will take place at a specific time in a specified place for a specified length of time.

■ Certain people will be expected at meetings. Procedures are agreed in the event of any one of them not being able to attend or if someone has to leave the meeting.

Once the contract is agreed, the consultation can proceed. However, in a health care setting, not all problems discussed between colleagues are negotiated formally or take place in a designated place, at a prearranged time. Consultations may be ad hoc and take place at the nurses' station, in ward meetings, in corridors, over the telephone or even in the staff room. It helps, however, to keep a contract in mind even if there is no formal agreement or definition that consultation is taking place. An approach to a counsellor by a GP who needs help with the wording of a letter to a highly distressed patient is an example of this.

Conducting the consultation – tasks

Consultation can help to define, clarify and solve problems through conversation between the consultee and consultant. The consultant helps to create an environment in which change can occur. While change may be sought, the consultant may have no control over the direction of change or any decisions made by the consultee. Questioning is particularly helpful for gathering information and exploring initial ideas. Examples of questions to a consultee in relation to general medical problems are listed below:

'What is the reasoning behind the shift in emphasis from in-patient to out-patient care?'

'What was happening at around the time this was upgraded from a unit to a department?'

'What are the particular aspects about working with this group of patients that might be different or stressful?'

'How is the handover to the new staff organized?'

'What do you think is unique to your work with this group of patients that sets your needs apart from other units in the hospital?'

'Who outside this unit most recognizes this?'

Formulating hypotheses

One task of the consultant is to consider carefully his place in the wider health care system. Sometimes, the consultant recognizes that it is neither appropriate nor possible to offer consultation. This may be because of his level of competence, position within the system, or decision not to work with a particular problem or consultee. It helps to make a hypothesis or calculated guess about such problems before each subsequent consultation session. This is based on available information (for example, who requested the consultation, and with what outcome in mind) and helps to focus the questioning for each consultation interview. It is helpful to reflect on how and why the consultants have come to understand the problem in a particular way. We ask the question: 'What has been happening to influence our own thinking in this particular way?' Hypothesizing can be of strategic value to both the consultant and the consultee. This in turn helps the consultee to reduce his or her bias towards any one person or idea, as the consultee, her context, and all those connected with the problem are taken into consideration.

Some initial questions to the consultee about the hypothesis in a first session may include the following:

'What has prompted the request for consultation?'

'Why now?'

'When did the idea of consultation first come about?'

'What is happening in and around the unit?'

'Have new staff recently joined the unit? Has someone recently left?'

'What will inform us that the case can be closed, and that we no longer need to discuss this problem?'

'Dreaded' issues

Identifying and talking about 'dreaded issues', or what people fear the most about their having a problem, is a technique used in consultation. The fear may be in relation to the consequences of the problem not being solved. Similarly, in a consultation there may be issues or outcomes that are 'dreaded' by the consultee. These may include a fear of dismissal, being ignored in decision-making, or not being put forward for promotion. Hypothetical and future-orientated questions are an effective way to address these fears ahead of time.

The following are examples of questions that might help the consultee to discuss his or her fears:

'Who is ultimately responsible for this case?'

'If this problem persists, how do you see things for yourself in relation to this unit?'

'What would be the worst possible thing you could imagine happening in this case?'

'What implications would there be if the patient were to die/ commit suicide?'

Ending the consultation and arranging follow-up

The process of hypothesizing, consulting, and reviewing the feedback and contract continues until there is agreement that the initial (or revised) goals of consultation have been reached, or there is agreement, for whatever reason, to end the consultation. At the end of the consultation, the consultant and consultee need to discuss:

- If, or how, they will work together in the future.
- What follow-up is to be arranged (if any).
- What changes there might be in their relationship. What will remain unchanged.
- What procedure will be followed if the problem recurs.
- What feedback (if any) about the consultation needs to be presented to a third party.

This process provides an opportunity for the consultant to avoid being drafted in again to carry out more work, even after the contract has ended, and for the re-creation of the appropriate boundaries between colleagues.

CONCLUSION

Counsellors working in health care settings may be called upon to consult with their professional colleagues. The consultant's relationship with the consultee is different from the one the counsellor has with a referrer. However, the consultant still draws on similar skills to those he uses when seeing patients. These include skills in developing a relationship, problem identification and exploration, examining different possibilities and outcomes, addressing significant concerns or 'dreaded issues', reframing, and using questions as a method of conducting the consultation interview. An important difference is that the consultant is usually a part of the wider health care system with which he is consulting. This has implications for whether he can reasonably be impartial and helpful.

Consultation skills make it possible for counsellors to have a broader remit to practise and, at times, to relate differently to their professional colleagues. Where joint consultation sessions are held with patients and doctors (as well as nurses), they learn more about counselling skills and techniques, and counsellors acquire a better understanding of complex medical issues. In turn, patients benefit from better co-ordinated care. This can reduce costs for health care (for example, a reduced bed occupancy in hospital; or improved compliance with treatment) and improve patients' quality of life.

Core Skills for Conducting Counselling Sessions

Chapter 5

Counselling Objectives in Health Care

INTRODUCTION

Patients may seek counselling because ill health or psychological distress has intruded into their life and affected their view of themselves and their relationships, as well as how they see themselves coping and adjusting, both in the short term and in the future. Irrespective of the route of referral to the counsellor or the theoretical framework used, there are several therapeutic tasks that guide the counsellor in therapy sessions. The main task of the counsellor is to engage with the patient in order to co-create with the patient new beliefs and ideas about a situation or problem that will enable the patient and his family to adapt to changes brought about by the current ill health. The initial goal in counselling is to determine whether there are problems, to discuss the context of those problems, and to explore ideas about how illness may affect people's beliefs and ideas.

This chapter highlights the therapeutic objectives in counselling and situates them in a health care context. Examples illustrate these objectives and ways of exploring issues in the context of counselling sessions. Counselling works best in the context of an engaged relationship; effective therapy cannot simply be a process of going through a check-list of interventions with a patient. The examples used are not comprehensive case studies but, rather, brief vignettes that link a theoretical idea with clinical practice; they also serve to illustrate levels of engagement with patients.

OBJECTIVES

The following help to achieve the aims of counselling with patients:

1   To determine whether any part, or which part, of the patient's caring system has defined a problem and to have a conversation about that problem (to elicit the patient's story).

A patient came to see a counsellor and stated: 'Dr Simpson says that I must see a counsellor because I have diabetes. But I don't have mental problems.' The counsellor responded by saying: 'What do you think it was that made Dr Simpson refer you?' 'He said that I wasn't looking after myself properly; my diet is bad and I'm not injecting regularly enough', replied the patient. 'And what do you think he was concerned about?' asked the counsellor. The patient replied: 'That I could end up in hospital, or worse. And he wants you to prevent that by "shrinking" me', replied the patient in a mildly challenging and sarcastic tone. The counsellor replied: 'I'm not sure whether I should be seeing you or Dr Simpson.' The patient then conceded: 'No, it's me. I'm not a "good" patient; I always buck authority. I don't like to be told what to do, and diabetes is the worst kind of problem to have with that state of mind.'

2   To elicit all of the problems, as the patient sees them, and then to discuss with the patient which need to be worked on first; that is, to assign priorities and an order to problems for resolution.

A young man was diagnosed as suffering from testicular cancer. He was referred to the counsellor working in the GP practice after he had been discharged from hospital following an operation to remove one testicle, as he felt overwhelmed by the news of his illness and its implications. In the first counselling session, he asked for advice about a wide range of issues. These included whether he should tell future girlfriends about his illness; whether the operation would prevent him from having children, and what he should do about his job. He also started suffering from symptoms of psychological distress, including insomnia, loss of appetite and being short-tempered with friends and colleagues. The counsellor felt overwhelmed by the large number of problems. The counsellor asked him to identify one or two of the most pressing problems, which is an important therapeutic intervention, in order to help both the patient and the counsellor to 'see the wood for the trees'. It would then be possible to consider how best to resolve them, rather than to try to solve all his problems in the limited time available.

3   To create a reality with the patient that fits with his current world-view and beliefs, to help sustain the patient through periods of change brought about by illness and loss.

In the case of a married man with advanced liver disease, one reality may be how he sees his role as a husband and a father, and how this will continue in view of his medical diagnosis, both while he is alive and after his death. Questions for consideration that help to reveal personal and family beliefs include: How will he continue in his role? Who else may take some of the role? What ideas or beliefs does he want to preserve? What will help him to cope with and adapt to the changes confronting him and his family?

4   To understand how the patient views his problems and help the patient to consider other perspectives about the problems.

Patient: *I am depressed. I find that having cancer of the prostate is getting me down.*

Counsellor: *I understand how difficult things can be. Who else has noticed that you feel depressed?*

Patient: *Sometimes my wife does, but then she tries to cheer me up.*

Counsellor: *What impact does it have on you when she tries to cheer you up when you are feeling depressed?*

Patient: *It can make me feel even worse. And angry too. I just want to talk about what's going on with me, and us.*

Counsellor: *What would you most like to talk about with your wife?*

Patient: *Believe it or not, not the prostate cancer. Or not that directly. But the treatment and the effects. I'm practically impotent now. I feel a sense of failure as her sexual partner. It's an awful thing after so many years of having an active sex life.*

Counsellor: *What would it take to have a conversation with your wife about these concerns?*

Patient: *It's embarrassing, but maybe if I were to explain to her*

> *why I sometimes feel depressed, rather than to snap at*
> *her.*
>
> *Counsellor:* *Yes, and maybe to do so at a time when you're not*
> *feeling as depressed, so you can talk to her without*
> *becoming too defensive or angry.*

5   To help patients feel that they have choices. As a consequence of being
    unwell, patients may feel that choices are being taken away from
    them. By reducing choices, one simultaneously takes away a level of
    autonomy.

> *Patient:* *The doctors tell me that the lymphoma is not respond-*
> *ing to treatment.*
>
> *Counsellor:* *What else was said?*
>
> *Patient:* *Nothing really. I know I'm going to die soon.*
>
> *Counsellor:* *If you were given the choice to be at home or in hospi-*
> *tal, and you were very unwell, where would you want*
> *to be?*
>
> *Patient:* *At home. I want to be able to look at the garden and*
> *have the dogs around.*
>
> *Counsellor:* *What decisions do you think you will need to make over*
> *the coming weeks?*

6   To retain a degree of neutrality in relation to the patient's lifestyle and
    decisions made about how he will cope with and adjust to his illness.
    This serves to enhance patient autonomy and self-confidence.

> *Patient:* *What's the use of taking these pills? They won't cure*
> *me. In fact the side effects are as bad as the illness.*
>
> *Counsellor:* *OK. What might happen if you chose not to take them?*
>
> *Patient:* *Probably the same as if I take them: I'm going to die*
> *and the pills may keep me going a bit longer, but for*
> *what?*
>
> *Counsellor:* *What has helped you to keep taking the pills thus far?*
>
> *Patient:* *'Help' is the wrong word. More like 'bullied'. The*
> *doctors say I have to take them. No 'ifs' or 'buts', just*
> *take them. I'm ready to die.*
>
> *Counsellor:* *Have you thought how you might persuade the doctors*
> *to see your point of view?*

7   To help the patient to continue to adapt and change (that is, to give hope where appropriate).

A young man was seriously injured in a road traffic accident and sought counselling after it became clear that he would suffer a permanent disability, possibly confining him to a wheelchair. He wanted to discuss whether to give up the offer of a place at university, among other issues.

Counsellor: *If I were to ask you what the most important implication is for you on receiving this news from the doctor, what might you say?*

Patient: *Going to university. I'm not going to university in a wheelchair. I might as well go for something different. Maybe weave baskets at home for the rest of my life.*

Counsellor: *I can understand how difficult it must be for you now to think about going to university and not being able to walk around freely as you once imagined you would do. How might it be for you, say, in five years from now, looking back, if you had decided not to go to university?*

Patient: *Sometimes I can't even think five minutes ahead, let alone five years. Maybe there would be some regret, though. I've still got my mind and that's as sharp as ever.*

Counsellor: *Yes, you do have that. How far ahead do you think you need to plan for?*

Patient: *Sometimes I have no idea. It depends on what a situation is like. If I was at university and it all worked out, then I could think about a future there. Maybe I need to try it out first.*

Counsellor: *Perhaps. And maybe that's something we could look at, and also talk about what it might be like in a wheelchair on campus.*

Patient: *Yeah. And some days when I'm feeling down I just don't even want to think about all these hassles.*

8   To place responsibility for problem-solving with those who define the problem.

Patient: *This is the worst decision I've ever had to make. The*

> *one doctor says there's a one in five chance that the baby will be born with a deformity. The other says the scan is 'inconclusive'. And now I've got only a week to decide whether to terminate the pregnancy.*

Counsellor: *That's an incredibly difficulty decision for anyone. Is there anything that would help you in reaching a decision?*

Patient: *If you made it for me! I don't want the responsibility either way.*

Counsellor: *I can understand that it might feel easier if someone else takes the responsibility. Is there anyone else you can discuss this with?*

Patient: *My boyfriend. But he's impossible. Doesn't care and would simply say 'do as you like'. Great source of support he's likely to be even as a father! Actually, I'm not prepared to take that sort of shit from him. He'll have to talk it through with me! It's about time he took some responsibility.*

9 To examine with the patient the impact of the problem on other relationships.

Patient: *I can't possibly tell my parents about the breast lump, they're old; it'll kill them.*

Counsellor: *If you weren't to tell them and something happened to you, how do you think it would affect them?*

Patient: *They would be equally as devastated. You see, I'm the youngest of the children. I've always had a special caring role in the family. Had it been my brother or sister, it would have been less of a problem. They're married. I'm not. The expectation is that one day I will take care of my parents. Not the other way around.*

Counsellor: *If your brother and sister were here today and had heard what you had just said, what do you think would go through their minds?*

Patient: *My sister would disagree because she's also very close to our parents. She would probably tell me I should tell our parents. She would say that they are stronger than we all imagine them to be. After all, my mom lost a*

> *sister during the war, and my father's first wife died in a*
> *car accident. I just hate it when everyone at home is*
> *emotional and cries. Perhaps telling them that it's a*
> *lump is not the same as saying 'It's cancer and I'm*
> *dying'.*
> Counsellor: *Maybe it's easier to take it one step at a time and to tell*
> *them about the lump and say that tests are being carried*
> *out to find out more about the lump.*
> Patient: *I'll think about it.*

10 To help a psychologically vulnerable person to cope with additional
stresses, thereby possibly preventing the development of major
psychological problems. This may engender addressing fears of death
and dying.

A patient became very depressed after being told by his doctor that he
would need to undergo heart bypass surgery. He was withdrawn,
stopped going to work, said little to his family and friends and could
not make up his mind whether to have the operation even though he
would probably die if he did not have it. He was referred to a counsellor and it appeared that his fear of dying had metaphorically immobilized him, preventing him from making any decisions. While the
doctors and his family had understandably tried to discourage him, no
one, it seems, discussed with him what might happen if he were not to
recover or he were to die. Once he had been able to talk about his fear
of dying and his worries about loss and how others in the family might
cope, he resumed his medical appointments. He soon reported that the
atmosphere at home had improved. Although he did not return to
work, he agreed to have the operation. He decided to spend the three
weeks before the operation with the family, 'in case things don't work
out'. The operation was a success and, in retrospect, he mentioned to
the counsellor that he was pleased that he had tried to prepare himself
and the family for the worst.

11 To help patients deal with unpredictability. A patient's concern about
unpredictability may be reflected in questions such as: 'Why should I
carry on?' 'How should I carry on?' 'How will the illness progress?'

(This example is based on an excerpt from a counselling session with
the patient with cardiac problems described above.)

Patient:	*What happens if the operation is not successful?*
Counsellor:	*I understand your concern about what could happen. What worries you most about what could happen?*
Patient:	*Maybe that I'd die.*
Counsellor:	*What would you most want to do if you knew that you might die, for whatever reason?*
Patient:	*Spend some time with my wife and children.*
Counsellor:	*I know that you have discussed these concerns with the doctor and that he told you that, although the risks are small, there is some risk. Is there anything that prevents you from spending time with them now?*
Patient:	*Not really, other than I get a bit morose and they always try to cheer me up. It cuts both ways; if I don't spend time with them I'm not preparing for the worst; if I do, they can annoy me with their cheeriness!*
Counsellor:	*Difficult decisions, I agree.*
Patient:	*I don't like uncertainty in my life. But it looks as if I should spend time with them. At least I would have done what they most would want me to do.*

12 To view medical problems as the entrée to other problems, such as relationship difficulties. Health care problems need not necessarily be the main or the most enduring difficulty for patients. How people cope with and adjust to medical problems may sometimes be viewed as a symptom of other problems.

A young man treated for a brain tumour found that he had become dependent on his family for support and care. He had always been strong-willed to the extent of sometimes defying his parents' wishes in order to assert his need for separateness from them. His illness and period of convalescence resulted in his becoming dependent on them. The family sought counselling to help address past patterns in relationships and the new circumstances. His parents felt uncertain as to how to care for their son and the patient in turn resented having to depend on his parents.

13 To help the patient maintain realistic hope and to affirm his coping abilities. This may entail examining whether there have been any positive changes in the patient's life resulting from misfortune or illness.

Counsellor: We have spent a lot of time looking at the difficulties you have experienced in many different areas of your life since the road traffic accident. This may seem a strange or insensitive question, but I was also wondering whether anything good has come of this?

Patient: Definitely. Yes. I now live life from day-to-day. I don't let little things get me down. I've got my priorities sorted out.

14 To normalize the views, feelings and experience of the patient, as this can help reduce a sense of isolation, exclusion and difference.

Patient: It feels so empty without my wife. Some nights I cry myself to sleep. I also think she could have been treated sooner had she told me about the lump.

Counsellor: It must be very hard for you after all these years. I am not surprised to hear that you feel lonely without your wife and that you miss her. That is normal. Sometimes it's easier to think how things could have been different when looking back afterwards.

15 To help the patient to engage with carers (family, friends and others), if this is what he desires, and at the same time to prevent health care professionals, who may feel compelled to 'mother' patients, from crossing professional boundaries. Failure to address this can lead to overdependence on staff and feelings of burnout. Supervision can help to recognize these boundaries, thereby increasing professional competence.

Patient: It feels so good when I come here for counselling. I feel safe and can save up all my feelings to talk about them here.

Counsellor: Apart from our sessions, where else do you feel supported and safe?`

Patient: With a few good friends, but we don't talk about my illness.

Counsellor: To whom do you feel closest?

Patient: My mother. But I wouldn't want to burden her with some of the 'heavy' feelings, like when I'm down.

Counsellor: If you were to share these feelings, do you think the two of you might get closer or become more distant?

Patient: *Closer. Definitely. But then I wouldn't need to come here as much!*

CONCLUSION

The therapeutic objectives described in this chapter consolidate a number of possible leads that counsellors can follow in order to identify and address patients' problems. Ill health can put severe stress on relationships as people face having to make significant choices, and may simultaneously experience a sense of diminished options. Throughout our lives, we are confronted with numerous situations where communication is difficult; and the process of communicating with a person who is distressed, unwell or even dying may be the most difficult of all. The barriers to effective communication affect not only the patient, but also the family, partner, friends and health care providers, each of whom may experience problems in communicating with the patient and with one another.

The complexity and unpredictability of different illnesses do not always allow for permanent solutions to be provided. Therefore, the counsellor may attempt, wherever possible, to introduce and create alternative views of the problem. The objectives of counselling are to bring out and define the problem, and become aware of the subsystems to be addressed in attempting to resolve the problems. Although it may be tempting to see the patient at regular intervals and throughout the duration of ill health, sometimes the patient's needs are best served by having contact only as the need arises, and by keeping an 'open door' in the counselling relationship.

Many different themes and beliefs emerge and recur when working with patients within health care settings. These include secrecy, uncertainty, dealing with threatened or actual loss, coping with reduced choices, a sense of shame, having to make many important decisions, fear of not coping and diminished autonomy, among others. It is probable that at some stage in the counselling process, one or more of these problems will arise. The main task and challenge to the counsellor is to help the patient and others to find an alternative view of the problem and to generate new solutions in what may be a brief or focused period of counselling. This can only be attempted and, one hopes, achieved in the context of an engaged relationship with the patient.

Chapter 6

Exploring and Defining Problems in Counselling

INTRODUCTION

The counsellor should consider from the outset of a new referral three main issues. These are:

- What is the psychological problem, if any; and what is the context in which this problem occurs? Who is most affected by the problem, and therefore who is it best to work with – the patient, or her relatives? Is a consultation with a professional colleague also likely to be of benefit? Is this a problem that can possibly be solved through counselling? Are there any contraindications to seeing the patient for counselling?
- What 'form' or approach to counselling should be taken? Consideration needs to be given to how the problem is described, current clinical practice guidelines, evidence supporting particular interventions over others and the setting in which the counsellor works. The approach may also need to be adapted as the problem changes during the course of counselling. Furthermore, the counsellor must decide whether a one-off assessment or consultation session is preferable to ongoing or intermittent contact with the patient.
- Who is best placed to provide counselling? The counsellor, nurse counsellor or other health care professional, inside or outside the health care setting?

Counselling should address the patient's defined concerns from the start of counselling sessions in order to build rapport, convey empathy and use the time effectively. Failure to address the main concerns early in the contact with the patient may inhibit the development of a therapeutic relationship. It is important to note that some patients may be reluctant to talk about psychological problems with their GP out of a fear that this will then be on their medical record and could affect future employment or insurance applications. For this reason, psychological problems may initially be presented as physical health problems. The counsellor should at all times be aware of patients' fear of the stigma attached to some conditions, which may make it difficult for them to be completely frank about their problems.

Counselling should cover a wide range of issues and concerns in the initial session, because: (a) the patient may recover, be discharged from hospital, deteriorate or even die before the cause of her concerns has been addressed; (b) opportunities to cope with problems or adjust to new circumstances may be lost and prove detrimental to the well-being of the patient and her family; and (c) the patient may wonder whether counselling can be of any benefit. A situation may arise in the counselling relationship in which the patient's main concerns and fears are never discussed. This may be the result of counsellor–patient 'collusion', which can take the following forms:

1   The patient is referred to a counsellor but is frightened to talk about her fears.
2   The counsellor 'respects' the patient's pace in counselling and senses that the patient 'is not yet ready' to talk about her fears.
3   The patient interprets the counsellor's reluctance to discuss fears as a signal that the counsellor has concerns about this. The patient does not want to 'upset' the counsellor, who seems friendly and kind.
4   The counsellor believes that avoidance of the issue of concerns and fears is a measure or sign of the patient's defences – which should be respected.

The importance of identifying and clarifying the patient's main problems has already been stressed. Exploring the patient's problems is an acquired skill. This task is made more complex when the problem relates to the patient's physical health. However, the converse is also true; and some patients fear psychological problems more than medical ones because of the associated stigma. The following section describes how to explore, define and address patients' problems.

FRAMEWORK FOR DEFINING PROBLEMS

The counsellor first needs to understand certain key issues about the patient's medical problem and personal circumstances in order to gain a clearer view of the nature of the problem. These issues relate to three frames that help to conceptualize problems within a psychological or psychotherapeutic framework, including knowledge about:

- *The medical or psychological condition,* its consequences and likely outcome.
- *The psychological effects* on the individual, couple or family of having the problem.
- *The context or setting* in which treatment, care and counselling are provided.

The problem is often defined initially by a medical term or a diagnostic label (for example, coronary heart disease, multiple sclerosis, a fracture). The counsellor needs also to consider the psychological implications of illness and contextual issues (for example, hospital, clinic, private practice); combined, these create a definition of the problem. We can illustrate the frames as follows:

The medical definition of the problem

Typology of illness

- Acute versus chronic.
- Life-threatening versus non-life-threatening.
- Stable versus degenerative, progressive, remitting.
- Contagious versus non-contagious.
- Inherited versus acquired.

Knowledge about treatment

- Is there an effective treatment?
- What does the treatment entail?

■ Is it curative, palliative symptomatically, short-term, long-term?

■ Is much known about this condition?

■ Is there much uncertainty?

The changing nature of health and illness

■ Advent of new illnesses, such as HIV disease in the 1980s.

■ Advances in medicine leading to different and/or more effective tests and treatments, with some conditions no longer being life-threatening.

■ An outbreak of a transmissible infection exacerbated by social conditions, such as viral haemorrhagic fever or MRSA, resulting in the rapid spread of infection.

■ Changes in the treatment of certain conditions, including greater use of day surgery or a shift in care from hospital to primary care.

■ More widespread early detection (genetic screening) for some conditions.

■ Limitations (rationing) being placed on the provision of health care.

■ Changes in the context of treatment (for example, the patient moving between NHS and private health care, or between the GP and the hospital specialist service).

Provision of care

■ Is treatment and/or care provided within a primary, secondary or tertiary health facility, or through private health care?

■ Will care require liaison between different doctors or carers?

■ Will treatment require frequent visits to the doctor or will it be home-based care?

The psychological definition of the problem

Developmental issues

■ What developmental stage has the person reached (for example, infant, child, adolescent, adult)?

■ At what stage of development is the person in relation to their family (for example, at home and dependent, left home, divorced, children left home)?

■ What effect does this illness have on this person in the context of their lifestyle and developmental issues?

Psychological issues

■   What is the patient's emotional and mental state?
■   What are the main concerns?
■   What dynamics are driving these concerns (for example, too much uncertainty, too little information about the diagnosis and prognosis, fear of loss)?
■   What losses are the patient and family facing?
■   How are they coping with loss or anticipatory loss?
■   What relationship and attachment issues are relevant?

The context of the problem

The problem presented is related to *the family system or cultural background of the patient*; for example:

■   A doctor refers a 'non-compliant' patient to a counsellor because the patient's family are against the patient taking prescribed medication.

The problem presented is related to *other systems with which the patient has contact*; for example:

■   A patient is required to undergo a pre-employment medical examination but is concerned that it will be discovered that she has had hepatitis B, and suspect that she may be an intravenous drug user or have acquired the infection through sexual contact. She seeks advice from a counsellor in a GP practice.

The problem presented is related to *other therapeutic systems with which the patient maintains contact*; for example:

■   A nurse with mental health experience on placement on an oncology ward thinks that a depressed patient 'is denying her illness and needs to work through her unresolved feelings towards her mother in order to come to terms with dying'.

The problem presented is related to the *system within which the counsellor works*; for example:

■   A doctor refers a patient to a counsellor 'to help the patient with her feelings'. In the course of counselling, it becomes evident that the patient feels confused about her care. She is being given treatment for her cancer, but no one discusses the prognosis with her. It seems that the medical team find it difficult to tell her that her condition is becoming untreatable.

These frames for exploring and defining the problem are useful for understanding the nature of the patient's problem. This can be further clarified by the counsellor asking some of the following questions of himself:

■ What is the problem?
■ For whom is this problem most a problem?
■ How does this problem present?
■ Is this a problem that can be dealt with by a counsellor, or should the patient be referred to another specialist?
■ Why is the patient talking about it now?
■ How does this problem affect the patient emotionally and physically?
■ Who else should be involved in the patient's psychological treatment and care?

Patients will sometimes describe a catalogue of problems to the counsellor in a single session. This is understandable, because the effects of illness may be complex and multi-faceted. Some problems may stem from inadequate information about the medical condition, the reason for specific laboratory tests being carried out and uncertainty about the prognosis. Concerns about how family and friends may cope during the period of illness or disability often present as practical issues such as loss of income or inadequate housing.

The counsellor's choice of words and use of language is important, and complex issues may need to be simplified in order to be meaningful to patients. Using language that fits with that of the patient and checking that the meanings of words used are understood may prevent misunderstandings, or assumptions being made. Anxiety, for example, is frequently expressed by patients in general and non-specific terms. Counsellors may find it useful to help the patient convey how he feels by asking him to describe behaviours. It is easier to consider therapeutic approaches for dealing with behaviours rather than categories of feelings such as 'depression' and 'despair' and diagnostic labels such as 'borderline personality disorder'. The following example illustrates how this can be done:

Counsellor:	*Can you say something about what it felt like when you went home from the hospital after you were given the test results?*
Patient:	*I felt really depressed.*
Counsellor:	*When you were depressed, how did that show? And how did it feel?*
Patient:	*I went quiet. I slowed down . . . like I switched off and curled up inside. I also sighed a lot.*
Counsellor:	*What ideas come to mind when you're slowing down, switching off, curling up and sighing?*
Patient:	*I suppose I wanted to be alone. I'm not sure that there are any ideas in particular.*
Counsellor:	*OK. What effect did that have on people around you when you needed to be alone?*
Patient:	*That's when things get even more difficult. My husband can't deal with my need to be alone. He's very kind and wants to help, but he keeps asking if there is anything he can do. That drives me mad.*
Counsellor:	*If you were to tell him that you needed some space, how might he react?*
Patient:	*You mean over-react! The last time I told him that, he started thinking that I didn't love him anymore. The tension that followed for weeks just wasn't worth it. So now I just don't tell him I need space.*
Counsellor:	*Can you think of a way of saying it to him without him over-reacting?*
Patient:	*I could start the conversation by assuring him that there is nothing wrong with the relationship. Then I could explain to him what I mean by 'space' and how long I may need, to give him some idea of what's going on in my head.*
Counsellor:	*That sounds a good way to start the conversation. Perhaps you could try that the next time. Let's go back to the day of the test results . . .*

It is useful for the counsellor to keep in mind a number of levels of problem definition that can be explored with the patient. The counsellor can explore the recursive link between ideas or statements, behaviours, relationships and beliefs in any order. This is consistent with humanistic, cognitive behavioural and systemic approaches. Figure 6.1 illustrates these different levels, and the recursive link between them.

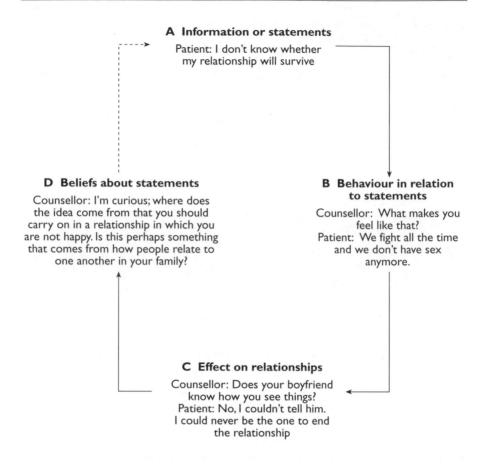

Figure 6.1 Establishing links between ideas, statements, relationships and beliefs

SHOWING UNDERSTANDING OF THE PATIENT'S PROBLEMS

Patients seeking help want to feel they are being understood by the professionals who counsel them. To do this, the counsellor may nod from time to time or reflect on what has been said. A strong confirmation to the patient that he or she has been heard is to use the patient's own words to form the next question or intervention, as in the example above. The framework illustrated in Figure 6.2 can be used for exploring the problem therapeutically.

SHOW EMPATHY
- Respect the patient's views and ideas.
- Do not invalidate or disqualify what the patient says.
- Use the patient's words and language in your conversation with him or her.
- Avoid making any assumptions.

VALIDATE
- Use cooperative and non-confrontational language.
- Try to convey that you are trying to understand her story from her point of view by directly soliciting this from the patient.

AMPLIFY
- Talk about the problem that the patient brings to counselling.
- Take care not to digress from this until that particular problem has been identified, reduced or solved, or a new problem becomes more pressing.

ADD COMPLEXITY
- Adopt a stance of curiosity (that is, not knowing) and ask questions of the patient. The answers to questions can lead to further questions. Sometimes, just hearing the question can stimulate new ideas for the patient.
- Complexity can be added by asking questions that expand or narrow the field, or both.

SIMPLIFY
- Complex ideas should be simplified. This intervention helps to give a new frame or perspective to the problem.

REFRAME
- Give new meaning to ideas and problems without disqualifying the patient's distress.
- Tentatively offer another perspective on a problem.
- Help the patient to view the problem differently.

ELICIT FEEDBACK
- Check with the patient whether you have understood the problem correctly.
- Ask for feedback as to whether you are addressing the patient's concerns.

MAINTAIN AN OVERVIEW
- Maintain an overview of the counselling process and a clear definition of the problem but avoid trying to make the patient's problem fit into some previously conceived theory about psychopathology.

Figure 6.2   Framework for therapeutic exploration of a problem

Problems for the patient change during the course of illness. At the pre-diagnosis phase, there may be anticipatory anxiety. During an asymptomatic phase, the patient may have to cope with uncertainty as to if or when symptoms may occur or recur. Later, the patient may have to adjust to new and unwelcome circumstances when symptoms of disease prevent her from working or engaging in family life as she used to.

The way in which patients view their illness or disability as a problem will in part be a response to how others view it. A person who has suffered a brain injury may find that the stigma attached to this is as severe as the problem itself. In other words, there may be times when the social implications are as pressing, or even more so, than the medical ones. There is a reciprocal and circular relationship between the problem and its context. One or both may change at any moment in relation to the other. The problem may therefore change from session to session, sometimes even within a counselling session. In health care, there are sometimes rapid changes and advances in approaches to treatment and care. The counsellor needs to be flexible in his working practice to accommodate these changes and the ripple effect they may have on the patient and her family. In one session, the counsellor may be discussing the patient's fear of undergoing an MRI (magnetic resonance imaging) scan, but in the next session, they may be talking about the possibility of the patient having to undergo major surgery.

With whose problem is the counsellor dealing?

The patient is just one part of the system with which the counsellor works. Invariably there are other systems, including members of the health care team and the support network of the patient. The immediate task is to obtain a definition of the specific problem and to try to identify for whom this is a problem. The patient's partner, a family member or someone in the health care team could all be affected, though each may have a different view of the problem and what should be done about it. The redefinition of the problem can start at the beginning of the session by exploring different people's views. For example:

Counsellor: Mrs Davis, what do you think is your husband's main concern?
Mrs Davis: I'm not sure, but I think that it may be that Tanya could die.

Counsellor:	*Mr Davis, what do you feel about what you heard your wife say?*
Mr Davis:	*I do worry about that, but my main worry now is how we will cope as a family during her illness. We're all very stressed and upset.*
Counsellor:	*Mrs Davis, were you aware that this was your husband's main worry?*
Mrs Davis:	*Yes, but surprisingly I find it easier to think about Tanya dying than her being ill for a long time.*

When the apparent solution becomes part of the problem

It is important to examine other sources of problems in counselling. In some cases, the referring person may create a new view of the problem in the light of his professional opinion, which might even exacerbate the problem. A man who has recently been discharged from hospital after being treated for leukaemia may, for example, be referred to a counsellor in a GP setting by a practice nurse who is concerned about the patient because he keeps checking his body for signs of skin problems – a possible side-effect of having to take immunosuppressive drugs. In addressing the problem, one task of the counsellor is to consider and discuss the nurse's concerns and beliefs about the patient and his 'obsessional' behaviour.

For any problem to exist, it must first be defined by someone as a problem. If others do not agree with the definition, the lack of consensus over problem definition becomes an additional problem. Many counsellors have the experience and expertise to assess psychological problems with a patient, where these exist. In no way wanting to minimize the patient's distress or close the door on a patient, the counsellor is also required to say when, in his opinion, there does not appear to be a definable psychological problem. In such a scenario, the patient and counsellor might meet for explorative work as opposed to focused or outcome-orientated therapeutic work. This can be illustrated by two statements of professional opinion: 'From what I have heard, I do not feel that this is an issue for which counselling is indicated, and I'm not sure that there is any further need for meetings unless there are other issues you would like us to discuss.' This conveys an entirely different message from 'This seems a very serious problem and we should meet on a regular basis for several months.'

A professional makes explicit or implies something about the *nature* of the problem when he makes a referral. The referrer may, for example, mention that the patient is 'depressed'. At the same time, a view is conveyed about *the person for whom this is a problem,* be it the patient, a family member or a member of the health care team. The referrer may also indicate *what should be done about the problem.* If the referrer suggests, for example, that a patient sees a psychiatrist, the message may be conveyed that there is an organic or biochemical basis to the behaviour; whereas, if the referral is made to a psychotherapist, there could be a belief that there were problems in the early development of that person, or extreme anxiety about the illness. No referral is therefore a completely neutral gesture. Some consensus about the problem between referrers and counsellors is needed in order to ensure that patients are managed satisfactorily. The case example below illustrates how lack of consensus was a problem with a patient in a GP practice, and how similar problems can be resolved. In this example, the attempted solution becomes a problem.

Case Study

Stephen, a 52-year-old man, recently had a heart attack. He did not have a history of heart disease and had had a reasonably healthy lifestyle. He was transferred from a cardiac intensive care unit to a general medical ward before being sent home to convalesce, where he was cared for by his GP. The practice counsellor had seen Stephen's wife soon after he was admitted because she was worried about what things would be like when he was back at home. She was concerned that he would want to go back to work too soon, and that she would constantly worry that he might suffer another heart attack and die. The couple were seen together by the practice counsellor shortly after Stephen was discharged from hospital.

After they had seen the GP for a check-up, Stephen asked to see the counsellor on his own. Stephen walked in, sat down and said to the counsellor: 'Doctor Mundy says that I should see a psychiatrist.' Apparently, Stephen had told the GP that he had become impotent and felt depressed. Although he wanted help, Stephen now felt that his problem was very serious. He had never seen a psychiatrist before and became very anxious at the suggestion, made without any explanation as to how a psychiatric assessment and treatment could be of help. Furthermore, he had read that these were common symptoms in men recovering from a heart attack and was somewhat reassured by this.

This situation presented the counsellor with a dilemma. On the one hand, the counsellor agreed that the patient's symptoms of depression and impotence could be related to his medical condition and treatment. But on the other hand, the patient agreed that he was depressed but did not want to take up a referral to a psychiatrist as he believed that this would compound his problems.

This case illustrates that it can be helpful to ask patients how they think some of their problems might best be solved before offering what may seem to be the right or best solution. There are several options for the counsellor in the above example. The counsellor might agree with the view of the GP and suggest that it is a good idea for the patient to be referred to a psychiatrist. A second option might be to delay offering treatment until the patient has been assessed by a psychiatrist, and then to do so in collaboration with the psychiatrist. A third option might be for the counsellor to disagree with the GP about the need for a referral to a psychiatrist. However, this might put the counsellor in conflict with his medical colleagues, which might also have serious consequences for the patient.

The counsellor might go back to the GP: 'Having spoken to Stephen today, there seem to be some issues that we need to discuss. How do you think the patient's psychological problems should best be managed? Later on in the discussion, the counsellor might also ask: 'If the patient were to see a psychiatrist, how do you think this might affect her view of herself at this stage?', and 'How do you see the work of a counsellor in relation to that of a psychiatrist with such a patient?' By asking questions such as these, it is possible to begin to examine the options open to the professionals, and the potential consequences of each option.

The counsellor may feel that the patient is coping despite her unhappiness. The GP may want the patient attended to by someone else because of his busy clinic, and suggests that the patient sees a psychiatrist in order to pass on the responsibility for assessing and managing the patient's anxiety and depression. On the other hand, the patient may express feelings of unhappiness but be content not to do anything significant to change the situation. The psychiatrist in turn may be faced with a 'resistant' patient rather than one who is depressed. It may be that the lack of consensus over the nature of problems and how they should be dealt with can lead to unforeseen difficulties in the management of the patient. These differences between professionals must be resolved first.

Problems arising from failing to define problems properly

Lack of agreement over the definition of a patient's problem, or about not consulting the patient about the referral, or indeed, over the purpose of referring a patient for counselling, can lead to additional difficulties for the counsellor, the patient and the referrer. Experience shows that those problems that can occur include the patient not keeping appointments; the patient 'resisting' counselling; the patient's problem becoming worse than it already was; conflict between the referrer and counsellor; and referrals being made at a time when little counselling can be done with the patient.

Whenever problems like these arise in the course of counselling, the counsellor should look beyond counsellor–patient interaction to the wider system for some understanding of what is happening. He may also look to the wider caring system, including the family and other professional carers, to determine whether different views or beliefs about treatment and care are at the root of the problem.

Problems in counselling relating to the experience of the counsellor

The practice of skilled professional counselling requires many years of supervised training and experience. All counsellors are expected to seek supervision or to refer cases that are beyond their competence, irrespective of their level of experience. Supervision provides an opportunity for support and professional growth. In some cases, barriers within the counsellor himself may stand in the way of progress in the course of counselling. This might stem from inadequate theoretical ideas, or a lack of therapeutic skills. A personal difficulty with particular issues or processes in counselling can impede the exploration or resolution of problems. A drive or mission to make people feel better, for example, may result in repetitive cycles of emotional 'first aid', which may not help patients to deal with anxieties about illness or death. Where the counsellor feels that the problem has become too difficult to deal with, there is a danger that he might become 'infected' with similar emotional problems as those of the patient unless more experienced help is sought.

CONCLUSION

The counsellor's task in exploring the patient's problems includes providing the physical and emotional setting and information that will help patients to make their own decisions. Decisions can be made and emotional growth sustained even in the face of serious psychological and medical problems. Patients can also be helped to examine difficulties before they become major problems, placing medical counselling in the domain of preventive medicine. By enabling patients to clarify their concerns, it is possible to begin to reframe them by asking questions that seek to place problems in context. Effective counselling depends on a clear definition of the problem. This guides the counsellor in his task and helps to determine when the problem has been solved or become more manageable.

Chapter 7

The Structure of the Counselling Session

INTRODUCTION

This chapter focuses on translating some of the theoretical ideas described in the book into counselling practice. Effective counselling about (or related to) medical problems needs clarity of purpose. To help achieve this clarity, a framework is described below that includes the principles and aims of the counselling. Having a 'map' or structure for the session can make it easier to achieve the tasks in any given time. This map can lead to:

- A better use of counselling sessions.
- Fewer misunderstandings about how counselling can help.
- Greater patient competence in dealing with distress.
- Increased patient satisfaction with the process of counselling.
- A clearer set of criteria against which the efficacy of counselling can be evaluated.

A salient feature of the approach to counselling described here is the *structure* of the counselling session, which helps to ensure that important issues are addressed in the context of busy medical settings (Quick, 1996) through a map of therapeutic practice.

USE OF QUESTIONS

The flow of conversation is guided by questions that facilitate the process of conversation between patient and counsellor, and provide a structure to the session.

Questions can:

- Help to keep a focus.
- Explore ideas or hypotheses.
- Avoid making assumptions about patient concerns, beliefs and problems, or perceptions of these.
- Identify knowledge, concerns, wishes and beliefs.
- Rank those concerns and wishes.
- Help people to be specific by clarifying the meaning of what is said; for example:

> 'You say you are depressed. Can you say more about that? How does it show?'
>
> 'Help me to understand what that is like for you?'

- Link people with ideas and other people they had not previously considered:

> 'If you don't tell your wife about the medication how will you manage to take it?'

- Address and inform about unfamiliar and sensitive issues, for example:

> 'When you say you are frightened of death, what is it about death that frightens you the most?'

Different types of questions are a cornerstone of a systemic focused approach (Tomm, 1987a, 1987b).

Linear questions usually lead to 'yes' or 'no' answers. Under some circumstances their use is appropriate, but they do not readily open up ideas for discussion. For example:

> 'Do you agree with the doctor that you should have this test?'

Those that show a *difference* between the present, past and future help people to make connections over time. For example:

> 'How have you coped with difficult decisions in the past?'
>
> 'What might help you to manage things in the future, and how might you cope right now?'

Hypothetical, future-orientated questions address future possible concerns, and also help to explore perceptions of others by linking ideas that might not otherwise have been considered. They are useful in helping people to address difficulties and prepare for the future, while the reality of these situations is some distance away. For example:

> 'If you were to become ill what might be your main concern? '
>
> 'Who or what would help most, or who or what might make it more difficult in relation to your concern?'

Circular questions link ideas, beliefs and relationships in a way that helps people to view problems from different perspectives or reference points. For example:

> 'What do you think your wife might most want to discuss today?'
>
> 'Would it be the same as you would choose, or something different?'
>
> 'Where did you get the idea that you always have to take the opposite stance to your wife?'

Reflective questions help to reframe problems, enable the counsellor to gain time and allow the patient to glimpse another perspective. For example:

> 'So maybe you see yourself as protecting your wife by not telling her that you are here today?'

GUIDING PRINCIPLES FOR FOCUSED COUNSELLING

Guiding principles form a theoretical background to psychotherapeutic practice and help to focus on the tasks. They include:

- Recognizing that there are different theoretical approaches that can be used. Some may be more relevant and applicable than others in health care and other settings where time is limited.
- Avoiding making assumptions about patients' knowledge, concerns, beliefs, possible reactions or views about their treatment, care or their approach to life.
- Having small, achievable goals, overall and for each session. This increases the likelihood of the counsellor or other health care professional and the patient agreeing about which issues are being dealt with and whether progress is being made.
- Using language carefully, as everything said during a session and in interactions with patients has an impact and may alter perceptions and responses.
- Accepting that patients cannot be reassured completely about a large number of issues, even though certainty and reassurance may be sought from the counsellor or other health care professional (in particular, from nurses).
- Being realistic about the patient's medical condition and what can be achieved from a medical and counselling point of view.
- Seeking regular consultation and supervision to enhance skills, avoid burnout, audit practice and determine effectiveness.

PRACTICE GUIDELINES

Having a check-list with a limited agenda for the first counselling session can help to keep a focus, especially in settings where patients:

- Are likely to have high levels of emotional intensity or distress;

- Are unfamiliar with counselling and therapeutic processes;
- Might have a diminished capacity to participate in counselling because of the effects of illness, treatment or the constraints of the setting;
- Are likely to have multiple or complex issues that may need to be discussed;
- May have only been offered a single, one-off session, or may be unwilling or unable to attend follow-up meetings.

The counsellor's check-list

1 *Discuss the referral,* including
   - ideas and perceptions about being seen by a counsellor;
   - issues about confidentiality;
   - special issues pertaining to the setting (will the patient be in bed; in an open ward; can the patient talk easily; is the patient in pain; is the patient likely to have visitors or other interruptions?) and how these will be managed.

2 *Aim to obtain sufficient information* to understand how the patient is affected by the condition and treatment, by
   - focusing initially on the story of the illness, the medical problems it presents and its consequences;
   - considering where the patient is in their 'life cycle' and the natural history of the illness;
   - identifying any critical events;
   - refraining from passing any opinion, giving a diagnosis or suggesting any treatment.

3 *Address the impact of the illness* on the patient and family, and how different relationships are affected. Use a genogram or family tree to:
   - obtain a map of family composition and relationships;
   - note life-cycle, developmental and medical issues that may be relevant to the patient and those close to him.

4 *Explore the patient's beliefs and wishes* about the illness, treatment, care and coping strategies.

5 *Address the patient's main fears and concerns.*

6   *Consider past strategies* for coping in order to address earlier adverse experiences with a view to identifying how the patient coped, develop ideas for managing current problems and discuss a treatment plan if appropriate.

7   *Facilitate discussion about the patient's relationships* with members of the health care team and identify potential problems. Discuss what should be fed back to other members of the team.

8   *Invite the patient to give feedback* about the session by finding out what was helpful, anything that was emotionally painful or difficult, and any ideas he has for further discussion.

9   *Provide a summary* of what was covered in the session, and highlight what might, and what cannot, be done in areas where problems have been identified.

10 *Arrange for future follow-up* and provide contact numbers that are readily accessible, should the patient require help.

The counselling session

The following steps form a 'map' that can usefully guide the interview. Although the illustration below is an example of a first session with the patient, many of the steps are equally applicable to follow-up contacts with patients. They can also be adapted for sessions that are held with more than the patient present (for example, couples or families). As the session develops, the exact order of the steps depends on the flow of conversation, which is guided by questions. The 'map' includes the principles, aims, skills and techniques that are woven into each step of the session (Bor *et al.*, 2004).

Think first before the start of each session, in order to anticipate issues and problems for each patient. Traditional approaches to counselling define the start of the counselling process as the first meeting between the counsellor (or other health care professional) and the patient. The systemic approach recognizes that this process begins when a referral is being considered or discussed (Selvini Palazzoli *et al.*, 1980b). An *hypothesis* is made about the impact of health problems and other related issues on the patient and his relationships, taking into account the stage of the medical condition, the stage of life of the patient, the patient's social, cultural and medical context, and the referral.

Introduce the session by clarifying:

- Who you are;
- Where you work;
- Your task in relation to the patient;
- The purpose of the meeting;
- The time available.

(This procedure should be followed, apart from introductions and location, in subsequent sessions.)

Engage the patient (build rapport) by asking questions to gain information rapidly about expectations; for example, who is the patient's support, and what types of difficulties might arise. This helps to settle the patient and focus the discussion on:

- What the patient understands about the meeting;
- What the patient wants to achieve, and his expectations for the session;
- Who else knows about the illness or that the patient is having counselling;
- Whether there is anyone he might want to be made aware of his illness or problems;
- Those areas in which the patient feels he is managing well.

Give a focus to the session by setting *small, achievable goals*; for example:

> 'If there was one thing you wanted to achieve from our meeting today, what might it be?'

Elicit and give information throughout the session, in different ways, by exploring the extent of the patient's knowledge about his condition. Sometimes it is the patient who wants information (about symptoms and prognosis). At other times, it is the doctor and/or counsellor who consider that there is information to impart. If the patient's knowledge is first explored through questioning, misinformation can be corrected and the gaps in knowledge can be filled at the patient's pace. It is useful to check what the patient has understood at the end of a period of information-giving.

Counsellor:	*What do you know about diabetes?*
Patient:	*Only a little.*
Counsellor:	*What is the little that you do know?*
Patient:	*I know that sugar is no good and you can have sort of faints.*
Counsellor:	*Where did you get this information?*
Patient:	*There is a man at work who was often ill and they said he had diabetes.*
Counsellor:	*From what you do know, what might be your main concern?*
Patient:	*That I might have to inject myself. I hate needles.*

Identify beliefs about the illness through questions; for example:

> 'What information do you want to be given about the laboratory and other tests that are being done?'
>
> 'Is there anything that you do not want to know?'
>
> 'What is your view about treatment for diabetes?'

(This last question can reveal the patient's beliefs and provides information rapidly about the likelihood of compliance.)

Elicit areas where the patient feels competent and able to manage before focusing on the difficulties, the aim being to help the patient shift his perception from being out of control to regaining some confidence; for example:

> 'You say are feeling very stressed. Are there any aspects of your life that you feel you are managing with less stress right now?'
>
> 'You say that you still manage to concentrate on academic work as a chemical scientist, and that you have confidence in your abilities in teaching this to the students. This seems to me important. I am reflecting, as you tell me this, as to how this confidence might help you at times when you feel a loss of confidence, such as at departmental meetings with colleagues who know less

▐▶

> about your area of work. As I understand it, you are a competent scientist but most of your other colleagues are more involved in organizational and management aspects of the academic curriculum and find speaking out in meetings easier than you do.'
>
> 'Might this idea that we all have different capabilities help to maintain your confidence, especially as you are now taking medication to reduce your embarrassment?'

Identify *the patient's main concerns early* in sessions to enable the most pressing issues to be addressed in the time available:

> 'If the doctors were to find that you *are* infected with hepatitis C, what might be your greatest concern?'

Rank concerns in order of importance or severity. This:

■ Reduces anxiety to manageable proportions;
■ Helps people to be specific;
■ Helps to set small, achievable goals, giving individuals a sense of control.

It is recognized that if problem-solving is applied successfully to one issue, it often highlights and provides insights about ways of tackling other difficulties. For example:

> 'Of all the worries about an uncertain diagnosis, who to tell, whether your wife could be infected, and your financial troubles – which worries you the most, and which is the least worrying today?'

Use language carefully to avoid or reduce misunderstandings. Using people's own words is a technique that:

■ Helps the counsellor, when feeling stuck, to gain time and to enter the patient's world-view:

> 'You say you are depressed all the time. How much of the day is 'all the time'?
>
> 'Is there ever a time when you are not depressed?'

- Builds rapport with the patient, because it confirms that he has been heard, and helps the counsellor to move at the patient's pace:

> 'You say that you feel depressed. How does that affect you?'

- Facilitates the discussion of sensitive or unfamiliar issues; for example:

> 'You say that you fear losing independence. What is it about being dependent that troubles you most?'

Help patients to manage concerns by, for example:

- Reframing problems, enabling patients to consider their predicament differently. This may ultimately help them to cope better on a day-to-day basis, while at the same time being realistic about the nature of the illness, the limitations it imposes on activities and its effect on relationships. For example:

> 'In choosing not to tell your mother, it seems that you are protecting her from hurt and disappointment.'

- Exploring resources available to patients (how they have coped with past difficulties, how they might cope in the future, who is around to help).
- Engaging the wider health care team whenever possible (team discussions; including other team members in interviews with patients and families). This also helps to relieve stress on staff, avoid burnout and increase the range of useful interventions.

Maintain clear boundaries between a professional and a friendship relationship. Enable the session to be therapeutic (the essence of the counselling relationship) by, for example:

■ Always being thoughtful about the impact of what is said and what happens during the session.

■ Maintaining a neutral stance (showing no surprise; asking questions). For example:

> 'You say that you feel like giving up all efforts to take your pills. How do you think that will affect your health?'
>
> 'Have you felt able to discuss this with your doctor?'

■ Sharing responsibilities with patients (concerns about them; diagnoses) and with colleagues (case discussion; specific consultations). For example:

> 'If you do decide to stop the medication, how do you think it might affect your diabetes? Who else do you think knows about your feelings? Is there anyone you think should know?'

Make an assessment towards the end of the session, based on what has been seen and heard, from emotional, social and medical points of view. Those hypothetical, future-orientated questions, which explore how patients might cope and who else is around, are especially useful if suicidal thoughts are raised as an issue.

End the session by summarizing the issues discussed. Ending the session well is as important as the beginning, and includes:

■ Decision-making for both the patient and the counsellor. The patient may have to decide whether or not to come back to the counsellor; whether to undergo tests or to talk again to the doctor; and may have issues to share with his family. The counsellor has to decide whether she is the right person to deal with the counselling; who to discuss the problem with in the future; and the frequency of sessions with the patient. Both the counsellor and patient need to decide on the follow-up, but ultimately the counsellor might have to suggest her own ideas if they differ from those of the patient and might be important to overall care and management. For example:

Counsellor: *What is your view about us meeting again?*
Patient: *I think I would like to meet with you again.*
Counsellor: *When do you think this should be – what interval of time?*
Patient: *In a week, isn't that the usual interval?*
Counsellor: *Well, we can, but from what I have heard you say and how you might manage between now and the results, we could even try 2–3 weeks if you want.*
Patient: *Yes, on reflection, that seems much better to me.*

■ Summarizing what has been seen and heard, focusing both on identified strengths and weaknesses. If emphasis is placed only on the positive aspects of the situation, it will not be realistic and the patient will not be supported effectively. For example:

> 'From what I've heard and seen today you have many worries, but seem to have people you could turn to for help. However, something is stopping you. Maybe you are protecting them. Maybe you are also protecting yourself from feeling dependent or facing up to your changed state of health. It seems that you will know when the time is right to take a move towards getting the support that is most helpful to you, like sharing your test results. Sometimes, knowing that others are there helps when you are adjusting to a new situation.'

■ Indicate what *follow-up* there will be, as this reduces the likelihood of unexpected phone calls or visits. If there is to be an ending and no follow-up, this should also be clarified. Details include:

(i)   Who can be contacted between sessions and how this can be done; and

(ii) Careful consideration must be given to the time between sessions. If patients are seen too frequently, they could be given a message that they cannot manage alone, which in itself undermines a feeling of competence. If the time between sessions is too long, then some helpful aspects from the session may become diffused or lost.

BRIEF, FOCUSED COUNSELLING

Focused counselling skills are valued in busy medical settings because of pressure on time, and because of the nature of many illnesses where symptoms and problems may change rapidly. The briefer the time available, the greater is the focus required to achieve an effective outcome for the patient. A short case example illustrates the main aims and how they can be addressed.

Case Study

A 60-year-old man was being investigated for the cause of extensive bruising. The in-patient haematology team saw him. Prior to the ward round the junior doctor told the team that the patient was extremely anxious. The counsellor recognized that it was important to clarify the patient's main concern and to develop an optimal relationship with him in the shortest possible time. In the following conversation, the counsellor was able to establish a rapid rapport and allow the patient to express his real concern in a few minutes. Doing this in the presence of the whole medical and nursing team was a way of demonstrating effectiveness and passing on skills to other colleagues.

Counsellor: I understand from Dr Black that you have been feeling quite anxious and tearful.
Patient: Yes. Very.
Counsellor: Can you tell us what you are most anxious about?
Patient: I want to be well. All this waiting for the results of the investigations is intolerable.
Counsellor: What is it you are most worried about?
Patient: Cancer. Actually I already feel a little better just having got the word out – said it.
Counsellor: Have you been able to discuss these fears with the doctor?
Patient: No, it would make it too real.

Eliciting and giving information concisely and effectively is also important in brief sessions.

Exploring and addressing main concerns and issues for patients and their contacts helps to get the underlying problems into the open and thus allows a greater understanding of the patient's behaviour. ▐▐▶

> Counsellor: What is your main concern about cancer?
> Patient: Dying, but first having to tell everyone.
> Counsellor: Who are you concerned the most about telling?
> Patient: Well, my wife and family.
> Counsellor: Have you told them about your worry?
> Patient: Not really, but my wife guesses. I find it hard to speak about it.

Developing, with the patient, an appropriate plan and identifying achievable goals helps to lead to some solutions and reduction of anxieties.

> Counsellor: As you will not get these results until next week, how do you think you can manage during this time?
> Patient: It will be hard, but I shall have television and my wife visits. That is not necessarily a help, as I try and not show all my worries.
> Counsellor: Would it be helpful if I came up and saw you, either alone or with your wife?
> Patient: If you could I would like you to meet my wife, as maybe she has some worries also.

The patient was more settled after this discussion and the medical team felt more at ease, as his behaviour was better understood. The patient agreed that the counsellor should come to the ward the next day when he knew his wife would be visiting. It was clarified that the patient would tell his wife that she had been invited to meet with the counsellor to have a chance to discuss any concerns she might have at this time. The option of having a meeting with his wife on that, or another, occasion was left to the patient. Giving him this option seemed to help him feel less worried, and he was more comfortable once a plan had been suggested.

CONCLUSION

Clarity about the principles and aims of counselling can give counsellors the confidence to focus on tasks when dealing with illness and its complex repercussions for patients and their relationships. Having a structure for the session enables the maximum to be achieved in a relatively short period of time. This can help both those who are trained counsellors and those who use counselling skills only as a part of their role.

Psychotherapeutic Skills in Health Care

Chapter 8

Promoting Coping and Resilience in the Patient

INTRODUCTION

Our belief that the 'heart and soul' of therapy is for the counsellor actively to seek out ways to engage effectively and differently with the patient, so that the patient can access her own competence and resilience. This chapter attempts to 'capture' and 'track' the interactional process between counsellor and patient from the beginning to the end of a counselling meeting, whatever the context, whether in primary care or in a hospital ward, and whatever the length of the meeting. It seeks to describe and illustrate relevant and appropriate interventions based on systemic and cognitive models of therapy, and attempts to embed them in the ebb and flow of this interactional process. The interventions themselves can be 'extracted' and utilized, either singly or together, at the discretion of practitioners during the course of their own counselling encounters. However, these interventions contribute to positive therapeutic change only in the context of an engaged and meaningful relationship between counsellor and patient. It is important to note that the quality of therapeutic engagement is not time-dependent. The bustle of the health care setting can often contribute an intensity that fosters engagement if time constraints are worked with positively. This chapter considers the implications for therapeutic practice when the patient is encouraged to be an active participant in the process of therapy

IMPLICATIONS FOR PSYCHOTHERAPEUTIC PRACTICE

To view the patient as one who continues to be resourceful and responsible even if distressed has major implications for the practice of psychotherapy in the health care setting. The very nature of the health care context in which we see patients contributes to prioritizing the problem and its cure, as opposed to seeing the patient as a person. Patients themselves also all too readily succumb to slipping into the role of passivity and inactivity in the presence of the professional. The first task for the counsellor is therefore to find ways that heighten the patient's own awareness of her current coping abilities that continue to exist despite her distress.

STARTING THE MEETING

The patient who is distressed and upset in front of the counsellor is invariably, and at the same time, displaying qualities that are illustrative of endurance, creativity, and decision-making capacities. A helpful belief to espouse is the understanding that a patient is only able to feel grief or pain because she has already experienced or had an alternative vision of life without misery. Allowing the patient to express this grief or distress is initially the most pressing task to be addressed in the counselling process. This is essential work and the traditional starting point of the counselling process. The therapeutic qualities of empathy, unconditional regard and being genuine, as outlined by Rogers in 1951, are as relevant now as then.

An invitation to the patient that may be utilized to begin the counselling conversation is as follows:

> 'What do I need to know about what's happening in your life right now in order to be helpful to you?'

This question challenges the patient to think, to work and to engage in an active way with the counselling conversation from the outset. Patients who are very distressed need to be given the sense that there is time to express how they feel.

The counsellor can continue by attempting to elicit a detailed description of the patient's distress or depression by saying:

> 'Depression means different things to different people. Some people get agitated, move about a lot, cry, or pull the blankets over their heads. What do you do when you feel low?'

Such a direct approach may startle the patient and at the same time help to engage her in the therapeutic process. The idea that she does not have a monopoly on how depression is 'done' may begin to erode the patient's conviction that her misery is complete and absolute. Encouraging the patient to give a detailed description of the problem in terms of behaviour can itself reduce the experience of the problem from seemingly over-whelming proportions to being more manageable. Any sense of the problem being reduced in size can help the patient to gain a sense of control in her situation.

How was the patient coping before the meeting?

Therapeutic opportunity arises from the moment the patient accepts the idea of seeing a counsellor. Research supports the view that once the decision is taken to begin counselling, considerable improvement in the problem or distress often occurs (Miller *et al.*, 1997). To find out how the patient was coping before the meeting is therefore important information for the counsellor to elicit. During the time between the initial contact between the patient and the professional and the first formal meeting, the patient may have tried to reduce the distress or to solve the problem. Whatever level of success (or lack of it) the patient has reached in this regard can be included in the counselling conversation. The following questions may help with this:

> 'How do you feel today in comparison with how you felt when you first made the appointment to see me on the day you got your medical diagnosis?'
>
> 'Has anything happened since then that has changed things for you?'

These questions invite the patient to be reflective. The whole of the patient's current situation and not just her problem is being validated and becomes the focus of enquiry. Time is also being used as a relative measure to elicit details of any changes or differences in the current situation. Changes may well have occurred and these should be acknowledged and explored. The most dramatic result could be that the problem has disappeared completely. If this has happened, we have found from our experience that patients will not necessarily volunteer this information at the beginning of a counselling meeting. They may need prompting to do so. Patients usually have a meeting with a counsellor to discuss 'a problem' and not their ability to cope! The counsellor needs to lead the conversation in such a way that the patient will share the fact that the problem may have diminished and that she may be feeling better. If this is so, the planned counselling may end sooner than anticipated. If the problem has become worse and the patient's situation deteriorated, this should also always be acknowledged.

How is the patient coping currently?

Utilizing the simple and powerful question "What bothers you most in this situation?" (Quick, 1996) helps the patient to organize her thinking about current experiences and may help to access the patient's own expertise. Answers to this question can target the patient's understanding of the problem, and the patient's definition of the problem can frequently surprise the counsellor. It is an invaluable question, as it can contribute to putting the counselling conversation on track and make it relevant – and it may save time too.

From the moment the counsellor encounters the patient, the counsellor needs to be on the alert for signs of coping and resourcefulness. Nothing should escape the counsellor's scrutiny. The fact that the patient presents herself to the counsellor can demonstrate the patient's ability to cope and take control of what is happening to her. If the patient arrives neatly dressed and on time for the appointment, this usually reflects a desire on the part of the patient to do something about her current distress. To make these observations explicit early in the counselling endeavour can have a powerful effect on the patient. The counsellor may chose to say something along the lines of:

> 'It impresses me that you made the decision to come to our meeting, and that you have taken such care over your appearance even here in the ward setting.'

This statement acknowledges the patient's distress; it also creates the context for a conversation where the patient is noticed and spoken to as a person, separate from her pain. Such an attitude introduces the basis of a respectful and collaborative relationship. The patient may benefit by being given a moment to process the above statement, a moment that can serve to slow the patient down and allow a pause. This may be therapeutic in itself. This kind of statement frequently takes the patient by surprise, which can contribute to engagement.

Operating from this stance, the patient can be encouraged to describe anything she is currently doing that relieves or moderates her distress, or that makes her feel less overwhelmed by the problem. The following questions may be useful in this respect:

> 'What do you do that helps to reduce your anxiety?'
>
> 'What have you done to bring about this improvement/change?'
>
> 'How did you learn to do this?'
>
> 'Is this something you've recently learned or have you always been someone who copes?'

These questions may take the patient by surprise, especially if they are asked with deliberateness, respect and with the attitude that what is being asked about already exists. The very certainty of such an approach challenges the patient's fixity of thought. When uncertainty emerges, hope may be generated. Movement usually indicates change. As the patient has probably been experiencing herself as hopeless and deskilled, she is unlikely to recognize or acknowledge any responsibility for the existence of change or improvement. The effect of such questions can be very powerful, as they attempt to highlight and commend the patient's efforts to cope and survive. They imply that attempts to cope already exist. The counsellor may need to encourage the patient in this regard. The following prompts may help to do this:

> 'You've told me that you manage to get yourself into work on time most days despite having to be at the hospital early for your treatment. What do you do that helps you to be on time?'
>
> 'How did you manage to get yourself up in time to come here this morning, given that you've been telling me that you lie late in bed on the days you don't go to work?' ⬛➡

> 'Has the conversation with your friend that you've told me about encouraged you to feel any more positive about your own efforts to work through this situation?'

While recounting her story, the patient will have given the counsellor plenty of material that can be used to construct the type of prompt illustrated above. If the patient responds and engages with these questions, it means that she is beginning to connect with this new version of herself. A sizeable step has been taken in terms of the patient beginning to see herself in a new way if she begins to contribute actively to the list of examples herself. The result of this may be that hope may be engendered in place of hopelessness.

PROGRESSING THE MEETING: ELICITING FURTHER EVIDENCE OF COPING

The initial meeting may be the first time the patient has been invited to recount all that is happening to her, allowing the 'jigsaw' pieces of her life to be put together and make sense of seemingly fragmented and unconnected experiences. During this phase, the counsellor may feel that he is not contributing very much, but in fact essential work is being done. He is validating the patient's distress. The work of counselling can often involve adding complexity to what the patient sees as a 'simple' problem. It is equally true that the work of counselling may at times be simple. Sometimes, the simple recounting of her story and having it validated may be sufficient for the patient. A parent may not want to burden a child with news of a terminal illness, and so hides her distress. A young person may not wish to disclose troubles she is encountering at school or college to parents who may themselves be enduring some emotional distress. An adult who has been sexually abused as a child may just need the space to recount the event, to enable her to come to terms with it. The recounting of the patient's story, with a few prompts or suggestions from the counsellor, may be enough for the patient to gain a fresh view of her current situation.

When the counsellor has gained enough insight into the patient's problem and situation, he may elaborate and move things to a different level psychologically. Certain questions may be useful in this regard:

> 'From where do you get your strength to keep going?'
>
> 'Given all that you've been through, how have you managed to survive/cope as well as you have?'

Such responses validate both the person and the pain, yet a distinction is drawn between the two. They are expressions of positive curiosity that do not coerce, but invite the patient to think differently about herself. Once again, the effect of such questions can be dramatic, as the patient may be surprised when her strength is referred to at a time when she feels vulnerable. Patients can be encouraged when the focus of the conversation does not limit itself to a discussion of their pain. Such questions can foster engagement early in the therapeutic encounter, which in turn can add intensity to the counselling process.

Sometimes too little attention is paid to the effect of any intervention on the patient. The counsellor needs to be able to recognize the moment when the patient ceases to be a 'patient' (as traditionally understood in terms of being passive and incompetent) and becomes a person actively engaged in the counselling conversation. The end of counselling may be indicated not when the problem has been solved but at the point where the patient considers that she is able to manage and solve the problem, or simply to endure her situation without the counsellor's help.

How has the patient previously coped?

One of the ways patients can get to the point of being reconnected with their own resourcefulness is by helping them to recollect other times in the past when they felt low and distressed. A patient can benefit from being asked directly to remember her role in contributing to the end of previous distress, utilizing such questions as:

> 'Have you felt like this before?'
>
> 'Have there been other times in your life when things have felt as bad as this?'

If the patient responds in the affirmative, the counsellor can ask for a description of these other occasions. Other questions the counsellor might utilize include:

> 'How did you manage to get through it that time?'
>
> 'How have you survived and coped?'

The patient may feel that her current distress is worse than anything that has happened in the past, and the counsellor needs to be sensitive to this possibility. The patient should always be given sufficient time to respond fully to any enquiry the counsellor makes.

How can the patient be helped to cope better in the future?

Cognitive-based models of therapy seek to identify problematical thought and behaviour patterns. The objective of counselling is to recognize, acknowledge and challenge these problematic patterns. However, our experience suggests that at such times the expression of pain, misery and depression is very pervasive. Too much dwelling on negative thoughts and behaviours may actually hinder therapeutic change. One possible and creative way of helping patients who feel stuck is to begin to talk about a future time. Much has been written about the well-known 'miracle question' (de Shazer, 1985). The belief is that future-orientated talk might encourage patients to think more creatively about how they would like things to be, and about what changes they would like to make to their current situation.

In our experience, patients have difficulty in talking in general terms about their 'miracle' or preferred future, which is not surprising. We have therefore found it more useful to ask patients about a particular situation or context that they find troublesome, rather than asking in general about a preferred future scenario. For example, a patient may want to change her angry response to her teenage son's refusal to get out of bed on time for school in the morning. She has tried her best to control her temper, as she can see it is not productive, but she has not yet been successful. Adopting an idea suggested by Mooney and Padesky (2000), we invite the patient to think of someone she admires. This can be a friend, a work colleague, or even a fictional character from film or television. We then ask the patient how she thinks that person would act in the situation she wishes to change. In our experience, her use of a role model can free up the patient's own creativity and enable her to conjure up a preferred behaviour or way of behaving or being in a given situation. When the patient in the example above was invited to think of an admired role model, she immediately smiled and exclaimed: 'I can just imagine what Toni would do in that situation. For one thing she would work out, in advance, a plan of action. She would also execute it with a sense of fun!' The very thought of this friend Toni seemed to introduce the patient to a variety of alternative behaviours applicable in the previously 'stuck' situation.

If the patient is asked to conjure up details of a miracle future, the question we have found most useful to ask is:

> 'Which bit of the miracle, if any, currently exists?'

This question helps to bring the future into the present and can rekindle a sense of hope.

QUESTIONS THAT HELP THE PATIENT TO EXPERIENCE A SENSE OF MOVEMENT

Any intervention that helps the patient to feel less 'boxed in' by her current situation and introduces the possibility of movement or other options is useful, even if the herald of this is an initial increase in anxiety. Any sense of movement the patient may experience can generate a sense of hope and the possibility that further change can happen, for both the patient and the counsellor.

A simple scaling exercise can be used to achieve this. Point one on the imagined scale represents the time when the patient felt at her lowest, and point ten the best she could ever feel. The patient can then be asked to select a point on the scale that represents most accurately where she judges herself to be currently. In our experience, patients rarely place themselves at point one or lower on the scale. Whatever point patients choose can be utilized. They can be questioned as to what they have done to get themselves to that position. This can take effort (and a good memory!) on the part of the counsellor to help patients recognize and acknowledge their own input to the situation. It took just such an effort to get Sam, who had been feeling low for a long time, to recollect that it was she herself who had taken the time to respond to an e-mail sent by a friend who was undergoing similar treatment as herself, and who later became a great source of support and comfort.

It can be useful to ask questions such as:

> 'How did you manage to get yourself to point 4/5 on the scale?'
>
> 'What did you do to help you arrive at that position?'

Such questions can challenge the patient to think of ways in which she has contributed to her own progress. Frequently, patients will require encouragement, even coaxing, to begin to think in terms of change or improvement as already having been accomplished, and their own contribution to that. Patients frequently attribute change to outside factors, such as medication, rather than to their own efforts. If the counsellor omits this rather painstaking 'tracking' of progress, an opportunity for considerable therapeutic change is lost. Such measurement of progress also provides feedback to the counsellor regarding the amount of ground that has been covered, and how much more work there is to be done.

The scaling exercise mentioned above can be used at different times in the course of counselling. It is helpful to utilize it towards the end of a meeting. Point one on the scale can represent the way the patient was feeling at the beginning of the meeting, with point ten, as above, representing the optimal position. Whatever point the patient positions herself at releases new information that can be utilized by the counsellor. If the patient is feeling a little better towards the end of the meeting, the counsellor can ask questions such as:

> 'What has made you feel a little better now?'
>
> 'What has brought about this change?'
>
> 'Was this change a result of some thought you had?'

Helping to make explicit how any improvement has occurred, even if it is simply the patient's ability to use something the counsellor has suggested, is valuable. It can be used as evidence of the patient's ability. If it is made explicit, this can be very affirming and can contribute to the patient's sense of mastery in the situation. If the patient is not feeling better, this situation also needs to be addressed, particularly if the patient has moved to a number lower down the scale during the meeting. If things are so extreme that the patient is actively suicidal, for example, medical colleagues may be asked to see the patient. Such an apparently simple measuring tool can be used in a number of creative ways in the course of any counselling encounter. Such measurements are essential to ascertain when progress is made, or when it is illusive.

THE TIMING AND SPACING OF COUNSELLING MEETINGS

The topic of timing and the number of meetings can be introduced at the beginning of the first meeting, when the counsellor can start the conversation by saying that he and the patient will have a discussion, and at the end of it they will decide jointly whether they need to meet again. Such a statement alerts the patient not only to the possibility that counselling may end imminently but, significantly too, that the patient has an equal part to play in the decision as to whether the counselling will continue or not. Such an approach can foster the patient's participation in, and responsibility for, the process early in the counselling encounter.

When invited to state her preference about whether to meet again or not, or when to meet, the patient's response should always be considered. A counsellor new to this approach might be surprised that, if invited, patients are well able to express that they think they have got what they want, and can manage by themselves for the present. This is especially true when the objective is directed towards eliciting the patient's ability to cope rather than to solving the problem.

Patients who leave counselling early frequently do so because they have got what they need from it (Talmon, 1990). Research suggests that change happens most frequently at an early stage rather than later in the therapeutic process. The alert counsellor who is confident in the patient's resourcefulness and ability to manage on her own is always vigilant to ending counselling earlier rather than later. This is both ethical and likely to be the most powerful therapeutic intervention he can offer the patient. It is a very powerful message for the patient to hear from the professional: 'I think you're OK; it seems to me as if you can now manage on your own.' This is the ultimate validation of the patient. However, such a decision is only ever taken based on sound judgement, clinical experience and appropriate skill.

Criticism is often levelled, suggesting that an approach characterized by actively seeking out patient competence is an approach that lacks rigour and discipline, but in fact the opposite is true. An approach based on true collaboration and mutual respect places high expectations on both partners. This can be exemplified by the subject of attendance at meetings.

Patients sometimes fail to attend meetings. Things happen to them: they oversleep; they become ill; their situation deteriorates; medical treatments fail. However, patients who are invited to participate as co-equal and responsible partners in the process of counselling, in our experience, rarely fail to attend prearranged counselling meetings. This of itself validates the collaborative approach. When patients are fully engaged in the process, they attend scheduled meetings. Time is used optimally by both participants. The counselling process becomes a working alliance that finishes when the negotiated targets have been reached as mutually agreed by both partners.

TOWARDS ENDING

The task for the counsellor towards the end of the counselling endeavour, whether that is a single meeting or a number of meetings, is to find ways to help embed the new story of competence and resourcefulness into the patient's thinking. The scaling exercise already described is one very useful intervention in terms of highlighting and reinforcing the patient's own contribution to any change or improvement that has occurred. This exercise is best placed at least ten minutes before the end of the meeting, to maximize its therapeutic benefit.

Another powerful way to reinforce changes a patient has succeeded in making is to ask the patient directly to search for evidence in her life that supports this new view of things. The patient could be asked:

> 'Has anyone noticed that you are different?'
>
> 'Who else notices the changes you have made?'
>
> 'Who else has said similar things about how well you are managing?'
>
> 'Who in your life would be least surprised at how well you are managing?'

Again, such questions often come as a complete surprise to patients, and their own answers to them even more so. Frequently, when change begins to happen in patients, it is often noticed by those living or working close to them before it is acknowledged by the patients themselves. People often remark on such changes, and yet patients themselves may not attribute significance to such remarks. It is a critical aspect of the counsellor's role to attribute positive significance to change. To avoid the omission of any serious relevant issues, the following questions can be asked:

> 'Is there anything you might have liked us to discuss in more detail?'
>
> 'Is there anything you would have preferred not to be mentioned at all?'

If a subject area is identified by the patient, she can be encouraged to think about how this issue or topic might now be addressed, or whom she might consult in order to resolve it. Such an attitude is not avoiding the issue, but is firmly grounded in the belief that the patient can cope, with or without the counsellor. In a health care context, the counsellor, as a member of the multi-disciplinary team, is not the only one who administers care. Patients are usually helped the most through collaborative care.

CONCLUSION

This chapter has attempted to illustrate the viewpoint that patients are capable and responsible despite being in distress. The objective of counselling in the health care context is directed towards uncovering what else besides the problem is happening in the patient's life that proves the patient's ability to be creative and resourceful. In our experience, one of the most therapeutic interventions the counsellor can make is to help the patient to differentiate between her distress at whatever has happened or is happening and her ability to cope and function.

Patients often feel a pressure to be seen to be coping, in both their family and professional lives. What this often means is that they do not feel free to manifest their distress. To be able to express distress and pain is in fact a measure of resourcefulness and is a normal response to pain and suffering. Conveying such a robust view to the patient can be profoundly therapeutic. To normalize negative emotions experienced by the patient is a powerful therapeutic intervention in itself and can help the patient to regain a sense of balance and control.

Attempting to work in the way described in this chapter, counsellors may feel at times as if they are going against the thrust of traditional treatment models and 'at odds' with the medical model. This is not so. The approach described here aims to combine the richness of traditional practice and evidence-based therapy while at the same time forging ahead with new attitudes towards the patient. With this new attitude, the patient is elevated to a position of competence and partnership, and the counsellor is freed from the position of being the expert. As a consequence, stress levels in the counsellor and his medical colleagues may be considerably reduced as the patient begins to regain control. The counselling encounter can thus be transformed into a dynamic experience. The objective of the whole process is for the patient to see and understand herself differently so that she may engage energetically with whatever demanding situation arises. When that is achieved, counselling may end, even when medical treatment continues.

Chapter 9

Reframing and Creating Balance in Patients' Beliefs

INTRODUCTION

Many psychological problems stemming from health-related concerns have their origins in personal beliefs about coping with adversity and disability. They may also arise where previous experiences, including people's upbringing, do not prepare individuals, couples or families well enough to cope with the changes brought about by illness or disability. These problems frequently relate to coping with uncertainty (about the course of the illness, the outcome, the effectiveness of any treatment and so on), feelings of hopelessness, a denial of the severity of the problem, fear of loss or abandonment and resentment by individuals towards caretakers for having to depend on them. Family members may perceive patients as brooding, depressed, passive, confused or agitated, which in turn may lead patients and health care providers to perceive the patients' family members as demanding or hypervigilant on behalf of their unwell family member. These complex dynamics may, in turn, affect relationships, as people either avoid talking about their fears or anxieties, or appear to talk about nothing else. Resilience may be related to the extent to which others are involved in the patient's care.

THE THEORY BEHIND REFRAMING IN COUNSELLING

'Reframing' is a psychotherapeutic intervention that can address complex relationship dynamics, especially at times when it appears that coping and adjustment are being thwarted by reliance on unhelpful beliefs. Reframing as an intervention serves to introduce new views and possibilities. The approach, firmly embedded in systemic theory, reflects directly the concept of the relativity of people's views and feelings. It is closely connected to Bateson's (1979) idea of 'difference', which introduces the concept of balance or complementarity. 'Happiness', for example, can only be comprehended in the context of, say, 'unhappiness' or 'despondency'.

A range of therapeutic themes can be discussed with patients. There are many possible views of reality. Counselling can introduce to the patient a different view of the problem; that is, it can reframe the problem. Campbell and Draper (1985) state that many families who are 'stuck' with a problem have lost contact with multiple views of problems or reality. The meaning they attach to symptomatic behaviour becomes lineal, that is, 'it is mad or it is bad'. One task of the counsellor, in such cases, may be to identify the patient's beliefs about his problems and to offer alternative views where appropriate. This is done by addressing both sides, or the complement, of a particular theme. Some of the most common themes pertaining to patients' concerns that arise in the context of illness, presented as complements, are shown in Figure 9.1.

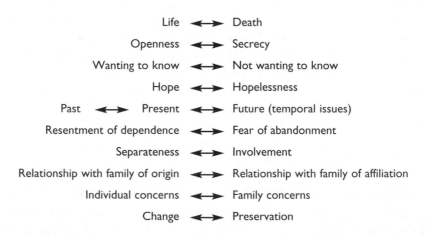

Life ⟷ Death

Openness ⟷ Secrecy

Wanting to know ⟷ Not wanting to know

Hope ⟷ Hopelessness

Past ⟷ Present ⟷ Future (temporal issues)

Resentment of dependence ⟷ Fear of abandonment

Separateness ⟷ Involvement

Relationship with family of origin ⟷ Relationship with family of affiliation

Individual concerns ⟷ Family concerns

Change ⟷ Preservation

Figure 9.1   Counselling themes as complements

Addressing the complement of a problem is the beginning of a reframe. The counsellor may be able to reframe one side of the problem in the context of the other. The need for separateness, for example, may be viewed in relation to levels of involvement and dependence, and vice versa. Some counsellors only place emphasis on one side of the problem, such as fear of dying, hopelessness, depression, dysfunction and pathology. Neither the counsellor nor the patient considers other possible views of the same problem, mainly because the initial problem presented by the patient may also reflect this one-sided emphasis. By addressing the complement, the counsellor may be able to amplify, add complexity to, and ultimately reframe, the patient's view of his problems. This may not only influence or change the patient's view of his illness, but may also have a ripple effect on other people's views, such as the family and health care providers.

By using circular questions and addressing hypothetical outcomes, new ideas, beliefs and connections may emerge. Discussing the complementary aspects of an idea can help to change a patient's perceptions of a problem, leading to emotional and behavioural change. This can be achieved where the patient comes to a different understanding of his situation by making new connections and recognizing alternative but plausible perspectives to a problem. In the seemingly hopeless situation of a fatal illness, a patient may, for example, recognize the extent of caring and closeness in his family for the first time.

The patient's sense of autonomy and capacity to cope may be enhanced by providing a context in which the patient is able to recognize that *he* is the resource for dealing effectively with difficulties, and the potential for confusion that may threaten his psychological stability. This can be done, for example, by validating *all* the patient's perceptions and adopting a non-oppositional stance, while at the same time carefully introducing ideas about the complementary side of the problem. This therapeutic task of reframing is rarely used, and yet it is especially relevant and helpful in a context where patients, their care-takers and professionals supporting them hold rigid views and beliefs. Reframing is a potentially powerful therapeutic intervention, but counsellors require training and supervision in order to prevent its misuse. The patient's view of the problem should not be invalidated.

EXAMPLES OF ADDRESSING THE COMPLEMENT IN PRACTICE

A number of complements may arise in the course of counselling. These are described below, and the method of reframing is illustrated with short examples.

Life and death

Some medical conditions are potentially (and sometimes inevitably) fatal. The theme of death, and associated fears, may be common in conversations with the patient. In thinking about death or dying and its implications for an individual, its complement, life or living, also has to be considered at some stage in the course of counselling. Thus, it is not possible to think about living with a serious illness unless one also thinks about the possibility of death. Thoughts about death and dying may need to be balanced by thoughts about life and living and the challenges they present. In this way, the counsellor highlights the focus between the two in order to help the patient gain a different perspective and perhaps to live in a better way with his illness. An extract from an interview illustrates this:

Patient: *The doctors have told me that I have a very high viral load and that my immune system is weakening rapidly. I really feel nervous about the future.*
Counsellor: *What do you feel most nervous about?*
Patient: *Most about dying. It's often on my mind nowadays.*
Counsellor: *This may seem a strange question, but I was wondering: are there any aspects of living that you are concerned about?*
Patient: *Having to face my parents with this news.*
Counsellor: *If they knew that, do you think that they would agree that you need to be concerned about telling them?*
Patient: *That's a good question. Possibly not. It's probably on their minds and we're all getting along by not talking about 'what if . . .'.*

Openness and secrecy

Some patients wish to protect others from so-called bad news. Others fear the ostracism, isolation and social stigma that may result from telling others about their illness. For these reasons, they may seek to keep it secret. In some circumstances, keeping secrets may prevent the patient from receiving adequate or desired social support, or interfere with co-ordinated management and care. The tension between secrecy and openness can be discussed in counselling, as illustrated below:

Patient: *I see no point in telling my mother that I will be having these tests. It would only worry her.*

Counsellor: *OK, but from where will you get support if you need it during the tests and while waiting for the results?*

Patient: *If I tell anyone, they will only worry, and that would add to my worries. I'd rather wait until the results come and then I'll decide what to do at that point.*

Counsellor: *I can understand your concerns about not worrying others. If, at a later point, you choose to tell your mother or others, do you think they would have wanted to be told sooner?*

Patient: *It cuts both ways. If I don't tell them, I'll be blamed for being secretive and uncaring. If I do tell them, they may add to my worries. It's still best to err on the side of hoping that it's 'good news' and that this was just a scare.*

Wanting to know versus not wanting to know

Patients will sometimes say that they want to know the results of clinical tests and investigations or other procedures. In reality, however, they may not want to know or they may be ambivalent. This problem may never be entirely resolved and can cause frustration to doctors and nurses. Patients and health care workers may have different views about how much information should be made known. Counselling sessions can be used to explore the patient's views about information and its dissemination, so as to improve communication between patients and the professionals caring for them. This theme is closely linked to the patients' view of themselves and their ability to cope. The patients can be helped to regain a sense of control by asking them (a) to clarify what they want to be told; (b) what they specifically do not want to know; (c) at what stages they want to be told; (d) whether anyone else should be present when they are given information; and (e) how they would indicate that their views have changed. For example:

Mother: *I understand what the doctor was saying about my daugh-*
             ter having diabetes, but I wonder if she is really too young
             to be told. What do you think?

Counsellor: *I can understand your reluctance to tell her too much at this*
             stage, especially because it is not yet clear how this will
             affect her and whether she will be on insulin. Maybe you can
             tell her gradually. Perhaps just some of the main details at
             this stage, such as an explanation for why she has to see the
             doctor. Then, as you are told more by the doctor, you can
             think about whether and how you would share the informa-
             tion with Susie. If your husband was here, what do you
             think he would want to do?

Mother: *Probably the same as your suggestion. Do it slowly, one step*
             at a time. Use words and descriptions that she'll understand.
             When she gets older, maybe tell her more.

Counsellor: *Seems a very good approach to me. We know that children's*
             reactions to illness and how they cope is directly influenced
             by how their parents cope. It's best to tell Susie only what
             you think she needs to know and in a time-frame that best
             suits the two of you.

Hope and hopelessness

With any serious illness, there is likely to be tension between feelings of
hope and hopelessness. These feelings are directly linked to the complements of certainty and uncertainty. The counsellor can seek to support the
patient's hope in the face of their life-threatening illness without invali-
dating or dismissing their fear of dying. This is not easily done. The counsellor can offer hope in relation to small goals and, at the same time, not
deny the reality that the possibility of illness is ever-present. The course or
outcome of an illness can never be predicted with any precision. It could
be said that, as long as there is some uncertainty in relation to treatment
and the outcome of the patient's illness, there is an element of hope. On
the other hand, certainty can also give rise to feelings of hope. A patient
who has been told that he is suffering from leukaemia, say, may be relieved
that some of the symptoms can be treated promptly. Clearly, the converse
is also true and, in other situations, uncertainty may erode a patient's feelings of hope. The introduction of the complements of hope and hopelessness into counselling is illustrated in the following example:

Patient: I feel really down . . . actually quite hopeless now that I've been told that in time I could become incontinent.

Counsellor: It must be very difficult for you to have to cope with more and more symptoms. Are there any areas in which you see some possible hope?

Patient: At least I can make some plans ahead of time and investigate what devices or contraptions I may need. Who knows, maybe things won't deteriorate too much, and becoming incontinent is just a worst-case scenario.

Counsellor: That is possible. What could you hope for in more personal areas, for example, with family and friends?

Patient: That they would continue to care for me, whatever the symptoms or problems.

Counsellor: Is there anything you might think about doing to ensure that this situation continues?

Patient: I need to keep them up to date with developments. I need to share this news with some of them.

Temporal issues (past, present and future)

Perspectives on time can be used to help patients gain a new perspective on a problem by linking past experience with the present and even with anticipated situations. At any given moment in counselling, a particular time period is being referred to. A patient may, for example, say that he currently feels depressed. The counsellor may then examine two other periods of time, asking the patient whether he has felt depressed in the past, his circumstances at that time, and how he coped then. The counsellor may also ask the patient, in thinking about the future, what would happen if he continued to feel so depressed and these feelings did not seem to go away, or how things might look if his depression lifted. In this way, the counsellor can always introduce a new view of the problem with a temporal theme.

Patient: I have felt so depressed for the past two weeks.
Counsellor: When last did you feel so depressed?
Patient: About two years ago.
Counsellor: Do you remember for how long it lasted?
Patient: No.

Counsellor:	*What were the signs to you then that you were feeling less depressed?*
Patient:	*I enjoyed my work more and went out with my husband and friends.*
Counsellor:	*What helped you get over feeling depressed?*
Patient:	*Time. It just went away over time. It took about a month to go away.*
Counsellor:	*Do you remember what signs there were that it was beginning to lift?*
Patient:	*I don't remember. But I do remember that my husband said that my sexual interest had begun to return!*
Counsellor:	*What might the signs be this time that you were beginning to feel better in yourself?*
Patient:	*At this moment, I have no idea. It just seems like I'm in a long black tunnel.*
Counsellor:	*If these feelings carried on, what do you think would most help?*
Patient:	*My husband. And some anti-depressant pills.*

Relationship with families of origin and affiliation

The patient's ideas about what his family of origin (biological family or blood relations) or social family (partner(s) and non-biological kin network) might think about a particular problem should also be discussed. He may already know their views, or be asked to imagine what these views might be. It is important to stress that, in counselling, it is the patient's perception of problems and beliefs that is important, rather than 'the truth'. An exploration of the patient's views about different family members helps to place a problem in the context of relationships. It gives a patient a reference point from which to look at difficulties, especially where there are different views within the family that affect the patient's beliefs. An excerpt from a counselling session illustrates this.

Patient:	*My girlfriend feels that I am too ill to continue working.*
Counsellor:	*What does she think you should do when you've stopped?*
Patient:	*Just stay at home and rest.*
Counsellor:	*Who else agrees with her?*
Patient:	*I think my parents both disagree.*
Counsellor:	*What makes them think that you should continue working?*

Patient: *They think it will take my mind off my troubles if I'm occupied or busy.*

Counsellor: *And what does your girlfriend think will occupy your thoughts while you are resting at home?*

Patient: *Perhaps how we can continue to have a good relationship and to cope with the difficult times that lie ahead.*

Dependence and abandonment

The nature of chronic and acute illness is such that there may be times when patients are able to look after themselves satisfactorily when out of hospital, and other times when they will need to be in hospital or rely on carers. This may present as a dilemma in the context of counselling, because some patients resent being dependent or even coming to counselling sessions. On the other hand, the patient may at the same time express a fear of being on his own or being abandoned. Such a dilemma may be played out through contradictory messages being given by the patient to the counsellor or other members of the health care team. There are times during counselling when it is important to discuss the patient's fears of abandonment and dependence. For example:

Patient: *I really don't think it's necessary for me to be here today.*

Counsellor: *How is that different from the last time you were here?*

Patient: *Then I felt really unwell and needed someone to talk to and to answer questions for me.*

Counsellor: *What sorts of things do you think you might want to talk about during periods when you feel well?*

Patient: *Perhaps if I could get more involved in my relationship while I was feeling better.*

Counsellor: *What do you think you would need to do in order to get more involved in your relationship?*

Patient: *I could see you less when I am feeling better and spend more time with my partner.*

Separateness and involvement

These dilemmas are similar to those of dependence and abandonment. When a patient becomes ill and understands the possible implications of his illness, he may wish to stay at some emotional distance from others. This may be, for example, because he does not want to infect others, perhaps feels too unwell physically to have close relationships, feels self-conscious or inadequate socially, or has a fear that a partner may desert him. On the other hand, at times of crisis, the patient may feel a real need for a significant relationship and a close emotional involvement. A similar process can occur in the course of counselling with patients either not wanting to keep appointments or asking for more frequent ones. For example:

Counsellor: *You mention that no one has been to visit you for the past two days. That sounds quite upsetting. I wonder whether you could say why that might have been?*

Patient: *I've told everyone I need some space to be on my own.*

Counsellor: *Can you say more about that?*

Patient: *I don't want to be a burden on my friends and family. If they visit me here in hospital, I think they're doing it out of a sense of duty.*

Counsellor: *Are there any benefits for you of them visiting even if it is out of a sense of duty?*

Patient: *I like the company, but get very tearful when it's time to say 'goodbye'. It's like I want them, and at the same time I don't want them.*

Change and preservation

One goal of counselling is to address the balance between helping people to adapt and change, but at the same time preserve a sense of stability and continuity in their lives. This goal addresses the therapeutic balance. The counsellor constantly thinks about psychological process in the session and may ask himself some of the following questions: 'What is the patient telling me? What is the problem? What does the patient want changed? What does he want to keep the same?' Sometimes the counsellor may try to generate too much change, which in turn can affect the balance of the therapeutic system. Through responding closely to the feedback, the counsellor can redress the balance by identifying whether the patient is becoming emotionally more stable, or whether he has become 'stuck'. In the face of the latter, the counsellor might ask herself: 'Am I pushing for change when change is not wanted? Am I trying to change the patient or system in a way that is inappropriate or too rapid?' The problems of change are addressed in the example below.

Patient: *I want to try to change some things in my life now the oper-ation is over.*

Counsellor: *I realize that there are some things in your life that you would like to change. Are there any aspects that you would like to keep the same?*

Patient: *How my parents look after me.*

Counsellor: *What does your boyfriend think you'd like to change the most?*

Patient: *The fact that I have so little energy to enjoy our relationship.*

Counsellor: *What would he most likely want to keep the same?*

Patient: *That I won't ever feel like leaving him.*

CONCLUSION

Some of the more challenging problems in clinical practice stem from strongly held beliefs and the management of views or feelings of hopeless-ness. These problems can affect communication between the patient and his family, and with health care staff. An approach has been described for counselling about patients' belief systems to enhance their perception of choice in how they view their relationships and what might be happening to them. This is not to suggest that, by creating balance in difficult clini-cal situations, patients will be relieved of their problems completely. Balancing techniques are a first step towards reframing a belief or problem. There may be some personal advantage, for example, in being in hospital, because it may encourage the patient to be more open about his illness than might have been possible while he was at home and able to mask problems. Complementarity can be introduced into counselling by asking hypothetical and future-orientated questions, such as: 'You say that the doctors only seem to give you bad news. Given your situation, what might be 'good' news for you? How do you think that good or bad news would affect how you see your illness and your relationship with your doctors?'

To make one last important point: there are potential pitfalls for the counsellor in the use of reframing, employing the ideas described in this chapter. It requires training, care and delicacy. Without training in this approach, the counsellor may use the technique as a means of avoiding the confrontation of problems with patients. The counsellor could also inadvertently deny or disqualify a patient's negative feelings and become combative with the patient by insisting on the 'good' or psychologically 'healthy' side.

Chapter 10

Working with the Family in Mind

INTRODUCTION

Most counsellors are trained to work with individuals and, consequently, focus in counselling sessions on intrapsychic processes, self-beliefs and the patients' feelings. When working in health care settings with people with health problems, issues pertaining to disclosure of illness, access to emotional, social and practical support and the impact of illness on other family members are also highly relevant. A genogram, also known as a family tree, pedigree or genealogical chart, is a clinical tool used for acquiring, storing and processing information about family history, composition and relationships. A genogram can be used to develop a map of family relationships with the patient, identify sources of support within the family, and explore transgenerational illness meanings. Genograms have been used in psychotherapy for years and are a natural fit for medical settings, especially when working with people who are coping with health problems.

This chapter is for counsellors with little or no experience of using genograms with patients and their families, or for counsellors and health care professionals who want to use genograms more effectively and imaginatively. A brief survey of the basic use of the genogram will show how it incorporates a patient's family, social and medical history in a temporal context. The family medical genogram can be used as a collaborative tool to incorporate patients' illness narratives and meanings of illness. These highly efficient diagrams share relevant information with other health care professionals in a way that can optimize the diagnosis, care and recovery of patients.

THEORETICAL BACKGROUND

The information contained in a genogram may include medical, behavioural, genetic, cultural and social aspects of the family system. This information can provide a rich source of ideas with regard to how a clinical problem may be linked to family history and relationships, and how a problem may evolve over time. Genograms help to reveal patterns and events that may have recurring significance within a family system. McGoldrick and Gerson (1985) explain that the act of constructing a family diagram with a patient or family, to map relationships and functioning patterns, acts in a way similar to language – to potentiate and organize thought processes. To this end, genograms can be conceptualized as both a therapeutic intervention and a part of the process of counselling.

Knowledge of a patient's family history is important in a health care setting, for several reasons. Information about a patient's family background helps in:

- Making a diagnosis of familial, biological and psychiatric disorders (for example, cystic fibrosis, heart disease, haemophilia, asthma, schizophrenia);
- Genetic counselling and the prediction of illness and disability;
- Evaluating somatic complaints;
- Understanding the family's role in the aetiology of illness (for example, in the case of diabetic ketoacidosis);
- Identifying psychological problems in different family constellations, such as stepfamilies; and
- Devising health promotion and treatment plans.

A genogram provides an immediate picture of the family and its medical history, and is a useful alternative to searching through thick files of patient notes for biographical and background information. Critical medical information can be highlighted and current medical and psychosocial problems considered.

A family genogram going back at least two generations will provide specialized information to act as a quick reference and to highlight choices so that health care teams can begin to construct a treatment plan (for example, smoking cessation, dietary changes, exercise) that will fit the patient's lifestyle. This can be done by:

- Discovering the patient's and family attitudes, beliefs and understanding of illness;
- Highlighting the emotional pay-off for different members when the patient is ill and when she is well;
- Identifying who else might be available to provide social support for the patient;
- Finding examples of the positive problem-solving skills of patients and their families in their historical accounts;
- Revealing the resources needed for patients to negotiate the challenges of current illnesses (serious, chronic, terminal) or disabilities;
- Providing a reference map that facilitates easy movement back and forth between the family's emotional and physical resources; and
- Discovering strengths and locating vulnerabilities that will affect medical situations; for example, the family structure, life cycle, generationally repetitive emotional and illness patterns, the life experiences of families, and the family members' relationships with one other.

From a counselling perspective, the family life cycle is an important variable to consider, since it will have implications not only for the patient and her illness but also for the family as a whole. To enable an individual to move on to the next stage in the family life cycle (for example, a parent facing an 'empty nest' after the children have left home), the family must reorganize itself at each pivotal point it encounters in the life cycle. These transitions can be difficult for some families, especially where one or more members suffer from a medical illness (Rolland, 1984). The listing of ages, dates and significant family events (that is, births, deaths, divorce) on a genogram enables the counsellor to examine with the patient whether or not life-cycle events occurred within expected parameters (McDaniel *et al.*, 1992). The genogram also allows for important anniversaries to be considered, especially those relating to change and loss within the family. This may be particularly relevant in the case of a death or a suicide within the family, or illness relating to distress, even though no conscious connection has been made between these events and illness. Josse (1993) describes the case of a man whose dyspepsia coincided with the anniversary of his uncle's death from stomach cancer. The man had not realized the extent to which his uncle's death had affected him until he began to discuss it while working on his genogram during counselling. The following example highlights the relevance of a genogram in patient care:

Case Study

Sally was an 11-year-old girl in fairly good health but suffered from recurring sore throats all winter. Her paediatrician explained to the girl's parents that removing her tonsils would greatly reduce her susceptibility to sore throats. Sally's parents decided on the surgery, which they understood would require two days' stay in hospital. Sally would then be able to recuperate at home and in ten days or so be able to return to school. The surgery for the removal of Sally's tonsils and adenoids was considered to be routine. Sally's surgery was scheduled over a break from school and between her recurring sore throats. However, during Sally's surgery, her respiration, blood pressure and heart rate dropped and she had to be revived. As the surgery team stabilized her and intubated Sally again, they lost her vital signs. Once Sally was stable and perceived to be out of danger, she left the recovery room for her hospital bed and was scheduled for release the next day. Some time during the night Sally began haemorrhaging and again her vital signs became unstable. She remained in hospital for several days. Sally eventually recovered and it was not until years later that she learned that her mother, grandmother and her mother's sisters all experienced similar problems to those she had had during surgery. A simple medical genogram tracking the illnesses, surgeries and recoveries of this family's female members would have been useful. The paediatrician might have noted the pattern and could possibly have taken steps to help prevent Sally's surgical trauma and the psychological distress to Sally and the family.

Genograms provide more than a quantitative measure through which clinical predictions can be made; they can be employed as a means of interpreting information subjectively about relationships and raising possibilities for exploration in therapy. By obtaining an 'image' of the current family context, the counsellor can assess the family's strengths as well as the possible links between the presenting problem and family relationships. Individual symptoms can therefore be recast in interpersonal terms. For example, a genogram might help to reveal that the onset of a child's asthma – possibly as a result of his feeling anxious and insecure – coincided with his mother starting an extra-marital relationship; this could lead to bringing the couple together to work with a counsellor to help their son to overcome his problem.

Although the origins of the genogram lie in family therapy, this tool can also be used effectively in individual and couple medical counselling. Indeed, it is especially useful in cases where:

- A psychological problem has implications for other family members, but they are not present in counselling;
- The presenting problem appears to stem from family relationships;
- Illness and issues of loss need to be addressed in counselling;
- Other care-givers seem to have inadvertently maintained or exacerbated the problem: a sociogram (genogram that also includes significant non-biologically-linked relationships) together with a genogram can help to map out all the relevant players and relationships; or
- The 'family' may be overlooked in individual counselling sessions; for example, with gay men, lesbians and people in individual counselling or therapy.

Genograms provide a means of helping patients to link their ill health with relational processes and even help to engage the whole family in the counselling process. The procedure of gathering information and mapping it onto the genogram helps the counsellor to develop a rapport with the patient. They can also be used to free the therapeutic process from an impasse. The patient or symptom-bearer (the person presenting with a psychological and/or health problem) is often viewed as the person with the problem, and therefore is the person who needs to be helped or needs to change. Viewing the presenting problem within the context of family relationships and within a multi-generational framework is a powerful way of reframing the problem and removing blame from any particular individual. The effect is to normalize the family's understanding of the problem, and perhaps also the reactions of different family members to it. Indeed, once the family patterns that may underlie problematic behaviour are identified, it is possible that the behaviour will change without the need for further psychotherapeutic intervention. Genograms can also help to focus questioning on significant family experiences such as births, marriages, leaving-home transitions and deaths – all of which may have some significance in the context surrounding family beliefs about illness.

CONSTRUCTING A GENOGRAM IN COUNSELLING

A carefully gathered and constructed genogram will provide clues to clarify the biological, legal, formal and informal relationships of the patient and other family members. The comprehensive medical and psychological information includes: with whom the patient lives, the family's past and current experience of illness and who copes best with anticipated or unexpected changes. A medical genogram can provide clarity about the biological and stepfamily members on both the maternal and paternal side of the patient's family, in addition to marriages, divorces, births, deaths, illnesses, and the current health of family members and siblings.

The patient is usually given the option of choosing where to start the genogram, but if this appears to be a problem, the counsellor can suggest the immediate household. The counsellor should be sincere, open-minded, interested and non-judgemental when constructing a genogram. Starting with straightforward questions is also a useful way of setting the patient or family at ease. Direct, linear questions are useful at the beginning for example, 'Who lives in your household?' – but the interview may later progress to questions concerning views about relationships, such as: 'Who in your family has the closest relationship to your father? How does this show?' The counsellor should not only identify the composition of the family or household, but also look out for unusual family configurations and significant developmental stages and how these are or have been managed. A transitional delay or a premature occurrence (for example, pregnancy or a young adult leaving home), for example, will be of interest. Major illnesses are also recorded next to the relevant family member. All this information may help to identify structural patterns and relationship similarities, such as divorce or overly close relationships, and the frequent occurrence of a particular illness, which may have a functional as well as a medical significance.

Constructing a medical genogram is not as unmanageable as it might first appear. Counsellors can use it as part of establishing the therapeutic alliance, and specifically during the joining process with patients and families, by asking respectful and well-constructed questions. It is useful to include, at the initial mapping session, three generations on the patient's maternal and paternal sides. Information should include, first, a list of parents, siblings and children; then grandparents, aunts, uncles and cousins from both sides. Patients might provide medical information only from one family side or the other, and what health information is provided may be incomplete. However, a medical genogram is a document that can be added to continually as patients and family members become more forthcoming with information. The medical genogram is constructed from the bottom row upwards, starting with the patient, the significant other and the patient's children. The second row includes the patient's mother, father and siblings, and the patient's position in the family. The third row lists the patient's grandparents, aunts, uncles and cousins. All rows indicate marriages, separations, divorces and remarriages, highlighting key people interacting in the patient's life. The symbols used in genograms to denote gender, family structure and emotional relationships are shown in Figure 10.1.

For each relative, the medical genogram records date of birth and, where applicable, date of death, cause of death, known illnesses, major medical events (for example, coronary bypass, tuberculosis), ages when these conditions occurred and lifestyle or occupational factors that may contribute to ill health. This information may also provide counsellors and health care professionals with relevant ideas about the onset of, and susceptibility to, genetically linked diseases. A medical genogram with such information will aid health care professionals with diagnosis, and help patients and family members to make informed treatment choices.

The counsellor fills in the medical genogram with psychosocial issues, typical emotional reactions, coping skills, problem-solving abilities, family interactions, and social and religious beliefs. All these affect the patient's diagnosis and ways of dealing with illness, treatment, rehabilitation and life-style changes. For example, McGoldrick and Gerson (1985) outlined interpretative psychosocial categories based on family-systems theory:

- Family structures;
- Life cycle;
- Repetitive patterns;
- Life experiences;
- Relationships, marriages, separations, divorces, estrangements;
- Attempted solutions; and
- Current problems.

Relevant information about these areas of concern make a genogram a valuable collaborative map for discerning:

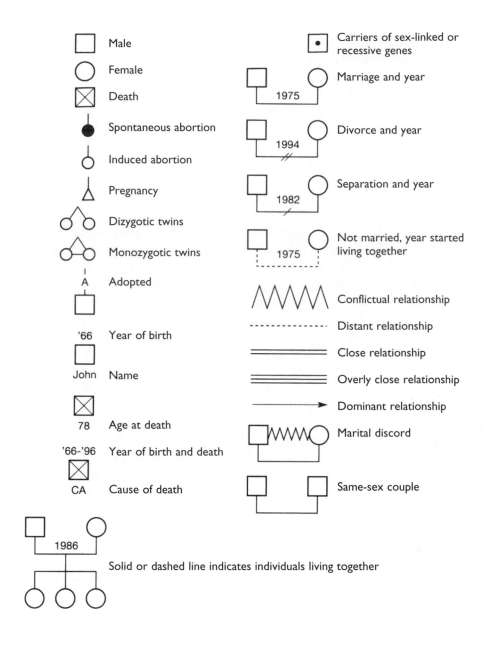

Figure 10.1 Basic genogram symbols

- The impact of a patient's illness on the family;
- Which family members contribute to the illness cycle;
- Who are supportive and who are not;
- Which relationships are stable;
- Economic influences;
- Communication patterns; and
- Appropriate referrals.

Questions should be asked concerning developmental stages and transitional life events, particularly where these coincide with the onset of, or changes in, medical conditions. Counsellors can use questions about the family's medical history to help patients and their families to regain a sense of control in a situation they had perceived to be unmanageable. Sharp (1994) suggests that counsellors and health care professionals encounter the most resistance while constructing medical genograms when patients and family members think the questions are too personal and prying – for example, those about sex, miscarriages and terminations of pregnancy. The best way for counsellors and health care professionals to avoid this perception when delicate questions are asked is to use extreme tact and sensitivity, clearly stating that highly personal information is confidential and will not be disclosed for any reason without the patient's permission. It is important for patients and family members to know and feel confident that medical genograms are not constructed 'to pry into your private lives [and there is] no need to be afraid to answer any question' (Sharp, 1994). Finally, counsellors need to assure patients and family members often during the process that all information is confidential between the counsellor and physician.

Patients and their families may view genograms as being too personal, or as airing dirty linen in public (Papazian, 1994). Counsellors need considerable skill with some patients and family members, because they may not wish to talk about sad, secret or stressful events. A useful approach for the counsellor with the reluctant talker or family could be to say simply, 'Because of your condition and the risks involved, any information that you or your family provide will be useful in treatment.' Counsellors and health care professionals can gather answers to medical questions by enquiring about familial medical conditions, physical characteristics, susceptibility to disease, hereditary diseases, chronic lifestyle conditions and illness patterns.

Counsellors can establish patient confidence in the value of the medical genogram by placing present health care issues in a context of how the family normally responds to illness and crises – by asking, for example, 'Who do you think has been most supportive at this difficult time?' or 'Who in the family was most surprised by your daughter's response to her grandfather's illness?' Patients and family members can be helped to understand the different ways they can address anxiety about illness. Counsellors can do this by reframing the current situation, normalizing the emotionally charged medical situation, and organizing a broad spectrum of information about the patient's illness, care and prognosis.

Basic genograms can be expanded to track multi-generational health, illness and emotional patterns found in families. The household depicted below is identifiable from the rest of the family by the solid line drawn around it.

Case study

James and Clare, aged 29 and 25 years, respectively, are a couple living together with their two young children, Stephen (5) and Gail (3) and a baby *in utero* (8 months). The couple were referred by Clare's obstetrician because Clare had become increasingly depressed and distant over the previous two months and James was also concerned in view of the impending birth. At first, her mood changes were put down to 'hormonal changes in pregnancy', but the couple were not reassured by this, because Clare's previous pregnancies had gone smoothly and had even brought the couple closer together.

Following an initial interview with the couple, the counsellor drew up a family genogram with them (see Figure 10.2).

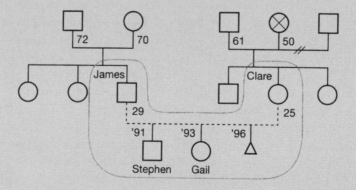

Figure 10.2 Example of a genogram as used in a counselling session

The counsellor observed from the genogram that Clare's mother was deceased, and on further enquiry was able to add to the genogram that she had died in 1993, soon after Gail was born. The discussion opened up after this, and the psychosocial importance of this death in relation to the new birth three years later became very apparent. The use of the genogram enabled the counsellor to discuss a bereavement which, having taken place three years before, had not been mentioned by the couple, but was evidently painful for Clare to talk about.

Combining a patient's basic genogram (current family composition and some basic social details) with their medical history becomes an effective tool to locate significant generational illness patterns and attitudes. This can provide counsellors with a clearer context for a systemic evaluation of how patients' families interact in problem-solving, respond to crises and emotionally saturated situations, and how the patient's family is likely to react to medical crises that have an impact on patient recovery. Discovering the lack or presence of coping skills for problem-solving will increase the counsellor's ability to bring to the fore whichever skills will be needed to alleviate difficulties, and interrupt anticipated behaviours that may hinder the patient's recovery in the current medical situation. Charting the evolution of a problem while discussing the genogram also invites the patient and his or her family to relate the family narrative and to participate in the domain of storytelling.

Constructing and exploring a genogram can be a very emotional experience for a patient or family, and may reveal issues that need to be addressed further, either in additional sessions or through referral. For this tool to be effective in clinical practice, it needs to be updated regularly during subsequent visits to the counsellor. As it is an unfamiliar tool to most counsellors, as well as being an emotional process, counsellors should first do their own medical genogram with a counsellor or colleague, to gain experience in its use and experience at first hand the impact of talking about family relationships by using this method.

CONCLUSION

The medical genogram offers counsellors a process tool for engaging in a different way with patients, with a focus on social support and on identifying transgenerational patterns. It can also help to open up new lines of enquiry with the patient and to place illness and health problems in the context of the patient's unique social milieu. In particular, it can boost the morale of both the patient and the family by highlighting each member's coping skills. The genogram can integrate a wealth of physical and psychological information into an inclusive diagnostic presentation, linking relationships with the medical and psychological problems in a more inclusive way that becomes a bio-psychosocial cycle. Tracking the family's social and cultural history will point out particular strengths and weaknesses that may otherwise be missed within the family system – factors that may be a resource for the patient's recovery.

Chapter 11

Cognitive Behavioural Therapy in Health Care Settings

INTRODUCTION

This chapter aims to give an overview of cognitive behavioural therapy (CBT) in health care settings and discuss some of the main concepts and techniques used in treating common mental health problems seen in health care; namely, depression and anxiety. We can only hope to give a brief introduction here, but anticipate that the references cited will encourage further reading.

Cognitive behavioural therapy has emerged as a useful form of therapy in many settings since the 1970s. Clinical trials have demonstrated its efficacy in the treatment of a number of mental health conditions, such as anxiety disorders, depression and sexual problems (Hawton *et al.*, 1999) and some personality disorders (Young *et al.*, 2003). The theory and techniques can also be applied to a number of health-related problems, including chronic fatigue syndrome (CFS) and chronic pain, and used in other medical settings such as cardiology, surgery and oncology (White, 2001). Some of the clinical outcomes achieved with CBT have compared favourably with those for psychotropic medication, and this has in part led to advocacy for the approach in a National Health Service (NHS) led increasingly by outcome research. The National Institute for Health and Clinical Excellence (NICE) has recommended CBT for the treatment of a range of conditions (NICE, 2004; 2005). As a result, many counsellors based in health care settings may benefit from gaining a greater understanding of the theoretical basis of this methodology and learning more about the practical applications of this versatile form of counselling.

This is not to say that CBT has a proven value over other forms of counselling and psychotherapy for every clinical problem, or that it will be applicable to all types of patients in all situations. However, it may be that counsellors schooled in other strands of therapy can gain from widening their skill base to include the cognitive behavioural framework. CBT can blend well within briefer approaches to therapy, for example (Curwen *et al.*, 2000). Also, many of the therapeutic interventions advocated by CBT can serve as useful supplementary techniques in various theoretical approaches; thus, it can also have a place in an integrative approach.

CBT embraces two principal philosophies: (i) that change is possible at any moment; and (ii) that the process of therapy belongs to the patient. In CBT, variations in behaviour and thoughts are seen as vital opportunities for therapeutic interventions. Such interventions do not need to be introduced by the therapist alone; indeed, one of the strengths of CBT lies in its collaborative approach. This joint effort is intended to empower and educate the patient so that he will be able to initiate and recognize change outside the therapeutic setting. The CBT approach is also goal-focused, using achievable objectives to maximize time and motivation. The behavioural techniques of CBT are used to accomplish these targets with small, manageable tasks, while many of the cognitive techniques focus on the language and thinking of the patient.

CBT cognitive work is based on the belief that the way in which we describe events has a powerful impact on our emotions. Our language and thoughts also help us to formulate long-lasting beliefs about the self, others and the world. The CBT approach encourages work to alter those beliefs, so that positive change in the patient may be long-lasting. However, the content of a CBT session remains focused on 'here and now' problems and immediate thoughts, so that patients are able to capitalize on the issues that are current in their lives.

THEORETICAL OVERVIEW OF CBT

The Stoic philosopher Epictetus is variously quoted as stating 'Men are not worried by things but by their ideas about things' (Powell, 2000). This concept forms the underlying principle of cognitive therapy, in that it is based on the premise that thoughts mediate and interact with emotions. This interaction is cyclical in nature: thoughts generate feelings and, in turn, feelings produce cognitions. When thoughts are consistently negative in nature, the resulting affect could be either depression or anxiety. In addition, behaviour and physical symptoms may help to maintain the cycle of negative thoughts and feelings. For example, a depressed patient may pass a friend on the street who fails to acknowledge him. Instead of thinking, 'My friend must not have seen me', the depressed patient may think something like, 'Oh, I am so awful that even my friends are ignoring me'. This negative thought could then generate feelings of sadness and despair, rendering the patient more depressed and even more likely to interpret the next benign event as being negative. Moreover, the patient may also initiate behaviours that would further validate these feelings. In this case, the patient may not call out to the friend, believing that the friend does not want to see him, and may start to avoid social gatherings altogether. The more isolated the patient becomes, the more compelling his negative thoughts will appear to be, and the depressed state is therefore maintained.

The role of cognitions

The thought patterns and beliefs (cognitions) that underlie our perceptions of the world are a major focus of cognitive therapy. These have been termed 'schemas' or 'core beliefs': extremely stable and long-standing patterns of thinking developed early in life that are added to through a person's experiences. Schemas are important beliefs about the individual and his environment that the individual accepts without question. They are self-perpetuating and resistant to change (Bricker and Young, 1993). Schemas are used unconsciously by people, to interpret the events in their lives and determine their responses. This is seen as a normal developmental process, helping us to order the world and our experience.

Problems occur when the schemas or core beliefs formed are unhelpful. For example, a person may present with an 'abandonment' schema based on childhood events, which may cause that person to interpret neutral events and interactions in a distrustful manner. A person with such a schema would have an exaggerated view that others will eventually leave or withdraw from them (Young *et al.*, 2003). Hence, in reacting to a cancelled date, the patient with an abandonment schema may have imme-diate thoughts such as 'I am so boring, people hate to be with me' or 'I am sure this person is going to leave me'. These thoughts are termed 'auto-matic thoughts' as they are generally immediate and occur without any conscious effort. They are seen as being generated by the negative schema or core beliefs. CBT is therefore often concerned with accessing and chal-lenging dysfunctional schemas, and developing more balanced, healthier perspectives on life. Similarly, the beliefs a patient has about illness and his ability to cope will have a profound impact on how that person deals with a diagnosis such as cancer or diabetes and may even affect the prognosis. Through gentle questioning at the assessment stage of counselling, the counsellor can begin to see how beliefs and thoughts influence the patient's experience, and use this knowledge to devise interventions.

Just as thoughts and beliefs can contribute to the development and maintenance of problems, so can people's thoughts and beliefs 'about' their thinking. These are known as metacognitions and they may be the target of therapeutic intervention. Where metacognitions are the result of thinking errors, they can contribute to the maintenance of problems such as health anxiety and generalized anxiety disorder (GAD). For example, a patient may hold a belief that anxious thoughts in themselves may be 'dangerous', and might eventually bring about mental collapse (Wells, 1997). The patient may then interpret the fact that he worries about things as indicating that he is going mad. The patient may then become more upset, possibly leading to the generation of more worrying thoughts. The counsellor working with this patient would encourage him to re-examine his beliefs about worry.

COGNITIVE FORMULATION

Counsellors make a thorough assessment of the problems brought by the patients. This helps them to devise a cognitive formulation that identifies core beliefs or schemas and dysfunctional assumptions (rules) developed from early experiences. These beliefs and rules are responsible for gener-ating the patient's negative automatic thoughts. The formulation also includes the critical incident that caused the patient to seek help ('Why now?') and the negative thoughts, feelings and behaviours that are main-taining the current affective state. The formulation is shared with the patients and is used to structure the progress of counselling. The example shown in Figure 11.1 overleaf offers a cognitive conceptualization taken from an assessment interview with a patient presenting with symptoms of depression. It shows how early experience can give rise to unhelpful core beliefs and dysfunctional assumptions about the world, which can be activated by an adverse event. This activation gives rise to the negative automatic thoughts experienced in response to a range of events. In depression, Beck (1967) observes that these form a 'cognitive triad' of negative thoughts about the self, the world and the future. Such thoughts produce the distinctive symptoms in depression, which serve both to maintain and increase the discomfort that is characteristic of this common condition.

Figure 11.1 illustrates the approach of the CBT model to the aetiology and maintenance of depression. It also illustrates the targets for intervention in counselling sessions. Intervention can take place at different levels. As stated earlier, one approach might be to encourage patients to re-examine their core beliefs about the world. Other interventions might be focused on negative automatic thoughts, encouraging alternative explanations for events. Behavioural interventions might tackle the inactivity and anhedonia so common in depression or in the case of treatment for a phobia, to help the anxious patient to cope with rather than avoid their fears. Some of these approaches will be outlined below, but we must emphasize that these interventions will only be successful if mediated by a sound, collaborative relationship between the counsellor and patient. Inviting a patient to change or challenge their ways of thinking may be perceived as threatening by the depressed or anxious client, and may even reinforce their negative view of themselves. Therefore, taking time to hear a patient's story using the skills of active listening and an empathic approach is essential. Further, when a patient presents with long-term problems of depression, anxiety or chronic ill health, a lack of hope about the situation may lead the patient to doubt the efficacy of counselling. In such cases, it may be advisable to work with small behavioural changes, with the intention of improving the patient's mood before moving on to the examination of core beliefs.

CBT TECHNIQUES IN COUNSELLING

CBT is focused mainly on the present. The history of a problem is explored only in so far as it helps to understand the development of the current problem and its maintaining factors. Although the cognitive

Early Experiences

Information about the client's early and other significant experiences that may have shaped core beliefs and assumptions.
As a child, the patient was often compared unfavourably with others in terms of achievement. Patient's father left home when the patient was aged seven and did not maintain contact.

↓

Development of beliefs about the self, others and the world.
Unconditional core beliefs developed from early experience:
'I am not good enough' 'I am bad' 'I drive others away' 'I'm a failure'

↓

Dysfunctional Assumptions or Rules for Living

Conditional statements, often phrased as 'if . . . then' rules, to enable the individual to function despite core beliefs:
'I'll be OK as long as I get things right every time'
'If I don't do what people want they will reject me'

↓

Critical Incidents that Trigger Problems

Situations or events in which the rules are broken or assumptions are activated.
The patient loses his job in a departmental restructuring despite good overall performance.

↓

Negative Automatic Thoughts

Problem and factors maintaining the problem
'I'm useless and this proves it', 'I lost my job because I'm no good', 'I'll never be any good', 'It's all my fault', 'I'm stupid', 'Everyone thinks I'm no good'

↓

Symptoms

Physical symptoms, thoughts, emotions, behaviours interacting in a 'vicious cycle'.

Physical: Poor sleep, loss of appetite and libido
Cognitive: Poor concentration, indecisiveness, self-criticism, suicidal thoughts
Emotions: Sadness, guilt, worry
Behaviour: socially withdrawal, lowered activity levels

Figure 11.1 Cognitive conceptualization

formulation of a problem does include early experiences, this information is used mainly to help generate the types of rules and negative thought patterns that may be sustaining the current situation. From a behavioural perspective, CBT advocates well-defined and achievable goals. In this way, expectations can be properly set. Clear goals also help to motivate patients: when problems are broken down into obtainable objectives, patients can more readily begin to experience success. Goals should be set by the patient and be relevant to his life. In the philosophy of CBT, small successes cultivate larger ones.

LINKING BEHAVIOUR, FEELINGS AND THOUGHTS

CBT is based on empirical research that supports the validity of its techniques. Similarly, the process of counselling encourages patients to test and validate their thoughts and behaviours empirically. Patients who are depressed or anxious cannot be expected to assess their own or others' actions objectively, or to incorporate appropriate feedback readily into their belief systems. For this reason, CBT uses a variety of techniques, both in and out of session, which help the patient to test the validity of his automatic thoughts and belief structures.

Tracking particular behaviour is a mainstay of the CBT approach. Because accurate recall of events can be affected by emotions, having patients keep a written record of activities and thought processes can be an effective therapeutic tool. The simplest form of tracking exercises are activity schedules. These are often used with depressed patients. Activity schedules simply have the patient record his activities for every hour of the day except when asleep. Through such an exercise, counsellor and patient can work together to pinpoint the times of the day that are troublesome for the patient, or particular activities that may be counter-productive to the patient's therapeutic aims. For example, a patient may return with a work week's activity schedule whose morning to midday schedule is as shown in Figure 11.2 overleaf.

Immediately, patient and counsellor have material with which to work. The routine of sleeping each day until 9 or 10 and then watching television would do little for anyone's mood. The simple suggestion of getting up for three days in a row at 8:30 and going for a brief walk could be the initial change needed for the patient to start making more changes himself. Seeing on paper one's use of time can be 'eye-opening', while scheduling

Monday	Tuesday	Wednesday	Thursday	Friday
7–8 Asleep	Asleep	Asleep	Asleep	Asleep
8–9 Asleep	Asleep	Asleep	Asleep	Asleep
9–10 Asleep	Asleep	Watched TV	Watched TV	Asleep
10–11	Watched TV	Watched TV	Got dressed	Watched TV
11–12	Got dressed	Got dressed	Read help ads	Got dressed
12–1	Lunch at pub	Read help ads	Lunch at pub	Collected dole
1–2	Watched TV	Lunch at pub	Talked with friends at pub	Lunch/grocery shopping
2–3	Talked on phone	Went to friend's house	Watched TV	Put away food

Figure 11.2　An activity schedule

changes can be a therapeutic intervention made by either the patient or the counsellor. These schedules can also serve to illustrate the links between feelings and behaviour for the patient.

Mastery and pleasure sheets are similar to activity schedules but also ask the patient to rate how well he felt he had mastered a particular activity, and how much pleasure had been derived from it. A ten-point scale can be used, with 1 representing no mastery or pleasure associated with the activity and 10 representing complete mastery or satisfaction with it. Two ratings are given for each activity. Mastery and pleasure sheets are particularly helpful with depressed patients who report no variation in their mood level or enjoyment of activities. The sheets quickly allow patients to see that variation does occur, even if it is minimal. For all patients, this exercise can clearly help to distinguish which activities and events are positive experiences and which are less satisfactory. The depressed patient can be encouraged to introduce more activities that bring pleasure and mastery into their week. Such methods can lead to an improvement in mood, which in turn can help to increase patient commitment to the counselling process.

THE ROLE OF DESENSITIZATION AND GRADED EXPOSURE WHEN TREATING ANXIETY (see Figures 11.3 and 11.4 overleaf)

CBT has been particularly effective in treating anxiety by using a combination of desensitization and graded exposure techniques. The human body cannot sustain a state of high anxiety indefinitely. At some point, the anxiety will reach a peak and then steadily decline. Unfortunately, because anxiety is by definition uncomfortable, most people never experience its declining aspect – they remove, or sufficiently distract, themselves from the situation before the decline occurs. In this way, the experience and memory of it remain distressing, that it was something that could not be handled, and this reinforces the patient's anxiety. Desensitization methods involve exposing a patient for long enough to his anxiety so that the anxiety would peak and then abate, thus teaching the patient that he can 'live through' that anxiety. Graded exposure methods manage the anxiety level of a given task, adjusting the level to the readiness of the patient and gradually increasing the level of difficulty as the patient progresses. Patients usually begin with a task they rate as moderately uncomfortable and work through a series of tasks with increased exposure to anxiety.

Imaginative rehearsal of an anxiety-provoking task or situation is a key component of desensitization and graded exposure work. Once a patient can 'see' himself accomplishing a task in his mind, he is much more confident in performing such a task in reality. Most of us imagine ourselves in different situations as a natural part of anticipated events: it is a normal coping method of everyday life. Thus, using imaginative rehearsal with a patient helps to normalize the experience within the therapeutic setting, and capitalizes on a method of learning that can be repeated by the patient outside the therapeutic setting.

Related to in-session desensitization, graded task assignments out of session allow patients to tackle their fears while in the natural environment. Patient and counsellor brainstorm tasks of various degrees of difficulty for the patient to perform outside the therapy setting. Tasks are organized according to the level of difficulty, and patients are usually encouraged to start with a task that generates the least anxiety (Padesky

Angela entered counselling for anxiety associated with having blood taken. She had become progressively fearful of needles to the extent that she was unable to have routine bloods taken for the monitoring of her medical condition. She started to sweat when anticipating a blood sample being taken and became panicky. She avoided going to clinic appointments, a situation that was beginning to have a detrimental effect on her medical care.

After establishing a solid therapeutic bond with Angela, the counsellor began desensitization training with her, explaining the theory behind the approach. The counsellor likened the exercise to jumping out of a plane. At first, to any novice, the thought of jumping out of a plane may be frightening, and the first jump may even be dreadful. But if that person were to continue jumping out of a plane repeatedly, after the 35th jump the experience would not be nearly so frightening. That person would have become 'desensitized' to jumping out of planes.

With this explanation, the counsellor and Angela then spent the rest of the session simply looking at and handling a needle and a blood collection bottle. At first, the exercise was rehearsed in the patient's imagination, with Angela imagining what it would be like to hold the needle and monitoring the level of anxiety she felt. When the anxiety level associated with that exercise decreased, Angela and the counsellor began to hold and examine the needle. Gradually, the difficulty of the task was increased; touching the skin with the needle, drawing the needle along the skin without breaking it and so on. Finally, Angela was coached through having her skin punctured by the needle. With practice, she was able to resume her clinic visits and felt a greater sense of control over her health.

Figure 11.3   The use of graded exposure in a case of a needle phobia

and Greenberger, 1995). This task is performed numerous times until the anxiety level associated with it is minimal. The patient then graduates to the next-level task on the list. The idea is to utilize the time between sessions for therapeutic gain and for the patient to experience success outside the therapeutic setting.

Coping statements, such as the one used by Jennifer, are a key component of exposure assignments. They help to mediate negative automatic thoughts and to keep the patient focused on a more positive outcome. For these reasons, CBT often uses flashcards to help patients remember coping statements during times of distress. In session, patient and counsellor generate a list of coping statements that target problem issues and recurring negative automatic thoughts. These can be written on a small card,

Jennifer was referred for therapy to deal with social anxiety. She experienced panic at the thought of going anywhere alone in public and had to be escorted to her counselling meetings by a friend. In the first session, Jennifer and the therapist came up with a list of activities that Jennifer felt uncomfortable in performing but that she would also like to accomplish by the end of therapy. The list and the associated level of difficulty looked like this:

Standing outside on her front porch	3
Posting a letter at the end of her street	4
Going to the corner shop for milk, etc.	6
Taking a walk in the park (without her dog)	7.5
Arriving for counselling unaccompanied	7.5
Having lunch alone at the local pub	9

The counsellor and Jennifer practised imaginative rehearsal of posting a letter at the end of her street until Jennifer felt comfortable with the idea. They also brainstormed various coping statements she could say to herself when her anxiety increased, such as, 'I will be OK. I may be anxious but that is a natural thing to feel since I haven't done this for a long time.' Her assignment for the week was to rehearse the scenario in her mind each morning and to post a letter by herself five times. She was also to begin imagining herself going to the corner shop alone. By the following week, Jennifer reported that she had not only posted her letters every day that week, but that she had also made three trips to the corner shop by herself.

Figure 11.4 Graded exposure in the treatment of social anxiety

such as an index card, and carried around in the patient's wallet. Thus, whenever and wherever a patient may be when they feel anxiety beginning, he is armed with effective coping statements. The patient is instructed to read through the coping statements as the anxiety occurs, and as many times as necessary to handle the situation. The statements should be generated together with the patient, and they should address directly the issues that the patient fears. A typical coping statement for anxiety might read:

Right now, I am feeling anxious. I am worried that I am going to have a panic attack. However, I know that this feeling could be faulty, just as prejudices are. Chances are I am going to be OK, just like everyone else here. I have been in much worse situations and I have managed to do just fine.

Statements need not even be this elaborate. Some patients may just need one or two lines of positive reinforcement, such as:

- I can make this speech. I am an expert in my field.
- Being nervous is just energy. I can use that energy to help me.
- I am the mother of five children. If I can handle them, I can handle just about anything.
- Thousands of people fly in planes every day. It is safer than driving in a car, which I do every day and I have never been hurt.
- I can ask for a rise. I am a strong and intelligent person and do my job well. The worst my boss can say is no (and if he does, he obviously doesn't know what I'm worth!).

Flashcards and coping statements are small interventions that can have a long-lasting and significant impact.

AUTOMATIC THOUGHTS

In CBT, automatic thoughts are those that seem to jump into a patient's mind with little or no effort at all. They are a spontaneous response to a situation and may defy logic. For example, if a person is depressed he might have automatic thoughts such as 'I am such a loser!' or 'I can never get anything right!' or 'Nobody likes me!' Examination and rewording of the language within automatic thoughts can be a direct and meaningful exercise. The flash cards and coping statements mentioned in the example above are two methods for intervening to prevent the adverse outcomes of negative automatic thoughts.

Because of their spontaneous nature, automatic thoughts tend to be both highly emotional and judgemental, and contain what is often referred to as 'thinking errors'. These biases tend to maintain or even exacerbate a problem by distorting information and by keeping the patient from processing new information. These errors include:

- All or nothing: a person sees things in black and white categories and misses the grey. If something is not perfect, it is a failure. After getting a poor grade in mathematics, a person might think, 'I am so stupid; I should just drop out of school.'

■ Overgeneralization: a person sees a negative event as a never-ending pattern of defeat. The person uses words such as 'always' and 'never'.

■ Mental filter: a person picks out a single negative feature and dwells on it. A person makes a great four-course dinner but dwells on the potatoes being slightly overcooked.

■ Discounting the positive: a person rejects positive experiences, demanding that they do not 'count' – 'Anyone could have passed that test.'

■ Jumping to conclusions: a person makes negative interpretations without facts to support them. The person 'mind reads' or engages in fortune-telling.

■ Magnification: a person exaggerates the importance of negative events or personal shortcomings – 'My dyslexia makes it impossible for me to learn.'

■ Emotional reasoning: a person assuming that his negative emotions are true/realistic and/or reflect something negative about himself – 'I feel so guilty. I must be an awful father.'

■ 'Should statements': a person tells himself things 'should' be a certain way, expecting unrealistic performance from himself and others.

■ Labelling: a person attaches a highly emotive negative label to himself. Instead of saying 'I made a mistake', such a person would say 'I am an idiot'.

■ Personalization and blame: a person sees himself as the cause of bad events for which he is not responsible – 'If I had only been a better husband, none of this would have happened.'

(Adapted from Burns, 1990, pp. 8–11)

All of these thinking errors keep a patient in a negative or counterproductive thought cycle. In counselling sessions, simply pointing out the errors being made and assisting the assessment of alternatives can help to set a healthier approach to the presenting problem. Thus, if a patient sighs under his breath, 'I am never going to overcome this problem. I am such an idiot. I may as well give up', the counsellor might intervene by directing the patient's attention to his own words and challenging the patient to express thoughts in a more realistic manner. The patient above can be redirected to think 'Sometimes, it feels as though I am not going to solve this problem' and 'I am able to solve other problems, so I may be able to solve this one.' The change is small but it diffuses the negativity and inevitability while still validating the patient's frustration with the situation.

Automatic thoughts, and the thinking errors often contained within them, are a ripe and fruitful area for change. They offer an immediate and accessible avenue to the patient's emotional and cognitive state. Thus, cognitive therapy recommends working with automatic thoughts when they are 'hot'; that is, as they occur. In this way, the use of time is maximized for the patient. Issues are handled as they are happening, because this is when issues can be explored with the most accuracy and detail. Thus, counsellors may ask patients to describe recent examples of difficult situations and, through gentle questioning bring negative automatic thoughts into consciousness where they can be open to re-examination via techniques such as verbal challenging. This involves eliciting alternatives to automatic thoughts from the patient rather than them being supplied in a didactic exchange. Thus the patient who has the negative thought, 'I can't go out, no one will talk to me' would be encouraged to ask themselves the following questions:

What is the evidence for this thought?

What alternative views are there?

What are the advantages and disadvantages of this way of thinking?

What thinking errors am I making?

Thus, the patient can start to see his thoughts not as facts but as statements that may be examined rather than accepted at face value.

Thought diaries are widely-used CBT tracking tools that help patients to realize the connections between automatic thoughts, feelings and behaviour. These are pro forma sheets completed by a patient between sessions. They provide 'hot' examples for future counselling sessions and begin the process of the patient learning to identify and correct his own thinking errors. This is aimed at supporting long-term improvement. A typical thought diary may be laid out as shown in Figure 11.5. Thought diaries are used to track difficult experiences and emotions for the patient during the week. Patients are asked to record undesirable feelings and the related events as close as possible to the time at which they occurred. This

How did you feel? (rate 1–10; 10 is the worst you can feel)	What was happening?	What were you thinking?	What did you do?
Miserable 8	My boyfriend hung up on me	'I am such a loser'; 'I always mess everything up'	Cried; ate a tub of ice cream
Lonely 9	Nothing. I was in bed by myself.	'I am always going to be alone'; 'I have been alone my whole life'	Cried; cried; called my boyfriend 20 times; watched TV until I fell asleep

Figure 11.5 Entries in a thought diary

allows the patient to recall the events and thoughts with much more accuracy.

Thought diaries open up several avenues of exploration and intervention for both patient and therapist. First, the diary demonstrates that the patient's automatic thoughts are likely to be a contributing factor to his mood. Calling yourself a 'loser' in a crisis is unlikely to elevate your frame of mind. Having the patient evaluate the validity of his thoughts after the situation can help him to reappraise the events. In the example given here, the patient's automatic thoughts contain many thinking errors that probably escalated the severity of the situation. In the CBT approach, patient and counsellor would work together to find more valid and/or beneficial statements. Eventually, the patient would be expected to find and correct, on his own, thinking errors closer to, or during, the actual situations. The diary also makes clear which solutions are or are not working for the patient. In the example in Figure 11.5, both patient and counsellor can readily see that the solutions attempted here, in the 'What did you do?' column, did not help to resolve the situation to the patient's benefit. As such, the patient and therapist are able to work together to develop alternative activities that would help to resolve or manage the difficulty in a better way. In brief therapy, where the focus of change may be to simply increase solutions that are working and decrease those that are not, the 'What did you do?' column of a thought diary may provide clear examples of each. Finally, thought diaries help the patient to break down a crisis into manageable pieces. By focusing on one element of a situation, patients can begin to deal with a crisis that might otherwise have seemed overwhelming to them.

WORKING ON CORE BELIEFS

It can be harder to identify underlying beliefs than negative automatic thoughts, because beliefs do not occur as one-off thoughts in word form, but often as non-verbal assumptions or general rules (Fennell, 1999). Many patients are unaware of their deep beliefs and will not have access to them. In the therapeutic setting, these beliefs may have to be inferred rather than observed directly. Themes may emerge in the nature of a patient's automatic thoughts or the things that a patient finds important; global evaluations of themselves and others can point to a patient's underlying rules and assumptions, or strong childhood memories of an event that seem to match the patient's current views of the world. Sometimes, therapists use belief questionnaires to identify underlying beliefs.

Beliefs can also be identified and explored through Socratic questioning. This is a gentle but searching form of questioning that attempts to guide the patient through a process of discovery (Padesky, 1993). Each question attempts to understand the patient's position at a deeper level, as if a layer of dust is being removed from the meaning of a problem with each question that is asked. In a very rudimentary form, Socratic questions continually seek to answer the question, 'So what?'. That is, 'What is the meaning of this situation to you?'; 'What does this or that say about you?'; 'How does that affect your life?' As a good counsellor cannot assume anything about a problem, Socratic questioning helps to ascertain the root of the problem; that is, why, at its very core, the problem is causing difficulties for the patient.

For example, a patient might enter counselling and say, 'Oh, it was awful. There I was in front of the entire audience of 500 enthusiasts and my mind went completely blank. I couldn't think of a word to say.' As a human being, one can certainly relate to the situation of feeling 'awful' – most people would feel that this scenario was indeed an undesirable one. However, a CBT therapist needs to 'go deeper'. She needs to uncover exactly what the patient meant by 'not being able to think of a word to say'.

A Socratic line of questioning might continue, 'Yes, that does sound difficult. However, I was wondering what in particular was the most awful aspect for you. What did you think might happen?' In asking the patient to theorize about what might have happened, the question directs his attention to relevant information that might be outside the patient's immediate focus (Padesky, 1993). Such information helps to define the situation better for both the patient and the counsellor. Consider these two answers:

Patient: *Well, everyone must have been thinking how stupid I was! I mean, I just looked so stupid and dumb. No one was ever going to talk to me at the convention. I could just picture myself being all alone once again, the loser, the outcast.*

Or

Patient: *Well, I might have lost my job! Five hundred people and not a word to say! That's not a sign of an expert! I was a complete failure.*

In the first answer, the patient has fears about being alone and disliked by other people. In a cognitive formulation, the core beliefs might be, 'I will always be alone', or 'I am inherently different from other people', or even 'No one will ever love me'. These are a different set of beliefs from those that could be extrapolated from the second answer. These seem to centre more on fears of failure rather than fears of being alone. Concerns about achievement might be at the core of this patient's fears such as, 'I will always fail no matter what I do.'

   These initial answers are just the first set of 'clues' to patients' overall view of their problems. A good therapist will need to explore these answers fully in order to build a complete picture of patients' fears. Socratic questioning is designed to help in the gentle probing for the deeper meaning of a problem so that the significance can be readily obtained and future problems centred on the same issue can be avoided. This method of questioning is useful in guiding therapist and patient towards readily understanding the meaning of a situation. This dialogue can also lead to a modification of a dysfunctional core belief. Some general guidelines to follow when using a Socratic approach include:

1   Ask questions that the client has the ability to answer.
2   Try to find relevant information that is outside the current frame of focus.
3   Generally move from concrete to more abstract levels of understanding.
4   Allow the patient to apply any new information to his understanding (Padesky, 1993).

This final point made by Padesky is an important one, especially when using a brief approach. As therapists attempting to use time in the most resourceful manner, it is easy to find ourselves directing patients towards a particular understanding of a problem. Although we may think our understanding of the problem under discussion is sound, a patient's self-discovery will always have the most profound effect. A good counsellor must allow her patient to put the pieces of the puzzle together. With Socratic questioning, we can pick up a piece and hold it to the light for the patient to see, but the patient will only feel that he has completed the puzzle when he chooses and places each piece.

Once dysfunctional core beliefs have been identified, it is possible to work with the patient with the aim of modifying the original beliefs into more helpful ones that will enhance long-term change and prevent a recurrence of symptoms. It should also be noted that direct work on the patient's core beliefs may not always be necessary in CBT. Successful work on automatic thoughts and the positive feedback provided by graded exposure or behavioural experiments can have a beneficial impact on beliefs. Also, any individual will have a range of core beliefs, many of which are helpful. An improvement in mood can lead to activation of these beliefs, which can help to maintain the reduction in symptoms of depression or anxiety. However, powerful core beliefs will affect the progress of therapy and such work will still be required.

Core beliefs are more resistant to change than the somewhat transitory negative automatic thoughts, although some similar methods can be used. The process of looking for more adaptive alternatives to negative automatic thoughts can help to demonstrate that thinking patterns are, to some extent, learned, and therefore alternatives can become integrated into a person's life. Core beliefs tend to be absolute 'I am a bad person'; 'I am unlovable'; 'Bad things will happen to me'; and lead to unreasonable demands: 'I must be perfect or they will reject me'; 'I must check my body for signs of illness every day or I will die'. Psycho-education about the nature of such beliefs and rules can help to provide grounding for a discussion of the types of belief that might be more realistic and helpful. The patient and therapist can then devise behavioural experiments in which the patient acts as though the more adaptive belief were true.

CONCLUSIONS

The CBT approach may not suit the desires and needs of all patients. Our approach with each patient must be tailored to meet the needs of that individual patient. Counsellors must listen to the language and expectations of their patients at all times. Patients who anticipate some exploration of their past or the meaning of their feelings may need to spend time on those issues. As stated earlier, the outcome of counselling will depend on the development of a good therapeutic alliance, and it is the responsibility of the counsellor to shift the focus and introduce techniques to build the counsellor–patient relationship. Furthermore, patients who are resistant to change may also be more resistant towards direct methods, such as out-of-session work. These techniques may need to be scaled down or approached more carefully with such patients. The balance between what is working for a patient and what is not will be different for every patient that walks into a counselling session and may even be different for each patient in every session. The more tools we have to hand, the more likely we may be to find the right ones to help our patients.

Themes and Issues Relating to Counselling Practice

Chapter 12

Dealing with Confidentiality and Secrets in the Course of Counselling

INTRODUCTION

Psychotherapeutic relationships are bound by confidentiality parameters. This is fundamental to the aims and principles of good counselling practice and the therapeutic relationship and process. The rules governing confidentiality in health care settings, and for counselling with people experiencing health problems, are no different from those that apply in other settings or for other problems. However, the issues are sometimes more complex. In health care, there is usually a need for collaborative working relationships with colleagues, and secrets may affect the patient's overall care and relationships when working within multi-disciplinary health care teams (Evans and Bor, 2005). *Ethical Framework for Good Practice in Counselling and Psychotherapy* (British Association of Counselling, 2002) sets out to define confidentiality. For example:

A counsellor should take all responsible steps to communicate clearly the extent of confidentiality he is offering to patients. This should normally be made clear in the pre-counselling information or in the initial contracting.

If counsellors include consultation with colleagues and others in the confidential relationship, this should be stated to the patient at the beginning of counselling.

The breaking of confidentiality is similarly subject to rules and guidelines. There are a number of circumstances where confidentiality can be broken. These are:

■ When the patient gives consent to the counsellor to break confidentiality.
■ When the information to be disclosed is already public knowledge (and as such is no longer secret or a breach of confidence).
■ When it is in the public interest to do so; that is, the public interest outweighs the individual interest (for example, the patient is a risk to herself or to the public).

Each situation has to be judged on its own merits, and the counsellor can use supervision and consultation to reach a shared decision about the need to disclose. But even the parameters of confidentiality within supervision and consultative relationships may be open to interpretation:

Care must be taken to ensure that personally identifiable information is not transmitted through overlapping networks of confidential relationships. For this reason it is good practice to avoid identifying specific patients during counselling supervision/consultative support and other consultations, unless there are sound reasons for doing so.

How do colleagues who are seeing the same patient, but are not aware that other colleagues are involved, come to share information and generate group ideas, if the person discussed is 'unidentifiable'? Does this really happen? An example from a health care setting illustrates this problem:

A patient with health anxieties kept phoning numerous health professionals within the same team in a hospital to discuss her symptoms and seek advice in a bid to allay her anxieties, albeit temporarily.

Without discussion within the team or with other affiliated health professionals, this individual continued to make regular telephone calls to different team members. This only served to sustain her health anxiety problem rather than treat it, and she felt she was being given slightly different information each time she spoke to a team member. Her calls (and worry) went on for several months before a member of staff eventually realized what was happening and started to compare details with other members of the team. It was only when the patient's name and clinical details were shared that a more appropriate way of managing this patient's problems could begin. Instead of offering limitless and differing reassurances, firm boundaries were set as to whom and when she could call, with the same information and intervention being used. This served to contain and reduce her anxieties so that problems underlying her health worry could be addressed and treated.

WHAT IS CONFIDENTIALITY?

Central to the concept of confidentiality is the sharing or withholding of personal information according to a set of rules or guidelines. Where rules are implicit, however, there is scope for ambiguity, assumption and idiosyncratic approaches to maintaining and breaking confidentiality.

Secrets

Confidentiality is sometimes understood to imply secrecy, which is not altogether correct. Secrets, like confidential information, may be withheld or shared selectively between individuals or groups. It is the withholding and sharing of secrets that creates alliances and boundaries between individuals and systems. A shift in the power dynamics and relationship between 'those who know' and 'those who don't know' can emerge, creating a context for power relationships (Campbell *et al.*, 1994). There are three main forms of secrets: individual secrets; internal secrets; and shared secrets.

Individual secrets are those in which a person withholds information from others in a system (for example, colleagues, family). An individual belongs to many systems, which may interrelate or function independently. For example:

> An elderly man decided not to tell anyone about his biopsy until after the results were known. He thought he might tell his wife if the results were positive, but at this stage, no relatives or friends were told that he was having the biopsy.

Internal secrets require at least one person in the system to be privy to the secret. Different levels of knowledge (about the secret) create two subsystems, those who know and those who do not. For example:

> A friend who assures the patient that everything said to her is entirely confidential – 'no one will ever know' – and therefore the information is shared between the two of them, has an internal secret.

Shared secrets are secrets that belong to the system organization but are withheld from external groups (for example, colleagues, the GP). They differ from internal secrets, where the information is shared with only one other person. For example:

> a patient told her mother, father and sister that she had cancer of the cervix, but asked them not to tell anyone else for the time being.

To ensure effective procedures are in place for managing issues and problems stemming from confidentiality, the rules need to be made explicit and disseminated to the target or affected audience. This may include patients as well as health care professionals, so that everyone has the same knowledge of what is meant by confidentiality within a given context or setting. This balances the power dynamics and creates a uniting context where 'everybody knows' (replacing the 'those who know' and 'those who don't' context and the perceived difference and power dynamic). Counsellors can help patients to reach decisions about the disclosure of information by addressing the reasons why someone needs to be informed, as well as the possible consequences of sharing personal and sensitive information.

The consequences of having secrets

The effect of keeping a secret may be either positive or negative. On the positive side, it might protect someone from painful information, such as a parent not being told upsetting news about his or her child. But on the negative side, it can lead to feelings of anxiety, dishonesty, suspicion and exclusion. It is not uncommon for people diagnosed with a serious illness to keep this information as an individual or internal secret, at least for a time, while they consider the implications or wait until symptoms show and they are no longer in a position to conceal the illness. While this might protect significant others, keeping the secret might produce anxiety and isolation in the individual. Also, there is a possibility that late disclosure will create further anxiety and complications, because the significant other might construe the withholding of information as a sign of a lack of closeness, fear of the significant other, or being lied to.

Another unforeseen problem might arise when the information withheld needs to be shared for ethical and safety reasons. For example, when a patient tells a counsellor not to tell her doctor that she is saving up her tranquillizers to take her own life, the counsellor is colluding with the patient's suicidal threat unless she discloses the threat to the doctor for the patient's safety. Similarly, if a patient tells a counsellor that she is not going to tell her sexual partner that she is HIV positive and will continue to have unprotected intercourse with the partner, the health of the partner is in jeopardy, raising ethical and legal dilemmas for those holding this information. In fact, the intentional infection of someone with HIV by not using protection during intercourse, or failure to disclose the diagnosis to a partner, is now regarded as a criminal act in the UK, for which there have been several prosecutions (Mears, 2007). Counsellors must not collude with a patient and turn a blind eye to such a criminal act; they should, at the very least, raise their concerns with the patient and document that they have done so, should the matter come to the attention of the legal system. Through counselling, however, individuals may be helped to find more constructive ways of addressing the dilemmas and complications of sharing and withholding information. It can provide a method for establishing communication and looking at the underlying issues. Within the wider clinical system, it may be helpful to promote team confidentiality and more comprehensive care, with health care workers working together rather than in opposition or in ignorance of others' involvement.

CONFIDENTIALITY IN HEALTH CARE PRACTICE

A two-tier approach

Confidentiality is an absolute term. Something is either confidential or it is not. In lay language, however, it has become common to refer to confidentiality in a graded format:

- Top-secret information;
- Very confidential information;
- Less confidential information; and
- Common knowledge.

In health care practice, it is not uncommon to observe a two-tier approach to confidentiality: the 'top secret' or 'very confidential' information is only disclosed under the strictest procedure, and the 'less confidential' information can become common knowledge among health care staff and anyone listening to their conversations or glancing at available records and forms. Examples of 'top secret' or 'very confidential' information include diagnoses of terminal illness, a history of sexual abuse, a history of alcohol abuse, depression and attempted suicide. Examples of 'less confidential information' or 'common knowledge' include details of a patient's blood group, marital status, number of children, profession, blood pressure recordings and medical procedures such as the extraction of wisdom teeth or tonsils. Whether patient information is deemed very confidential or less confidential often depends on the degree to which the information is thought by the health care professional to be private or associated with stigma. Of course, the move towards computerized medical records in the NHS, and the long-standing right of patients to access their own medical notes, means that – whether intended or not – information about a patient might become available to more people than just her counsellor and doctor. For guidance on how to record clinical notes, and the rules pertaining to access to a patient's record, readers should consult Du Plessis and Hirst (2006).

Differences may occur over the need or requirement for information between health care professionals, particularly between the medical and nursing team and allied therapy professionals. This is especially apparent for counsellors, who see the confidential relationship as a therapeutic relationship based on trust. Only in rare cases would these health professionals disclose patient information. This is in contrast to the medical team approach, which relies on 'shared confidentiality' and open discussion about patient details, including name, age, relationship status and so on, as well as their physical and mental state of health.

The open flow of information within a team is essential in order to provide consistent medical care. The above differences in perspective may be the root cause of conflict in a health care setting, where communication between health care professionals may be impeded by different notions of confidentiality. Counsellors need to be aware of this potential source of ambiguity and seek to clarify team confidentiality boundaries, so that everyone involved can develop a common view of what is meant by confidentiality for individual patients and sets of circumstances.

Management of secrets

The following suggestions provide a practical approach to managing secrets in clinical practice:

- Identify whether there is a secret.
- Identify whether there is a problem related to the secret, and for whom this is a problem.
- Clarify dilemmas and problems associated with maintaining this secret; for example, consider the advantages and disadvantages and the implications (using future-orientated and hypothetical questions).
- Obtain written or verbal consent to liaise with other relevant health professionals. Keep a record of such conversations.
- Reflect on your involvement in the process; that is, are you *colluding* with the individual by agreeing to keep the secret, or *challenging* the individual by not agreeing to keep it? The patient should be advised at the outset that it may be necessary to break confidentiality for legal/ethical reasons. Or should you *opt out/refer* – for problems that do not have legal implications but, rather, create an impasse in therapy that might require treatment to cease, or for the patient to be referred?

Secrets, families and children

Secrets in families are common and may involve outside agencies in their maintenance and disclosure. The counsellor can play a role in helping families and professionals to acknowledge secrets in families, particularly transgenerational secrets between parent and child. Such transgenerational secrets may involve professionals working on behalf of the child, and represent 'conflicts of interest' and dilemmas. The following two examples illustrate this difficulty:

Case study

A parent wanted to be told everything about her 16-year-old daughter's visit to a GP, but the GP refused to discuss the consultation because of 'patient confidentiality'. The counsellor helped them to overcome the impasse by addressing the key dilemmas of parental versus medical responsibility for the girl's welfare. Mutual concern for her welfare and the wish to respect the girl's independence, while acknowledging her need for professional and parental help, was introduced as a theme that united both parental and medical interests, and led to collaborative working.

Case Study

At the outset of counselling, the counsellor explained to his patient that 'confidentiality' meant giving some feedback to the GP who had referred her to the counsellor. The patient had agreed to this. When the patient disclosed that she had given her daughter some of her sleeping tablets in order to help her to sleep, it was possible to discuss her reasons for doing this and the consequences, and to remind her that her GP might need this information in order to best care for her daughter. The patient was unhappy about this, and concerned that her daughter would be taken into care. However, since she had consented to the GP knowing, she was resigned to the outcome rather than feeling let down by the counsellor. They were also able to discuss openly the mother's concerns about the involvement of social services in their situation.

The following excerpt from another counselling session further illustrates how a counsellor can explore dilemmas associated with how information is disseminated between family members.

Counsellor: *You say that you can't tell your children about your motor neurone disease. What do you think they have already noticed about your health?*

Patient: *Well they must see me hesitate and have difficulty walking. I also slur my words. Jack even joked about my being drunk . . .*

Counsellor: *What do you think they think is going on?*

Patient: *I know Pat is concerned, she keeps telling me to go back to the doctors . . . I think she is worried.*

Counsellor: *What do you think she is most worried about?*

Patient: *That I have something serious, something incurable . . . that I'm not doing anything about it . . . but what she doesn't know is that there is no cure for my disease . . .*

Counsellor: *Do you think it would help her to know this?*

Patient: *Yes I guess so . . . and Jack, I don't want him getting the wrong idea . . . but I don't know how to tell them.*

Counsellor: *You know them very well; how would they suggest you tell someone some difficult news?*

Patient: *They would say just do it straight . . . no frills, to the point . . .*

Counsellor: *How could you do it in a way that they would appreciate?*

Patient: *Just say it . . . say I've got a disease which affects my nerves and that it can't be cured, and take it from there . . .*

Secrets in families may present as a communication impasse, in which a professional feels immobilized and unable to help the family break entrenched communication and behaviour patterns. Unpacking the secret can remove an obstacle to change for the family, the health worker and the counsellor.

Preventive methods

The counsellor can play a key role in preventing problems and improving patient care by facilitating communication between agencies and individuals. In particular, the counsellor can identify situations in which themes of 'impasse' or 'over-protection' occur. Examples would be, for example, when a doctor informs the relatives about an individual's terminal diagnosis before discussing it with the patient; or where a counsellor does not involve other members of the multi-disciplinary health care team for fear of breaking the confidentiality of a therapeutic relationship.

To avoid ambiguity and enhance patient care, it is also helpful to develop a confidentiality policy that details who needs to know what, when, why, and how. Where there is an explicit confidentiality policy available to health care workers and patients, open communication is more likely to take place. This is because people know in advance what are the possible implications of disclosure. They are also less likely to withhold information based on fears, assumptions and fantasy. If patients feel more able to be open and honest about their problems, health care workers are in a better position to address their needs and to generate appropriate solutions. A sample confidentiality policy is outlined below, to suggest ways in which an agency could develop guidelines to govern communication within health care teams and between groups (members of a GP practice, teams, departments and organizations). Such a policy is different from a professional code of conduct. Codes of practice and ethics are often drawn up with a particular professional discipline in mind. A confidentiality policy should take into account how information should be *shared across* disciplines and between departments and external agencies.

A sample confidentiality policy

1   The organization needs to have a set of written rules that are accessible to all members of staff, governing the way in which personal information about patients is obtained, stored and used.
2   It is necessary to specify how information is to be passed between agencies (computer network, papers and so on), how letters should be posted and received, who should read them, what discussion is necessary and with whom.
3   Rules need to be identified for storing information on computer disks (in accordance with the Data Protection Act), in paper files and so on. Access to and storage of information should be limited to those who really need to know.
4   Who needs to know and who does not should be made explicit. Procedures must be set up to ensure that access to information is limited only to those who need to know (this will include security procedures). Written consent for sharing information on a 'need to know' basis should be obtained from the patient. A written record should be kept of all conversations about the patient with other professionals, other agencies or the patient's relatives.
5   Strict guidelines need to be set out about how information is to be used. This must also include how the information should *not* be used, in order to protect patients from discriminatory practices.
6   Information that needs to be shared with other agencies should be detailed in the document. This would include how, when and why information might be shared with other health care workers, family, employers, occupational health or human resources teams, the patient's GP and so on.

CONCLUSION

Confidentiality is a much used but misunderstood concept because it is ambiguous and open to interpretation. It always relates to the passing (and withholding) of information between people and has to be interpreted in terms of its context. In health care settings, confidentiality is such an important and integral aspect of patient care that it is often 'taken as read', without due care and attention being paid to its meaning within a given context. Consequently, patients, families, health care workers, employers and others may have different views about what is meant by confidentiality, and this can create difficult and confusing situations. Breaches in confidentiality often arise from a lack of clarity about policies and practices and a lack of openness between individuals. Counsellors are well placed to consider, with the patients, the advantages and disadvantages of secrets, how they differ from confidentiality, and how to share information in the interest of optimal patient care.

Chapter 13

Giving Information and Breaking Bad News

INTRODUCTION

This chapter highlights relevant issues for counsellors and other health care professionals when they give information to patients, including imparting bad news. Consideration is given to the different emphases placed on *who* gives information (for example, counsellor, nurse, doctor, physiotherapist, dietician); *to whom* it is given (for example, patient, relative, child, adult, elderly, friend); and *how* information should best be given (everything at once, bit by bit, to the patient on his own, with another colleague present).

Giving information (imparting knowledge; telling about facts such as test results) is an integral part of the role of all health care professionals, including counsellors in specific specialized contexts such as in cancer care, infertility clinics, genetic screening, sexual health clinics and HIV antibody testing. The impact of a doctor giving information about illness and treatment to a patient and relatives may precipitate referral to a counsellor, or requests for counselling from patients. In the context of 'informed consent', doctors have to ensure that patients understand and agree to the taking of particular medication or undergoing certain procedures, and that any side effects or adverse consequences are clarified.

There is a difference between giving information (imparting knowledge and facts) and giving advice (an opinion and recommendation about future action) (Edwards *et al.*, 2001). This chapter concentrates on the issues, procedures and dilemmas related to the topic of giving information to the patient and responding to situations where the patient seeks the counsellor's professional opinion. The counselling approach described encourages patients to reach their own decisions about treatment and health care by enhancing perceptions of choice and promoting competence to do this. The sensitive issue of giving bad news is examined later in the chapter.

SPECIFIC ISSUES FOR COUNSELLORS ABOUT GIVING INFORMATION

Giving information is part of the routine task of most health care professionals and is an important aspect of clinical governance in all health care settings. Some counsellors may be uncomfortable with information-giving as part of their task, because:

- It can be at variance with counselling approaches that focus on responding to the patient's emotional state and avoid giving information and advice.
- There may be confusion between giving information and advising patients.
- There can be dilemmas about how much specialist medical knowledge counsellors may require for the task.
- There may be lack of clarity about the role of the counsellor in giving information in settings where the doctor has ultimate responsibility for the patient.
- There may be legal implications if counsellors give incorrect information.

Despite these potential difficulties, counselling training usually includes acquiring knowledge about human growth and development, loss and bereavement, interpersonal relationships, illness processes and how people cope with adversity. Core counselling skills of listening, engaging with patients and assessing problems are well suited to information-giving in health care, not only in those specialist settings where it is well developed, but in almost every health care encounter and every setting.

Information-giving is one specific component of the communication between counsellor and patient in certain health care contexts. The information imparted may encompass a range of issues about specific illnesses, tests, diagnoses, prognoses, treatment options, and the impact of all these on patients and their significant relationships (Harrington *et al.*, 2004). Furthermore, 'information-giving' suggests a single direction in a health care relationship, whereas we recognize that it involves listening, processing and responding, all of which make the activity an interactive process.

Particular aspects of communication with regard to the processes involved in information-giving that need to be considered include those listed below:

- Information-giving always has a context (hospital, specialist clinic, GP surgery) that influences the nature, content and extent of how information is given, and therefore conveys different meanings. Each context implies different relationships with patients; for example:
  - a patient returning for test results;
  - a patient in a general practice with a common psychological problem such as anxiety or depression; or
  - informing a relative that someone has died.
- Information-giving in the medical context can sometimes imply a monologue (the patient being lectured to, or just given information); however, in the context of counselling it is always an interactive process.
- One cannot *not* communicate in a counselling relationship; even if no information is given, all actions and behaviour have a meaning to both patient and information-giver.
- Information-giving includes the *content* (what is said) and the *process* (how it is said, or what is being conveyed/implied).

RATIONALE FOR EFFECTIVE INFORMATION-GIVING

The main rationale for enhancing the practice of giving information is to achieve a better outcome for patients by promoting their competence to make informed decisions. Frustration, anger or withdrawal can be experienced by both the giver and receiver of information if it is given without due concern for a patient's wishes, beliefs or ability to understand. In addition, there may be a lack of compliance with treatment regimes if the patient is not fully informed about his or her medical condition. Many patients come from different religious, social or cultural backgrounds and hold beliefs that may be at variance with the way that traditional Western medicine is practised. Language differences contribute great complexity to the whole issue of imparting and exchanging medical information. Patients who cannot read or write English cannot give informed consent. It is not unusual for such patients to hide their difficulties with understanding English from the health care professional.

The reason or requirement for giving information may seem obvious, but a lack of clarity about the main goal can cloud how it should be given. The following are some reasons for giving information:

- Patients themselves may increasingly request information and wish to be actively involved in decision-making about treatment and care. This is particularly the case in the current climate of increased patient participation in decision-making;
- In an age when medico-legal issues assume increasing significance, it is important for patients to be best informed about their health care and well-being;
- Understanding the implications of a particular medical condition can help patients to adjust to and make decisions about a range of issues, including:
  - behaviour and life-style restrictions (infectious transmissible diseases such as HIV, hepatitis and tuberculosis; or diabetic, cardiac and neurological conditions); and
  - life-stage decisions (marriage, having children, change of job, caring for others).
- Legal and financial considerations such as declaring inherited conditions to a partner in the context of having children, or taking out insurance.
- The patient's family may request or require information about the medical condition to help them plan care.

THE COUNSELLOR'S ROLE IN INFORMATION-GIVING IN HEALTH CARE SETTINGS

In most medical settings, there is a hierarchy over who gives what information to whom, and who receives what information from whom. In terms of physical illness, it is most frequently the doctor who considers what information needs to be passed on to the patient and determines when and how to do this. However, increasingly it is the counsellor who takes the lead in some health care settings, such as primary care, with regard to information-giving about common psychological problems. Clinical nurse specialists may also take on this type of responsibility, as do other health care professionals in their realm of practice. When giving information in health care settings, the legal implications of the doctor's responsibilities must be taken into account. In most circumstances, doctors give information to the patient alone. It is helpful to encourage medical and other colleagues to invite other appropriate health care professionals, including the counsellor, to be present from the outset, as this can help in dealing with any repercussions for the patient and, in turn, assist the doctor in time-limited situations.

A counsellor working in a health care setting may be strategically placed to:

- Reinforce information given by other members of the health care team.
- Clarify aspects that were not understood, or where information has been misinterpreted.
- Identify where patients' beliefs, both cultural or religious, may be at variance with the information given.
- Explore whether there may be language barriers or other circumstances (learning disabilities) that might reduce comprehension of information.
- Offer some support to the patient through difficult periods of time.
- Help patients to formulate questions to obtain the information they need from doctors and nurses, which may also help in decision-making.

When relatives request information about patients, it is optimal practice to clarify with the patient, wherever possible, whom he wishes to be kept informed or to be part of decision-making. This avoids breaches of confidentiality and misunderstandings that can arise in the information-giving process. For example:

A 40-year-old Nigerian woman attending an antenatal clinic for tests for abnormalities of the foetus was invited to discuss this alone with the midwife. She sat silently, not answering any questions. After some time, the midwife asked the woman if there was a problem. The woman then said that she wanted these tests and understood the risks, but that she had to leave it to her husband to make the final decision, as this was their tradition, he being the head of the family. This patient was therefore encouraged to discuss the situation with her husband.

Counsellors may also be able to supplement information about patients' social and psychological situations to help the doctor and other members of the health care team, but obviously always gaining the patient's consent first before doing so. This passing on of information can be done through ward rounds, writing letters, making entries in medical records, or giving verbal feedback to the doctor. Information about the patient's situation, which can sometimes affect medical care, may emerge during counselling sessions. In other circumstances, doctors may require a psychosocial assessment before making decisions about a patient's care. The following example illustrates this:

Mrs Grey, a 38-year-old married woman, was referred by her GP to the counsellor for a psychological and social assessment. The GP wanted this information prior to further investigations for chronic fatigue and vague abdominal discomfort, which she had experienced for two years. During this time she had undergone a number of routine tests and consulted a number of specialists, but nothing abnormal had been found.

The counsellor's objective was to elicit Mrs Grey's views about what she considered could be done to help her and her main concerns and expectations; and to consider the GP's underlying uncertainty about the aetiology of her symptoms.

It emerged that Mrs Grey had been married for ten years, and that she and her husband disagreed about having children. She had a successful career in advertising and, until recently, had not wanted to forgo her job to have children. The dilemmas about keeping her career and giving in to her husband's wishes to start a family had become more acute since they both recognized that she would soon be past childbearing age. She had not been able to talk about this either to her husband or to her GP, and she had become increasingly anxious that she might not be able to conceive if she decided at a later point to have children. The counsellor gained Mrs Grey's agreement that her GP needed to have this information in order to understand her situation better. This in turn helped the doctor to raise the subject with Mrs Grey and consider what steps should be taken. Mrs Grey was relieved to be able to talk about her dilemmas and agreed to see the counsellor again before any further tests were carried out for her abdominal pain. The counsellor and Mrs Grey discussed the point that, if her tests found nothing abnormal, there might be a symbolic link between the abdominal pain and the dilemma about having a child, which was causing emotional pain for her and her husband.

SOME THEORETICAL CONSIDERATIONS

The way that information is given has a major impact on patient care (Lloyd and Bor, 2009). The patient's level of stress and anxiety can be reduced in most cases by giving adequate information prior to investigations, surgery and entry into drug trials. False hope and unreasonable expectations may be reduced if, for example, patients are given the opportunity to discuss their concerns and are informed about what might happen to them in the course of their illness and care (Miller and Telfer, 1996). There is even evidence to suggest that, if patients are fully informed before undergoing surgery, they have a shorter recovery period and may require fewer pain-relieving drugs. Patients are found to be more satisfied with their care and more likely to comply with advice if they have received clear explanations about their problem and its management.

The traditional method of giving information by the medical professional is in the form of a 'lecture' – in other words, to resort to a monologue rather than a dialogue. For example, 'You have diabetes and will need to have daily insulin. The nurse will show you how to do the injections.' This is sometimes done without checking whether the information is understood or has relevance to the person receiving it. This approach in health care stems from the traditional, hierarchical doctor–patient relationship, with the doctor in a powerful, knowledgeable position. The patient may not be invited, nor expected, to participate in decision-making. Anxiety can therefore be created for both patient and health care professional if patients do not understand or absorb the information given to them, or if it is misinterpreted (Paling, 2003).

Counsellors in health care settings have an important role in furthering good practice, as well as teaching and demonstrating specific counselling skills to other health care professionals in their daily work with patients, and contributing to communication skills teaching in medical schools. Some difficulties encountered in giving information may arise where counselling training and practice is insufficient and there is pressure on time in busy clinics. In some health care settings, these difficulties are overcome by counsellors working alongside doctors as an integral part of specialist teams. The counsellor can meet the patient together with the doctor, ensure that information is understood, and encourage the patient to seek clarification where necessary.

Giving information, as with any other aspect of counselling, is likely to be accomplished more easily and effectively if due thought is given to the overall principles, aims and tasks of counselling.

The following are the *main principles* for counsellors in giving information:

- Clarify *what* should be communicated *to whom* and *by whom* and *when* to communicate information.
- *Avoid making assumptions* about the patient's knowledge, concerns, beliefs, wishes, expectations, need or desire for information.
- *Choose words carefully*, being mindful that everything said can have an emotional impact and consequences. This occurs particularly when patients are very anxious and have to be given unsought or complicated information.
- *Share responsibility* for decisions with patients by eliciting their views about what they want to be told, by whom, and if there is anything they do not want to be told.
- *Record* in medical notes a summary of the information given to the patient, what information patients wish to be passed on to relatives, and what is important to pass on to other doctors, as well as anything that patients say they do not want to be told about.
- *Maintain clarity about the role of the counsellor* in any information-giving session with the patient. Sometimes the counsellor is part of a team, acting as a consultant for the patient and/or the medical team; or the counsellor may sometimes be the first person to give information. This affects how information is given and how the counsellor relates to the medical team.
- *Discuss with the patient the potential for an impasse* between the patient and the medical team, such as a patient not wanting to be told a diagnosis, and therefore being unable to benefit from certain treatments or to enter relevant clinical trials, which requires their consent, as in this example:

Counsellor: *I understand from the nurse that you do not want to know the results of your latest liver tests, as you fear what might happen to your liver in the future.*

Patient: *That is right. My philosophy is just to live day-by-day. I don't think of the future.*

Counsellor: *If the tests indicated that it might be important to offer you some treatment now, what should the doctor do with this information?*

Patient: *I'm not sure right now. I hadn't thought of it like that.*

Counsellor: *Did you realize that you might be able to be offered some treatment?*

Patient: *I have heard that the treatment is worse than the condition, but I haven't heard what that treatment might be. I need to think away from here.*

Counsellor: *That is a good idea. You can call this number if you have anything you want to discuss before your next appointment with the doctor.*

GUIDELINES FOR GIVING INFORMATION

Giving information requires knowledge on the part of the person giving the details, and a willingness by the patient to be informed. Thus, it is essential to determine who wants the information and the use to which it will be put.

The *counsellor* should:

- Start by finding out what information is sought. This helps to avoid assumptions being made, gives an indication about the patient's ability to understand issues and helps to ascertain the language and style that are best suited to the discussion, and whether translators are needed.
- Ascertain the extent of prior knowledge about the issue being discussed.
- Be knowledgeable about the information and understand it well enough to be able to convey it accurately and simply.
- Give the information gradually, in small amounts, avoiding jargon and technical words.
- Allow sufficient time for discussion.
- Respond to the patient's questions as far as possible, and with honesty if the answers are not known.
- Be sensitive to, and prepared for, the possible impact the information will have on the patient and close relatives.
- Have resources for dealing with different situations that might occur (colleagues to consult for disturbed, suicidal patients, for example).
- Address the impact of information on the patient's own support systems.

The *patient receiving the information* should generally be:

■ In a fit state of physical and psychological health to receive the information (conscious; not too critically ill).
■ Able to listen to what is being said, and not be distracted by other overriding anxieties or physical symptoms.
■ In a situation where the patient is either seeking information or is willing to be the recipient of unwelcome but necessary information.
■ Wanting to, and being able to, communicate. Some patients are withdrawn, anxious, angry and aggressive. Others have hearing and speech difficulties.
■ Able to understand the information (children, the elderly, individuals who have learning difficulties, or cultural or language barriers may need particular and individual arrangements put in place for the accurate exchange of information to take place).

AN EXAMPLE OF AN INFORMATION-GIVING SESSION

The following case demonstrates the steps taken during a counselling session when the way that information was given was important.

> Mrs Green, aged 45, had experienced chest pains and discomfort for some months. She finally consulted her GP, who sent her to a cardiac specialist. The specialist planned to investigate whether the patient's arteries were blocked, by doing blood tests and performing an angiogram (an invasive procedure). Following the first appointment, he referred Mrs Green to the counsellor on the team as he was concerned about her level of anxiety and wanted this explored before carrying out invasive tests. He found it difficult to get her to respond to his questions during consultation and she appeared withdrawn.

The following 'map' for giving information helped the counsellor to cover all the important aspects. Snapshot discussion examples from the above case are used to illustrate some of the points.

1 *Think first* about who made the referral, and for what reason; what information is intended to be given; and the age, gender, and medical and social context of the patient. These all have an influence on the

start of the session and help to focus the discussion. In the case example detailed above, both the GP and the medical consultant cardiologist were unhappy to proceed without more reassurance about Mrs Green's emotional and psychological state. Her age and marital status were also relevant.

2   Find out *what the patient perceives the problem to be,* and what he wants to know.

> *Counsellor:* *Following your meeting with Dr Brown, what is your view of your situation now?*
> *Mrs Green:* *I just feel trapped.*
> *Counsellor:* *Trapped in what way?*
> *Mrs Green:* *Trapped because I have this pain and it worries me, but I also fear being told that I've got a heart condition.*

3   *Explore concerns, beliefs and wishes.*

> *Counsellor:* *What is it that you fear most about the possibility of having a heart problem?*
> *Mrs Green:* *That there really is nothing that can be done, and that I may not be able to do all the things I do now.*
> *Counsellor:* *Where do you get the belief that there is nothing that can be done to help you?*
> *Mrs Green:* *I'm not sure. Perhaps because my father died unexpectedly of a heart attack.*

4   *Outline the information to be given.*

> *Counsellor:* *What did you understand about the tests Dr Brown suggested?*
> *Mrs Green:* *Not too much except I'd have an investigation that is done with a local anaesthetic and I have to be in hospital for the day. But he didn't say much. You know what doctors are like: rushed, looking at notes and the computer screen, and bleeps going off.*
> *Counsellor:* *Do you know why he wants to do these tests?*
> *Mrs Green:* *He said something about calligraphy. I just 'shut off' at that point. I was so scared.*

5   *Use understandable language* devoid of jargon and present the information in clear short parts, being specific. Vague information can raise anxieties.

> Counsellor: *I think he means angiography. Do you understand what Dr Brown means by angiography?*
> Mrs Green: *Not really.*
> Counsellor: *Tell me what you do know.*
> Mrs Green: *It means a tube is put in so they can look to see if the veins are blocked.*
> Counsellor: *That is correct. So you did understand some of what Dr Brown told you.*
> Mrs Green: *Yes, but I didn't really want to hear any of it.*

6   *Give important information first.*

> Counsellor: *Dr Brown says he can't help you or make any decisions until he has done some tests. The most important is to insert a tube through a leg vein to your heart to see what is happening. This usually means a day in hospital and a local anaesthetic, but he will discuss this with you. He will also need your consent to do this.*

7   Use *diagrams* or drawings to clarify information if appropriate. It might be easier to explain some things diagrammatically than to try to do it verbally.

8   *Use genograms (a family tree)* to obtain a family history; this is important in some conditions to reach a diagnosis or to calculate the risks of transmission (heart disease, rheumatoid arthritis, diabetes) and can help in establishing current relationships.

> Counsellor: *Is there anyone else in your family who has had heart problems apart from your father?*
> Mrs Green: *My mother has angina.*
> Counsellor: *Who else knows that you have had this pain?*
> Mrs Green: *No one except my doctor.*
> Counsellor: *What might your husband say or do if he knew you were here?*

Mrs Green: *He'd be more worried than me, and that would be too much for me.*

9   *Negotiate how the next steps are to be managed*, and share responsibility for decisions with the patient.

Counsellor: *For Dr Brown, an angiogram is an important first step and will help him to confirm whether or not there is a problem with your heart. He said that he would also feel happier if you told your husband, or if someone else close to you knew about what is to happen.*

Mrs Green: *I'll have to tell my husband if I'm to stay in hospital. I suppose that I'll have to do what Dr Brown says!*

10 *Check the patient's understanding* of what has been said.

Counsellor: *Before we go any further I would like to hear from you what you understand about what we have discussed so far.*

11 *Acknowledge the patient's ambivalence and 'reframe'* the patient's viewpoint. Both are important techniques for giving advice and information in a way that is consonant with the patient's viewpoint. 'Reframing' may mean taking time to understand the patient's situation, while keeping the balance of imparting those aspects of the diagnosis, treatment and prognosis that are important for the patient's health, and maintaining hope.

Counsellor: *I can hear that it is very hard for you to decide what to do right now. It seems that you are protecting your husband from the worry and at the same time also protecting yourself from a certain diagnosis, fearing it is your heart. This means that although you want to ask advice you are stopped right now from doing so.*

Mrs Green: *You're right. I think I want to know and at the same time I don't want to know. Dr Brown thinks it is my heart, I'm sure.*

Counsellor: *Yes, he didn't deny that there might be a problem because of your symptoms and the family history. However, do you think it might give you more discom-*

> *fort to continue with the pains and uncertainty, and no*
> *diagnosis? Or do you think it would be easier to know*
> *for sure one way or the other?*
>
> Mrs Green: *I hadn't thought about it like that.*
>
> Counsellor: *If the doctor found out that you had a problem with*
> *your heart, what might be the advantage of knowing?*
> *How might it be different from what happened to your*
> *father, who had no idea that he had a problem?*
>
> Mrs Green: *I hadn't thought about that either.*

12 *Obtaining informed consent* is the responsibility of the doctor performing the procedure and includes the nature and purpose of what is to be done, as well as the benefits and any risks there might be. A dilemma for many doctors, especially if the patient is anxious or appears not to understand fully the medical issues, is how much information about risks should be given and how much a patient needs to know in order to give informed consent. To overcome such problems, patients should be encouraged to ask questions and discuss fears. Counsellors can check perceptions and correct any misunderstandings prior to consent being given. Patients should also be given written information and, whenever possible, not be rushed into making a decision. They should also have the opportunity to discuss issues with another person, such as a relative, friend or counsellor.

13 *Summarize* what has been said and what will be the next steps. Asking the patient to do this is also a useful way of correcting misinformation and misunderstandings before ending the session. In some circumstances, it can be equally effective for the patient to hear the summary in order to confirm information. Summarizing the points made during the discussion can help to slow down events that seem to be going too fast for the patient, clarify the medical terms and procedures, and address anxieties.

> Counsellor: *From what I have heard in our discussion it seems that*
> *you've suffered for some time from this pain and now*
> *worry that you may have some heart trouble. This is a*
> *special worry because of what happened to your father.*
> *It seems that you are afraid to ask Dr Brown for his*
> *views about your heart and so you feel trapped. You*

> *will know when you are ready to remove the uncertainty by asking questions and facing what has to be done. It just might be different from what you fear and expect.*

Language barriers are also a challenge when giving information. All attempts should be made to have a skilled, suitable translator present. However, the risk in using translators is that they may interpret information rather than merely translate it, and meanings can be changed. Care needs to be taken that this does not happen. As in the above example, the described steps used with Mrs Green are the same. As translators are usually lay people, there needs to be some prior clarification with the translator about the reason for the meeting with the patient, and how the health care professional wants the session to be conducted. Such interviews may need more time, and information has to be given in small steps. Other aspects for consideration are that the patient might be embarrassed to talk in front of the translator because of the content of the discussion (sexual difficulties, personal problems), especially if they are of the same nationality. These hurdles need to be examined and overcome, as far as is possible, with both patient and translator, before the start of the session. We now turn our focus to the sensitive issue of giving bad news.

GIVING BAD NEWS

Imparting bad news is an inevitable part of information-giving in health care settings (Ptacek and Eberhardt, 1996; Baile *et al.*, 2000). Counsellors may have a role either in giving bad news or, more frequently, in helping the patient and others to deal with the consequences of the bad news they have received. The problems associated with giving bad news and the potential difficulties and barriers this can create within the doctor–patient relationship are not new to medicine (Dosanjh *et al.*, 2001; Simpson and Bor, 2001). The skills required in giving bad news are similar to the basic counselling skills of listening, observation and reflection, all of which are used in giving information. Additional skills focus on dealing with specific problems in communicating bad news of any kind, such as techniques for maintaining hope and creating balance in adjusting to illness; obtaining compliance with treatment; or dealing with extreme situations (accidents) or emotional reactions (anger or crying). The focus of the remainder of the chapter is on the additional skills and techniques needed for imparting information that constitutes bad news and dealing with the reactions of patients and their relatives to the news. The ultimate objective is to leave the patient and/or relatives, feeling competent enough to cope in their chosen ways with the news they have been given.

Doctors with medico-legal responsibility are, traditionally, the professionals who give bad news about health to patients. Ideally, a multidisciplinary care team connected with patients can provide back-up, but often this is not the case. A counsellor might be the designated person in the team to deal with the impact of the bad news given to the patient, but other members, such as nurses, can also contribute to patient support in this regard. Counsellors' appreciation of the issues associated with giving bad news can enhance their contribution to multi-disciplinary care. Even if they do not have to pass on the news themselves, they may frequently be required to deal with its consequences.

The meaning of bad news

Conventionally, the concept of bad news is perceived in situations where there is:

■ A message that conveys to the individual that there are fewer choices in his life;
■ A threat to an individual's mental or physical well-being;
■ A risk of upsetting an established lifestyle; or
■ No hope.

It is tempting to make assumptions about whether news is *good* or *bad* for an individual. However, news of whatever kind is only information, whereas the idea that it is either good or bad is a belief, value judgement or affective response from either the provider or the receiver of the information in a given context or situation. It is personal perceptions that define whether news is good or bad. There are also degrees of bad news from very bad to not so bad. There are many situations when health care providers might preface giving bad news with 'I am sorry to tell you that . . .' or good news with 'I am pleased to tell you . . .', illustrating how value and meaning are attached to information from the outset by the conveyer of the information. Such preconceptions about what is good or bad news associated with any medical condition may influence or constrain the patient's range of responses to the information. A patient, for example, who is given so-called good news in the form of a negative HIV antibody test by a relieved doctor, may feel ashamed to cry or to discuss other problems he has. For that person there may also be an element of bad news; the patient may now feel that there are no excuses for risking failure in a new sexual relationship, whereas his fear of HIV had previously protected him from meeting new partners. Similarly, a patient who feels some relief about getting a confirmed cancer diagnosis may be concerned that the doctor will misconstrue this as denial, emotional blunting, or be suggestive of a psychiatric disorder. Clinical experience highlights the value of eliciting from the patient what would be bad news, or waiting until the patient attaches meaning to the information before defining the news as being either good or bad.

It is important to seek an understanding of what patients' fears might be about their health and the implications for relationships, sleep, work, and future hopes and expectations. Bad news is closely related to loss, whether physical, emotional, or social. The responses to loss are similar to those in bereavement. Clinical experience has shown that common fears include:

- Loss of physical well-being and its impact on relationships, work, finance and social life.
- Loss of mental ability and ultimately being unable to make decisions for oneself.
- Lack of control and increasing dependence on others.
- Loss of a sense of future, and living with uncertainty.
- Disfigurement and pain in the course of illness.
- Social stigma resulting from disfiguring or infectious conditions.
- Living with a reduced quality of life from a personal and relationship perspective.
- Death (what it ultimately means) and dying (process, pain, isolation).

Patients also have fears related to the development of symptoms, how these will manifest themselves and how they will be recognized. Some patients may especially fear symptoms that will be visible to others, such as a disability or disfigurement, which affects self-image and others' perceptions of them. There are also invisible manifestations of symptoms, as revealed through tests and internal examinations, such as some gynaecological symptoms. Infectious or transmissible diseases (tuberculosis, herpes, hepatitis A, B and C and HIV infection) raise fears about disclosure and the effect on relationships. Symptoms of neurological impairment, such as epilepsy, may be especially frightening to patients because they may be equated with loss of self-control and 'madness'.

Patients' psychological responses to such fears are mediated by a number of personal, social and cultural factors that might determine the extent to which they are distressed by their changing physical condition and appearance. Some patients find that psychological problems become more pressing after they have been discharged from hospital to convalesce, because the hospital provided a protective social environment.

What apprehensions do health professionals have about giving bad news?

There are a number of factors that might make it difficult for health care providers to give bad news to their patients.

- Some health professionals may be concerned that they will distress patients if they either tell them bad news or talk to them about any fears they may have in relation to their health. This could stem from the myth that to talk about the potential for bad news is to 'tempt fate' or to destroy any feelings of hope the patient may have.
- Uncertainty about how to respond to the reactions of patients who display their emotions openly (showing anger or crying, for example) or seem to display no feelings at all may make health professionals unsure as to whether their own responses should be personal or professional. Should they be clinical and aloof, or more engaged by showing that they are also upset?
- Some may identify strongly with particular patients and their specific problems, especially if their ages and lifestyles are similar, or they may have the experience of a similar health problem.
- Not knowing all the answers to questions that patients might ask and having insufficient counselling skills or experience may arouse anxiety, resulting in some health professionals delegating to colleagues the task of giving bad news.
- Working alone can also increase stress and tension, with no 'sounding board' or outlet for discussion.

- Giving bad news can lead to time-consuming conversations with patients, and this may deter some doctors from being more open with their patients in busy clinical settings. This inevitably leads to less open communication and more dependence on other health professionals, such as nurses and counsellors.
- Conflicting information and differing responses to the diagnosis or treatment proposals, resulting from a lack of communication between the different health professionals, can create problems for both the patient and health professionals.
- If the patient's self-confidence and hopes for the future are eroded by bad news, the health professional may feel guilty and fear being blamed for this.
- Giving bad news may also involve discussion with patients about sensitive topics, including sex and sexuality, procreation, chronic ill health, dying and death, all of which are difficult issues to discuss, and require advanced training and supervised experience in communication skills.
- If patients are young, an implication of a serious diagnosis is that they are being told that they may have a shortened life-span and this is a hard task for many health professionals.

Approaches to giving bad news

Doctors can take various approaches to giving bad news. These include:

1 *Non-disclosure*, where the doctor decides what the patient should be told, is based on assumptions that patients need to be protected from bad news; that they invariably do not want to know bad news about themselves; and that it is appropriate for the doctor to decide 'what is best' for the patient without reference to the individual concerned. This 'model' is untenable in times of increased consumer pressure for information, and can be seen as a violation of the right of human beings to have access to information about themselves.

2 *Full disclosure*, where all available or known information is given to every patient, whether or not the patient has been asked if they are agreeable to this. It is based on the assumption that the patient has a right to full information and the doctor has an obligation to provide

this; that all patients want to know bad news about themselves and are better off knowing; and that it is appropriate for patients to determine what treatment is best for them, since they have to live with the consequences, and to do this they must have full information.

3   *Individualized disclosure*, where each patient is considered separately. This is a model where the amount of information and its rate of disclosure are tailored to the needs of the individual patient through patient–doctor negotiation. It is based on assumptions that people are different in the amount of information they want and in methods of coping; that most people need time to absorb and adjust to bad news, so disclosure can be given over time; and that a partnership relationship between doctor and patient is the basis for decision-making founded on mutual trust and respect and is in the patient's best interests.

There are three options for when to give bad news and how to manage patients' concerns:

1   *Reassure the patient, potentially colluding with denial*

The counsellor can reassure the patient that his fears are probably worse than in reality. This option may be difficult to resist, because it can result in the immediate reduction of a patient's anxiety and emotional distress. It is a form of supportive emotional 'first aid'. It may be indicated when patients appear to be vulnerable, isolated and in extreme distress. Sometimes, there are areas of information where there is much uncertainty and where the outcome of either the disease process or the suggested medication is not known. Reassuring patients may serve to 'sweep the fear under the carpet', only for it to resurface at a later date. If patients are reassured repeatedly, the counsellor or doctor takes on some of the anxiety of the patient by assuming responsibility for some decisions that could be shared with the patient. This is more likely to result in feelings of stress for the doctor and dissatisfaction on the part of the patient. The counsellor might also be colluding with the patient's denial of the severity of the problem, or potential problem, if false hope is offered. It is not consistent with the understanding of an optimal patient–counsellor relationship as understood in this book; namely, one that is characterized by an adult-to-adult partnership.

2 *Impose views on patients when it is too late and possibly face resistance*

A second option is to wait until a crisis occurs before discussing bad news. The patient may be seriously ill before his concerns are elicited. This has certain limitations. Patients may be unprepared for bad news; they are not only anxious about their physical condition, but will inevitably have fewer ideas about how they might cope. They may present as anxious, depressed and withdrawn, and some may even express suicidal thoughts. Counselling is less likely to be successful if the referral and intervention are made when patients are already seriously ill. If referrals for specialist counselling are made at a time of crisis, patients may then appear resistant to any intervention by the counsellor. Referrals made when patients are still well tend, on the whole, to have a better outcome. In some cases, however, giving bad news at times of crisis may be the only option.

3 *Use hypothetical and future-orientated questions; avoid denial and resistance*

The third option is to address the potential for bad news and concerns about the future with patients, using hypothetical and future-orientated questions, at appropriate times while patients are still relatively well. There are several advantages to this approach. Patients are some distance from potentially serious conditions or situations that concern them. If issues are raised and addressed at this stage, patients can plan ahead of crises; they can be helped to view their situation more objectively; and it may help to increase their future options. The ideas can be put across in a non-confrontational way, through the use of questions. Nevertheless, denial can be a vital coping strategy with some patients and should therefore not always be viewed as being dysfunctional. Thus, patients who indicate that they find it too unsettling to talk about their fears for the future should not be pushed to do so. However, finding out what patients know, what they want to know, what they do not want to know and what might be their main concerns is central to this approach, rather than challenging or laying bare a patient's psychological defence.

The task of helping patients to deal with uncertainty may be made easier by the use of hypothetical questions such as 'If you were to get ill, what might be the most difficult aspect for you?' Such questions can protect patients against extreme stress in the future by having them think about possible problems and how they might cope with them before they occur. The main concerns of the patients are thereby addressed and this can also lead to a more efficient use of clinical time. Hearing the questions may be as important in changing perspectives for the patient as the answers given at the time. All questions convey an idea or imply a statement. Questions are also a way of giving back to the patient some responsibility for finding solutions to concerns at a stage when they can be acted on realistically. This use of questions may prevent health professionals from becoming overburdened with the patient's needs and worries. The approach emphasizes helping patients to cope on their own, which may lead to the need for less patient contact, and is a key way of enhancing the patient's ability to cope.

Who should give the bad news, and to whom?

It is important from the outset that there is clarity about who has medico-legal responsibility for giving bad news. If this is not agreed and understood, the process may become confused and messages to the patient may be unclear. Thus, a first step in preparing patients for bad news is to clarify who will give them this news. If this is not clarified, there are inevitable problems, many of which relate to the difficulties of the referring person.

It is generally considered that patients over the age of 16 have rights as well as responsibilities (BMA, 2001). This includes the right to give 'informed consent'. However, even if the patient is considered able to give informed consent and receive information, there are often relatives involved as well. Good communication with patients has to come first, but in various situations and at different stages of illness, communication with those closest to the patient is also important and they can become vital members of the caring team (McLaughlan, 1990; Brewin, 1996). An early part of any preparation should thus be to clarify whether patients have shared their illness concerns with anyone, who that is and to what degree they wish them to be involved. An opening question is: 'Who else knows that you are here today, or about your problem?' When dealing with children, consideration has to be given to the views of the parents about how much information should be given to the child.

Consideration has also to be given to any conflicts that might arise between a child's right to know and to be involved in decisions about his health care and the health care of the parents. For example, a child might have the ability to understand about an illness such as leukaemia at the age of 8 or 9, but the parents may want to shield the child from the knowledge of the severity of the condition, the prognosis and the details of possible treatment protocols. However, the child may ask questions that cannot be answered unless some facts are given about his condition.

Preparing patients for bad news

Preparing patients for bad news can be a discrete activity; nevertheless, all information-giving embodies aspects of preparing to give bad news. Unlike those involved in accidents or those dealing with unexpected medical crises, patients with chronic illness can be helped to make practical changes and prepare themselves emotionally for bad news. Talking to patients about their fears, which often relate to the future, is one of the most important psychotherapeutic interventions. It provides an opportunity to help patients to cope with any anxiety and uncertainty about what might happen to them over the course of their illness. Sometimes, seemingly small practical steps (making a will and a living will; arranging enduring powers of attorney) help to settle some anxieties and concerns. If this is done satisfactorily, the counsellor may even have helped to prevent some psychiatric symptoms in those patients who seem very anxious about addressing their fears. Deterioration in a patient's clinical condition affects his relationships, feelings of hope and view of himself in the context of the illness. For some patients, it may mean being open with people about the diagnosis. For patients who are neurologically impaired, an important additional issue may be dealing with loss of control in relationships and an increasing dependence on others for support and care.

Preparing patients for bad news can be seen as an opportunity to initiate communication between health professionals, the patient and his family members by enabling views about care and treatment to be expressed. Identifying the patient's views provides an opportunity to challenge beliefs and enables the meaning of bad news to be viewed from a different perspective.

GUIDELINES FOR GIVING BAD NEWS: THE STRUCTURE OF THE COUNSELLING SESSION

While there is no right or wrong way of giving bad news, some principles and techniques may make it easier for the health professional to prepare patients and their families more effectively for bad news.

Guiding principles

The guiding principles are similar to those of any counselling session, but some should be re-emphasized. These are accompanied by brief examples to illustrate the points, and include:

■ Make *no assumptions* about what might be particular concerns or bad news for any individual, and recognize that these concerns can change over time. For example:

'When I last saw you your greatest worry was how you would cope if you began to get ill. Now that you have started medication, is this still a worry, or is there anything else of more concern today?'

■ *Consider the timing* of how and when to impart 'bad news'. Assessment of a patient's physical, psychological and social circumstances, available resources, and the clinician's readiness to discuss the news with the patient provide guidelines for resolving this key counselling dilemma.

■ *Maintain some neutrality* by responding thoughtfully and professionally to a patient's reactions, and not making value-laden judgements such as: 'There's no need to be so upset; there is lots that can be done. It's not the end of your world.' Neutrality enables patients to respond more freely, without the feeling that certain responses are expected of them. For example:

Patient: I can't believe that I have breast cancer. It's the end. (Patient sobs)
Counsellor: You say 'the end'. Help me to understand what you mean by that.
Patient: (Sobs)
Counsellor: Let me try again.
Patient: (Looks up and stops sobbing)
Counsellor: What is the hardest for you to believe right now?

Patient: (Continues to sob loudly)

Counsellor: (Pause, passes patient a box of tissues). What would help you the most right now?

Patient: Nothing. Though I wish I could think straight.

Counsellor: Well, tell me first about the things that you can think straight about.

Patient: (Stops sobbing and hesitates) I'll be all right in a minute ... (pause) ... This is the day I've feared the most. Actually things look a bit clearer now. Could the lump just be eradicated without cutting off my breast?

Counsellor: That is a possibility. So you are thinking straight about what questions you might ask of the surgeon. What else are you thinking straight about now that we are talking?

Patient: Well, that it all feels rather pressurised and maybe I have to just take one step at a time.

Counsellor: Is there anything that would help you to do that?

Patient: Well, yes. Just having this chance to talk about it alone without pressures from family and friends.

■ *Share responsibilities* with patients whenever appropriate. This may mean helping patients to talk about and live with the uncertainties, and often the certainty, of their condition and even their death, by showing them that the health professional is not afraid to discuss their concerns.

Guidelines for the session

The following guidelines can act as a check-list to ensure that important aspects are covered when imparting bad news:

■ First, *attend to some practical details*, which can make it easier both for the health professional and for the patient. These include ensuring that there is privacy, a reasonably comfortable ambience, sufficient time available and established links with other colleagues who can support the patient afterwards if necessary.

■ *Give the news* immediately in order to leave the maximum time for discussion.

■ On hearing bad news, many people are unable to absorb anything further and do not hear what is being said. Take care not to flood patients with 'helpful' information. Rather, *check what they have remembered and understood* about the investigations and laboratory tests that have led to the diagnosis. Also, check again what they want to know about the subsequent test results. Identify any things that they say that they do not want to know about so these can be returned to at appropriate times.

■ *Identify* who else may be available to support the patient. This helps patients to look to their natural support network outside the health care setting and reduces dependence on professional staff.

■ *End the session* by asking patients to summarize what they remember, particularly about the options for treatment and care. It is easy to assume that patients have retained and understood what they have been told. If this is not done, the patient may leave only having heard the bad news, which increases the risk of depression, anxiety and even suicide.

■ Make an agreed *plan for future contact or referral.* Give patients realistic contact numbers in case they want further information or help before the next appointment; this provides a 'safety net'. Avoid giving home telephone numbers, as this draws the patient into a one-to-one relationship, which may exclude other social and professional support. It is also contrary to good professional practice.

■ *Discuss with colleagues* the essential components of the patient session. This can make the task of giving bad news easier by increasing professional support and sharing the care of the patient appropriately.

Skills for giving bad news

■ *Facilitating communication* (establishing rapport and trust) by introducing yourself, defining the purpose of the meeting, maintaining eye contact and being aware of body postures (leaning forward). Convey information without disguising it in language that is either vague or ambiguous; for example, by not using coded words or euphemisms such as 'immunosuppressed' for a condition such as HIV infection, or 'breast lump' for cancer of the breast. Be clear that there are treatments for many of the associated infections, but no cure for HIV itself; and, in the case of breast cancer, that there are different options but it is malignant and needs radical treatment.

■ *Showing empathy* by introducing the topic of bad news sensitively and demonstrating respect and care. This will influence, to some degree, how the patient responds. It is sometimes helpful to embroider a little and use prefaces such as 'I was wondering whether you had ever thought about how things might be if this infection does not clear up as quickly as last time?' Taking an empathetic position also encourages the patient to talk more freely. For example, 'You may think that some of my questions seem a bit intrusive but I can't help wondering whether . . .'. Showing patients that the counsellor is not afraid to discuss their concerns, no matter what these might be, is a way of showing empathy and closely tracking the thoughts of the patient.

■ *Using future-orientated and hypothetical questions*, which can help patients to think about situations, and even solutions, while they are some distance from the real problems. Such questions also link people with ideas and other people whom they might not otherwise have considered in relation to the problem or concern. For example:

> 'What is the smallest step you could take to help you feel less anxious right now?'
>
> 'What might help you feel more confident and less anxious in, say, six months' time?'
>
> 'What if you did become ill, who might you turn to for help?'
>
> 'What might be the effect on your wife if you decided to tell her about your heart problems?'

■ *Placing emphasis on how the patients have coped* with difficulties in the past, and helping them to consider how they might cope *now* and in the *future*. This stimulates people to consider how they might manage if the news turned out to be bad for them. For example:

> 'Have you ever had news in the past that made you feel very frightened and unsure how to respond? How did you manage to overcome it?'
>
> 'How might that experience help you right now?'
>
> 'Is there anything from the way you managed then that might help you if you had a problem in the future?'

The final question above can help people to reach a sense of competence by referring to their normal coping strategies. Most people are able to find something that confirms competence, coping strategies or beliefs.

CONCLUSION

The consequences of how information is given to patients can have a profound effect on the way they subsequently react to illness, engage with and adhere to treatment regimes and use the resources made available to them. In some situations, there might be less need for specialized counsellors if more thought, time and skills were devoted to the way patients are given information about their condition by doctors and other health care workers. A range of health professionals, including counsellors, can use their particular skills and knowledge about illness and its effects on individuals and relationships to enhance effective, satisfactory information-giving to patients. There are dilemmas about whether counsellors in health care settings need to have specialist knowledge about particular conditions in order to give information. However, it seems that having skills in dealing with one disease can usually be transferred to other situations.

Having to give bad news and helping people to cope with it is an important aspect of health care. How bad news is conveyed may determine, or at least influence, how the patient copes and adapts. The approach to giving bad news described in this chapter needs to be used with thought and sensitivity. Asking the patient questions should serve as an invitation to a conversation about difficult issues. The use of hypothetical questions is an approach that requires a high level of training, because it focuses on the most painful aspects of living and coping with disease. It may be damaging to patients to ask hypothetical and future-orientated questions, which raise their anxiety, without addressing the patients' feelings and how they might cope.

Chapter 14

Counselling for Loss, Terminal Care and Bereavement

INTRODUCTION

Loss and bereavement can be experienced in a wide range of situations where there is change or transition in relationships or status. Loss may be experienced when someone gets married and leaves the family home, or after redundancy or divorce. Lack of the 'healthy state' can lead to a state of psychological and emotional loss. The loss of health and the accompanying decreased physical or mental ability is central to counselling in health care settings. An understanding of human growth and development, of psychological processes as well as of specific illnesses and their impact at different stages of life, is essential to the practice of counselling about loss. Counsellors also need to be especially mindful of the impact of differing cultural and religious beliefs.

Death is part of the life cycle: it is the most feared loss associated with a period of serious illness, though long-term disability and diminished health status together with changed body image and a threat to a habitual life-style are also feared. While there may be a special emphasis on counselling dying patients and the bereaved, this is just one aspect of the counsellor's or other relevant health professional's task in relation to loss.

Clinical practice has shown that ideas about and feelings of loss may start from the moment a person believes that he is ill, or receives a specific diagnosis of illness. Others may perceive themselves as being ill or vulnerable to illness when they have not yet sought medical advice. Both groups of patients can experience anticipatory loss and this may be the initial focus in counselling sessions.

UNDERSTANDING LOSS

Most clinical approaches to loss are based on theories about the psychological aspects of death and dying, and Elizabeth Kübler-Ross (1969) is perhaps most recognized in this regard. Views about bereavement and approaches to counselling the bereaved are usually related to a theoretical understanding of change and loss in relationships (Carter and McGoldrick, 1981). As a function of emotional growth and development, individuals are challenged to process change both in relation to their own life and to the lives of others. Death and dying are just one point on the arc of the wider life cycle, which, in the context of family, social relationships and belief systems, continues after the death of an individual.

Terminally ill patients, their families and other close contacts are faced with life-cycle changes brought about by dying and death; these can be made more difficult if there are unresolved relationship problems. Terminal illness can also evoke reactions from health care professionals about their own mortality, making it especially important to understand the implications of loss for the individual and for family relationships.

Ideas about loss and dying may be introduced at an early stage of counselling. Even if they are not expressed openly, people may have fears, anxieties and misconceptions about a range of losses (family member, life-style, body image, independence), and these are accentuated by illness. Addressing them is one way of preparing patients for loss, and of helping the bereaved to deal with loss itself when it occurs. The focus of counselling initially may be about the loss of health, changes in life-style brought about by illness and consequent changes in relationships. As illness and debilitation progress, patients may experience additional losses, including the ability to participate in decision-making and the loss of body image and function. Counselling can lay the groundwork for further discussions about the impact of these changes on others, and help the patient to retain a sense of control in different areas of his life for as long as possible and to make arrangements for the future (setting up enduring power of attorney, living wills and anything else relevant to the patient's peace of mind).

Illness can lead to physical, psychological, economic and social losses. The losses brought about by acute, sudden illness or trauma are different from those that come from chronic conditions, where some adjustment over time is possible. Beliefs and perceptions about certain illnesses, as well as personal and family responses, may influence adjustment, and for this reason the typology of illness is relevant when counselling patients about illness and loss (Rolland, 1994a, 1994b). Where illness has periods of remission (arthritis, leukaemia), adjustments to this fluctuating pattern of health and illness may be difficult but may be anticipated. There are common losses and fears experienced over a range of illnesses and diseases, and all these losses can be of concern to patients in different ways over time. There are losses connected with both chronic illness and acute illness, and some patients may suffer greatly from anticipatory loss, a reaction that can be as complex and emotionally painful as having to cope with loss itself.

COUNSELLING ISSUES IN TERMINAL CARE

The terminal phase of illness holds special challenges for the counsellor. There may be physical, practical, psychological and emotional concerns that patients want to discuss or settle. As the patient's health deteriorates, the counsellor may need to focus more attention on the close family and friends. During the terminal-care phase of illness, some management and psychological issues can arise that might need to be addressed with patients and their close contacts:

■ *Confidentiality and secrets.* Although issues of confidentiality – who should know about the patient's condition – require attention at all stages of disease, they become more complex and pressing in the terminal-care phase of illness. Foremost among these is the question of who should know about the diagnosis, especially for conditions such as HIV infection, which carry stigma, or those inherited, such as Huntington's disease. Problems are less likely to occur if confidentiality issues have been discussed before the patient's health deteriorates. Patients' views about who should be kept informed about their condition should be recorded in the medical and nursing notes and must be reviewed periodically.

■ *Resolution of past relationship conflicts and difficulties.* It is sometimes assumed that it is imperative for the family and other close contacts to resolve past conflicts, or settle 'unfinished business' between them, before someone in the family dies. While it may be appropriate to facilitate this process, it is equally important to assess when *not* to pursue 'tying up' loose ends and, if necessary, help people to adjust to, and cope with, 'unfinished business'. The following dialogue illustrates how the counsellor can help a family to leave some business unsettled:

Patient's sister: *I read a book once, which said that secrets between people are harmful. But my brother and I worry that if he were to be open about his drug problem, it would upset my parents so much that they would reproach themselves and might even reject him.*

Counsellor: *Are you both happy to keep this secret from them?*

Patient's sister: *As happy as one can be in keeping a secret from one's parents.*

Counsellor: *Do you have other secrets from your parents?*

Patient's sister: *No. We are open about everything else. They know he's ill, they know it's hepatitis but they don't know he has septicaemia. It would be awful for all of us if my parents got very upset now about drugs when there is nothing we can do.*

Counsellor: *What will help you to manage to keep this secret without stressing you so much?*

Patient's sister: *It won't be easy not to just let it slip out, but we'll have to watch out not to. Maybe I'll tell them after David dies. Talking about it like this helps to be clearer about what to do.*

Counsellor: *So, reviewing what you've said. It might help you to think about whether just telling your parents, or letting it slip out, might relieve you, if not your parents.*

■ *Pre-existing conflict between family members and partners or spouses.* This can emerge in the terminal-care phase of illness, or when a newly diagnosed illness brings changes in daily living activities.

Counsellors may find that they have to deal with conflicts about keeping the diagnosis secret or taking responsibility for important decisions. Ideally, such difficulties should be pre-empted in discussions with the patient about how professional carers should best respond to these situations. An extract from an interview with a male patient about his boyfriend illustrates how this may be approached:

Counsellor: *What does your mother know about your relationship with Tim?*

Patient: *She thinks that he is just a friend. I've never told her more.*

Counsellor: *Would you now like her to know more?*

Patient: *Yes, because they may meet.*

Counsellor: *If your mother meets Tim and she asks him about your diagnosis, do you think he would tell her?*

Patient: *If he is stressed he might just 'blow it'. I think he feels angry that I won't tell her about us.*

Counsellor: *How do you think your mother would react if she did know about your relationship with Tim?*

Patient: *I don't know, but I think it may be better for all of us.*

Counsellor: *Does Tim know this?*

Patient: *No.*

Counsellor: *What stops you from talking to Tim about this?*

Patient: *Once I talk to him I may not be able to avoid telling her and I am afraid that she may reject him.*

Counsellor: *So your biggest fear is that your mother might reject Tim. It seems to me that you are protecting her and Tim, but giving yourself the burden of this. Maybe each in their own way, and time, will find a way to accept each other.*

■ *Next-of-kin and decision-making.* In cases of acute, unexpected and terminal illness, decisions may have to include next-of-kin and this is more complex when no precise discussion has taken place about this topic. In the terminal stage of illness, the focus of attention in counselling may broaden to include joint sessions with the family and close friends. In some cases, relatives may seek ways of engaging support by giving clear messages of distress, such as avoiding visiting the patient. In other instances, they may complain about the patient's care as a way of venting feelings that may be difficult to express elsewhere, particularly within the family. Some understanding of what is happening for the relatives and what prompts their behaviour can make the terminal phase less painful psychologically for all concerned. Relatives and close contacts may seek help from a range of health care professionals, or the patient's counsellor, without the knowledge of the patient. In such cases, the discussion should be limited to concerns or difficulties that relatives themselves may have in relation to the patient's illness, rather than engaging with personal details about the patient, unless the patient's permission has been obtained. For example:

Counsellor:	*Does your brother know that you have asked to see me?*
Patient's brother:	*No. I wouldn't want him to know.*
Counsellor:	*If he did know, how do you think he might react?*
Patient's brother:	*I'm not sure, he might be pleased.*
Counsellor:	*What might he be pleased about?*
Patient's brother:	*Well, it might be of some relief to him that I have someone to talk to about my worries.*
Counsellor:	*I am happy to talk to you about your worries but, as with any other patient, I cannot give you any information about his condition, as we do not have his permission.*

■ *Organizing and settling legal and financial matters.* Making a will is a practical step that acknowledges the possibility of death. Experience suggests that a will is better made when people are well. However, the task of making a will is neither routine nor familiar for many people and they may need help to discuss the implications of this task. Opportunities should be taken, either as part of their medical care or within counselling sessions, to encourage patients to consider the benefits of making a will while they are still mentally competent to do so.

While the act of contemplating a will, or indeed writing it, may prompt some people to think more about dying, the psychological benefits of 'getting one's affairs in order' should not be overlooked. An extract from a conversation between a counsellor and a 40-year-old divorced woman with acute leukaemia, who had a long-term female partner, illustrates this:

Counsellor:	*You mentioned that you feel that you need to make a will, but that it is difficult to do so because it would*

	make things seem 'final'. Is there anything that might be made easier for you and others if you were to decide to make a will?
Patient:	*I'm not sure. I might feel a bit more settled.*
Counsellor:	*More settled in what way?*
Patient:	*Well, I'd know my family and ex-partner would be taken care of, and I could also say exactly what things I would want my mother to have. Then sometimes I think what might happen if I didn't leave a will. The worst thing I could think of would be relatives fighting with one another if there was no will. Having had this conversation I'll consider doing one, but not until just before my next treatment.*
Counsellor:	*Is this something you've discussed with your partner?*
Patient:	*Sort of, but not very frankly.*
Counsellor:	*From what you've told me, I get the impression that you will somehow know when and if you want to talk more frankly.*

By neglecting to make a will, some patients at times may be communicating indirectly that they would prefer others to make decisions for them about their estate. The effect of this lack of action may be to give rise to tensions and feelings of ambiguity in relationships, and this may be either the patient's deliberate choice, or an unforeseen consequence of not having made a will. The counsellor's task in such situations could be to anticipate these outcomes with the patient in the course of counselling sessions.

■ *Other practical issues that might be raised in counselling.* These include the provision of financial and social support; availability of home care; and who should make important decisions if patients are unable to do so for themselves. Counsellors can also help patients to obtain advice from legal or financial advisers.

■ *Dependency.* Patients who are very ill or dying can feel a loss of dignity, especially from the inevitable dependence on others for basic activities (going to the lavatory, bathing, brushing teeth). Nurses usually take on some of these intimate tasks in hospital and sometimes in the community. Reassuring statements to the patient, which do not ignore the embarrassment or annoyance at being dependent, may help to put them more at ease. Offering some choices to the patient can help to maintain hope and restore a measure of dignity.

■ *Talking to people about dying.* Telling people that no more can be done to alter the course of an illness is possibly the most challenging aspect of health care, especially when talking to patients who seek hope and reassurance. For some doctors, it may be hard to shift from curative to palliative care. For other members of the health care team, including counsellors, it is easier to respond to patients' questions about their prognosis when doctors have taken the lead and clarified treatment plans about terminal care. It is then possible to explore the patient's concerns and wishes against a more realistic background. It is common for patients at this stage to seek support for their relatives in the form of counselling. They perceive this help as relieving them of the strain of having to provide emotional support themselves by 'putting on a brave face'. Some relatives and friends may show their reluctance to 'allow' patients to die by encouraging them to fight on, to keep eating, and by willing them to live. They may also attempt to 'inflict' 'cheeriness' on them. This can be stressful and upsetting for some patients who, after an extended period of failing health, may welcome the relief from pain and suffering. Other patients are ambivalent about wanting to know the 'real' answers to their questions. They may ask questions of nurses or counsellors that they do not put to doctors. This may be because the patient may perceive them to be more approachable members of the health care team. Sometimes, patients do not really want the answer, so they avoid asking the doctor. An extract from a conversation illustrates this point:

Patient: *Just keep me out of pain and make sure that I'm not alone.*

Counsellor: *If the doctors and nurses know your wishes they will do all they can to keep you comfortable. You will have to let them know when you are in pain. You say you don't want to be alone. Who would you most want to be with you?*

Patient: *My mother.*

Counsellor: *Does she know this?*

Patient: *Not really. I haven't spoken to her in that way.*

Counsellor: *Do you think you could talk to her more easily now?*

Patient: *I might today if I feel like it when she comes.*

> Counsellor: *It is important to only talk when you feel ready. You can still have some control about what you want to do, even in this small way.*

■ *Coming to terms with death.* Health care providers and family members may assume that 'coming to terms with illness and death' – a phrase that is commonly heard – is necessary and desirable for the patient's psychological well-being. This notion emanates from theories that view the denial of problems as being detrimental to psychological health. This quest or belief may inadvertently cause more psychological problems for those patients who resist discussion about painful issues. Dying patients may connect the process of 'coming to terms with dying' with an attempt to come to terms with how they have lived. The following are examples of some ideas that can be used in counselling if patients want to talk about death or dying:

> 'What aspects of how you have lived might make dying easier?'
>
> 'In whose life did you play a significant role?'
>
> 'Whose beliefs and ideas about living and dying are most similar to yours?'
>
> 'What one thing would you most like to be remembered by?'
>
> 'Who do you think will miss you the most?'
>
> 'Have you talked to your sister about how you would like her to cope with you not being there?'

Many patients adjust to deteriorating health in ways that differ from how they imagined it would be. This may be due to their own inner resources and possibly unexpected support from family and friends, or their beliefs. It is vital to explore and clarify patients' and their relatives' beliefs, especially for those with strong convictions.

> 'Help me to understand what the hardest thing is for you at this time?'
>
> 'What might help you the most?'

As the patient's health deteriorates, providing opportunities to talk about the changes in their condition and relationships over time might be helpful. Uncovering the patient's coping and resilience is possible even when death is close:

Counsellor:	*I'm wondering how you have managed this long period of illness as well as you have. What is it that helps you to keep going in this way?*
Patient:	*I just live from hour to hour and day to day. I've decided that if I let myself think about the future it makes it hard for me to be calm about what is happening to me now.*
Counsellor:	*So how do you manage to keep out thoughts about the future?*
Patient:	*I keep busy by seeing friends, and watch television a lot of the time.*
Counsellor:	*What is one thought you might have gained from this conversation?*
Patient:	*I've actually managed quite well.*

■ *Feelings of hope and hopelessness.* Two distinct aspects of hope in the terminal phase of illness, physical and emotional, may stem from the certain knowledge that the 'end will inevitably come'. Questions such as 'Will it be slow or quick? Will I be in pain, and how uncomfortable will I be?' reflect physical fears. Some measure of hope can be maintained at all stages of illness but careful choice of words is important if patients are not to be falsely reassured. One entrée into discussing the inevitability of death and introducing some hope is to find out from patients what they know about their condition and how they want to be cared for. For example:

Patient:	*I have a feeling the doctors have given up on me.*
Counsellor:	*What makes you feel that?*
Patient:	*They don't come to see me any more.*
Counsellor:	*Would you like them to come more often?*
Patient:	*I suppose so.*
Counsellor:	*Has anyone else given up hope?*
Patient:	*I'm in a daze now. I don't know what to think.*
Counsellor:	*I understand that – let's take things slowly. Is there anything you hope for?*

Patient:	*Some quiet on the ward at night so I can sleep. More honesty from the doctors!*
Counsellor:	*How do you think you can influence the doctors to be more honest?*
Patient:	*Ask them more questions. Actually, I hope they don't say to me 'It's the end'. It's OK feeling it; I just don't want to hear it.*
Counsellor:	*In some ways you are preparing yourself for the worst. You are willing to not ask questions fearing what you might hear. However, in this way you feel abandoned. The doctors might somehow have decided to wait for you to ask questions.*
Patient:	*You are right there. The last time they did a ward round I avoided a discussion by telling them the porter was waiting to take me to X-ray.*
Counsellor:	*So in that way you can control when you are ready to talk and hear what they have to say.*

The second aspect of hope relates to the patient's emotional concerns. A patient's hope that she will be remembered after death and how she will be remembered is very different from the hope that she might live longer, have a less painful death and not lose control. One way is to encourage patients to talk about how they want to be remembered. An excerpt from a conversation illustrates the use of future-orientated questions:

Patient:	*It bothers me that I'm still frightened in some ways.*
Counsellor:	*Can you try and say what is frightening you now?*
Patient:	*Not having control now.*
Counsellor:	*Would talking to people about how you would like to be remembered help you to feel you had some control?*
Patient:	*Perhaps. I want to be remembered like I used to be, when I felt very much in control of my life.*
Counsellor:	*By whom would you most want to be remembered like that?*
Patient:	*My son, also my parents. I hate them seeing me like this.*
Counsellor:	*Maybe they feel the same and telling them about your wish might help them too. This is just an idea.*

■ *Saying 'goodbye'.* There are rituals for ending relationships. Saying 'goodbye' to someone who is dying can be the most painful farewell. It may be at this point that relatives and friends may seek the counsellor's support or advice. Brief but frequent visits by the counsellor to the patient may be all that is appropriate at this stage. If patients indicate that they might have any concerns, they should be helped to express them. This is an example of a conversation with a 25-year-old Pakistani man dying of lymphoma, with devoted parents:

Counsellor: *You say that your main concern is your worry that your father will 'go to pieces' after you die. Is there anything that would help you to feel less anxious about this?*

Patient: *No. I am ready to die and he won't let me go.*

Counsellor: *Have you been able to say this to him?*

Patient: *No. I couldn't.*

Counsellor: *Do the two of you usually have difficulty in saying what you want to each other?*

Patient: *Yes.*

Counsellor: *Do you think your father might 'let go' in his own time when he is ready? If he does it too soon, it may not be right for him.*

Patient: *Maybe I'll die before he 'lets go'.*

Counsellor: *Do you think that would be more difficult for your father or for you?*

Patient: *For him.*

Counsellor: *What would he have to do to show you he had 'let go'?*

Patient: *Not keep pushing food at me.*

Counsellor: *Do you think a father could ever let his child 'go'?*

Patient: *No! Maybe I should tell him I'm ready; that may help him a bit, which may help me.*

Counsellor: *You've touched on an important idea there.*

Relatives can be reassured that just being there with the patient, sitting, holding a hand or reading conveys closeness and a sense of relationship. In some instances, relatives and friends feel afraid and do not wish to be with the patient at the time of death. They may need 'permission' not to witness the death. The nurse in the following example does not put any pressure on the husband of a dying patient to stay at her bedside (Brewin, 1996):

> *Nurse:*   *Sarah is not very well tonight. What do you want us to do if her condition deteriorates further?*
>
> *Partner:*   *I would like to know, of course. Actually, in my mind I have already said 'goodbye' to her. I don't know if I want to see her worse or dying.*
>
> *Nurse:*   *That is OK. It's been a really tiring day for you. Why don't you leave things with us for a while? We will give you a call at home if things change. You can decide then what you want to do.*

Death ends a relationship in one sense but, at the same time, memories and ideas about the deceased may continue and remain part of the lives of those left behind. This paves the way for bereavement counselling, if required.

BEREAVEMENT COUNSELLING

It can often be that at the point of the patient's death that counselling for those left behind starts as a discrete activity. The process of grieving can last over months or years. Recovering from a loss can take place gradually, or might in some cases change rapidly in response to some unexpected change of view or perspective for the bereaved. Being pressured to recover and take part in life by comments like 'Are you not over it yet?' or 'You need to get on with your life' can be unhelpful and add to distress. For some bereaved people, one counselling session may be sufficient to clarify thoughts and feelings and reassure them that their reactions are normal. For others, several sessions may be more appropriate, spaced over time and possibly with increasingly long intervals between them. Sessions over a few years may be indicated at important anniversaries (birthdays, holidays and the anniversary of the death itself).

Timing is a crucial aspect of bereavement counselling. Friends, relatives and health care professionals may sometimes complicate reactions to loss and bereavement by 'pushing' people to confront loss when they are not ready to do so. It may be the painful feelings that come from loss and change leading up to or following a death that prompt people to seek professional counselling. Others do not seek counselling and help, but may be identified by GPs as suffering from the bereavement. Patients themselves may consult their doctor about physical ailments (chest pain, shortness of breath, insomnia, lack of appetite) that indicate a grief reaction. While death is a part of every life cycle, no assumptions should be made about the bereaved person's possible reactions; what is a loss for one person may not be so for another.

Bereavement can have a profound impact on psychological and physical well-being, leading to increased mortality and the use of medical services in the weeks and months after a death (Stroebe *et al.*, 2007). Bereavement counselling will not be appropriate for everyone, as grief is a natural process. However, it may help to mitigate the occurrence of bereavement-related depression and stress disorders. A counsellor can help people to identify the emotional effects of the death and address the loss, which is a way of looking towards the future. Although this process is distinct from that of 'coming to terms with the loss', it can at least help the bereaved to understand the loss in the context of day-to-day living.

The point at which people come for professional help for bereavement may signal that they have become 'stuck' in their loss or, in contrast, wish to resolve difficulties and move on in their lives. Often, talking about the future may be as painful as talking about the past. Bereaved people can feel isolated because they are alone, or because others encourage them to 'look on the bright side'. Counselling can facilitate the expression of thoughts and fears that otherwise might not be spoken about. Where a death has been unexpected or difficult to accept, talking about it may help to make it more real for the bereaved.

Reactions to loss through death include feelings of grief, anger, guilt and sadness, which may be expressed in different ways. However, reactions that may be 'abnormal' in one culture, society or religion, may be the tradition and normal in another. Some people find that they cannot stop crying; while others have a desire to be left alone. These are by no means the only responses commonly associated with the death of a loved one. While still grieving, some may experience a measure of relief when death finally occurs, ending both the patient's suffering and the carer's distress associated with approaching loss. While death may bring an end to the suffering for patients, it may also give rise to new and unanticipated problems (financial change, unaccustomed self-dependence) for the bereaved. Loss may also be complicated by the reality or fear of social stigma when the cause of death is revealed. Cirrhosis of the liver from excessive alcohol use, or liver failure following an overdose of paracetamol, for example, may carry with them an additional stigma not normally associated with loss.

Grief reactions may also be masked. If there is no open display of grief, it is difficult for others to know how a person is feeling and they may therefore be uncertain about how to comfort or relate to them. Sometimes, the bereaved continue to live as though the relative or friend has not died. If this apparent denial of reality is not addressed, it may become a problem that requires the professional help of a counsellor or psychotherapist. The person may find it too painful to think about the loss and may fear becoming overwhelmed by his feelings. Such reactions to loss and death can, over a long period of time, affect people's ability to manage their daily lives. Delayed grief reactions can occur at any time after the initial period of loss, though the onset is most commonly associated with anniversaries such as birthdays and other significant dates and the occurrence of other personal losses. Some people may never completely come to terms with a loss, particularly if it is the death of a partner or child.

TASKS IN COUNSELLING THE BEREAVED

Clarity about the aims and tasks of bereavement counselling enhances its effectiveness, covers all approaches and can be used with different cultures. The main tasks include:

- Helping the bereaved person to *identify and address their main concerns.*
- *Enabling appropriate mourning* to happen without undue difficulties in daily living.
- Helping the bereaved person to review what has happened in the past and *develop ideas about the future* in such a way that the loss is balanced with some hope.

The guidelines for bereavement sessions are similar to those described for other counselling sessions, but with some additional considerations, including:

- The events leading to the death;
- Talking about the death and subsequent rituals;
- Previous experience of loss;
- Issues pertaining to how others have coped with the loss;
- Beliefs about life and death;

- Views about the past, present and future; and
- The mourning process.

All these can be woven into the conversation in a way that is appropriate for the individual, the nature of the problem and the stage of bereavement that the individual has reached.

It may be difficult for the counsellor to know what to focus on in a bereavement counselling session. The following issues might be of help in conducting the session:

- *Start the session* by identifying what made the bereaved seek an opportunity to talk, or what it was that prompted a referral. The counsellor may also ascertain what the bereaved person's expectations are for the session. Recalling memories and thoughts about the deceased can sometimes help the bereaved person to start talking about her own feelings.
- *The events leading up to the death* and the circumstances of death affect people in different ways. Thus, seeking information about the facts surrounding the death can help to start the discussion. It may be therapeutic for the bereaved person to talk about the events surrounding the death from a new perspective and to explore some of the following:
  - how long the deceased person was ill before dying;
  - who else the deceased and the bereaved people talked to about the illness;
  - from whom the deceased and bereaved people got their support;
  - whether it was an anticipated or a sudden death;
  - how the dying person prepared others, if at all, for her death; and
  - what beliefs the deceased and bereaved people had about life and, if known, about death and dying.
- *Talking about the death.* The way in which an individual died may leave memories that have an important effect on those who are bereaved. If, for example, the deceased person choked to death, the bereaved person may metaphorically remain 'choked with grief'; or, if the person died peacefully, the memory might be of a 'good' death. In circumstances where the death took place surrounded by those the patient most loved, the view might be that she was not 'lonely'.

Conversely, if the person died alone in the night, it might be more difficult for the bereaved person to accept the reality of the death, especially if it was a sudden death with no warning of previous ill health.

■ *Rituals and events immediately after the death.* Bereavement counselling can, in its own right, take the place of a ritual for some people, as the conversations in counselling may keep alive memories of the deceased and provide a set time for expressing grief. Rituals that surround death and the period after a death help people to confront and deal with the pain of the event. Such traditional activities provide a context in which mourning can take place, as well as assembling friends and relatives who provide social support. Religious ceremonies and customs have their place in coping with loss. In the Jewish religion, for example, people mourn actively and with varying degrees of intensity for a year. The period of bereavement is circumscribed and the bereaved person is expected to stop mourning and resume a normal life after this period. Keeping a lock of hair or maintaining the deceased person's possessions are forms of memorials. Other rituals include visiting the graveside or place of remembrance, or planting a tree in a favourite place.

Carrying out rituals may help some, but not all, to deal with overwhelming and incapacitating grief. An obvious ritual is for the person to visit the graveside with an explicit task (for example, to read a letter in which important ideas and feelings are conveyed); while other rituals may be uniquely appropriate to the person and their loss. These might include standing on a bridge and throwing a symbolic article into the flowing water, or returning to a place that was significant for the bereaved person, or reciting a poem. The possibilities are endless and the therapeutic effect is in terms of the power of the symbolism and association, rather than any objective criterion.

Grieving can be prescribed with the aim of both intensifying and constraining thoughts about the deceased. One way is to suggest to someone overwhelmed by grief that she sets time aside each day to think about her relationship with the deceased person. This ritual helps to give expression to feelings of sadness and helps the person to begin to cope better at other times of the day. The counsellor can further help the bereaved person by encouraging her to undertake small, practical tasks when she is not focusing on feelings of loss, and so begin to change her routine. The aim is not to disqualify the person's feelings, or to prevent her from grieving, but to help her to give expression to her grief as well as to continue with important daily routines. Information from the genogram will help both the bereaved person and the counsellor to identify other possible sources of emotional and practical support. Rituals may not be necessary or appropriate for everyone. Open discussion about how events were managed after the death can be therapeutic in itself.

■ *Assess how the bereaved person has been coping* by enquiring about how time is being spent. Giving the bereaved person the opportunity to decide on the frequency of counselling sessions is one way that the bereaved person's perception of how she is coping and the level of anxiety being experienced may be gauged. It is important to be alert to the ways that the bereaved person attempts to cope with the loss. It is not unusual for people to increase their use of alcohol at night, or to rely more on sleeping pills or other medication, or even to neglect themselves (personal hygiene, or not eating, for example). Some examples of questions that can be used to help in this assessment include:

> 'How much of the time do you think about John?'
>
> 'If you allowed yourself to forget his death for a while, what would you think about?'
>
> 'You say you'd feel disloyal if you didn't go to the cemetery. Where does this idea of disloyalty come from?'
>
> 'What memories of John do you most want to keep alive?'
>
> 'When you find it hard to sleep, what do you do?'

■ Consider *previous experience of loss*, which may influence how those who are bereaved deal with a current loss. Helping them to make a connection with how they previously managed such a loss may give them more confidence in their present ability to overcome the grief. Often, the response is that they have never experienced a death. In this case, links can be made with other important losses (divorce, emigration, pets, favourite belongings).

Where there have been multiple losses either in a family or of friends (an accident or infectious disease, for example), 'shell shock' and emotional numbing may result. Helping the bereaved to express feelings and concerns, as well as linking them with their previous experience of dealing with loss, can help them to emerge from the shock.

Counsellor:	*What makes it so difficult for you to talk about John?*
Bereaved partner:	*Just that he had to die.*
Counsellor:	*If you were to let yourself talk about John, what might be the easier things to talk about, and what might be the most difficult?*
Bereaved partner:	*It is easier to talk about our relationship, which was really good. But it's also hard because there have been so many deaths among my friends and it might be Jeremy next.*
Counsellor:	*What have you learned from your experience of other friends that now might help you to deal with John's death?*
Bereaved partner:	*That somehow it seems that people are not afraid when it comes to the end.*
Counsellor:	*Then how might this experience help you with your own feelings?*
Bereaved partner:	*Knowing that people I have known were not afraid at the end gives me some strength.*

■ *Present and past relationships* influence the response to a death. It is common for the bereaved person to feel initially that it will be impossible to enter another enduring relationship. Sometimes, they are trapped by feelings of guilt that they should even consider future relationships. Helping the bereaved person to identify and express beliefs, fears and guilt can be the start of enabling them to view these from different perspectives, and thus help to form the basis of release to move on in the future.

Counsellor:	*Sarah, you tell me you feel quite lost without Clive. How do you see yourself carrying on without him?*
Sarah:	*It is hard to think that I could ever make a close relationship again. I have a few friends. One in particular.*
Counsellor:	*How does Clive's death affect your present relationships?*
Sarah:	*I'm frightened to get involved again in case I have to lose that person again.*

> *Counsellor:* What was learnt from your relationship with Clive that might help you to decide to have a new relationship in the future?
>
> *Sarah:* We were such good friends, even before we became lovers, and I know that is important. So maybe it is worth the risk.

■ At the time of death, connections with the *family of origin and choice* may reappear. This in itself can be a source of pain if the relationships were not good. Against this background, it is important to be alert and aware when such customs are eroded as a result of emigration and family dispersal, which can make a loss more difficult to manage. Using genograms to identify relationships and patterns of relationships across and between generations can be a powerful therapeutic intervention with bereaved people. It is a method of opening discussion about change, loss, and patterns of support and can generate interest in people's past and present and make them curious about their future. Young children as well as adults can be readily engaged in this task.

■ *Beliefs* about loyalty to family members, sex, marriage, and parent-child relationships may be re-evaluated when there is a death and may influence a bereaved person's perception of how to manage relationships and live from day to day. The rituals surrounding death can serve to reveal, confirm or challenge these beliefs. Counselling can help people to express a belief, its origins and how it affects the bereaved.

The following dialogue illustrates a way of identifying beliefs:

> *Counsellor:* You say that you feel bad about feeling some relief that your sister has died. Where does the idea come from that you cannot show some relief after her death?
>
> *Bereaved sister:* It wouldn't seem right after all her suffering. My mother cried for six months after my father died. She was inconsolable.
>
> *Counsellor:* What do you think that meant for all of you?
>
> *Bereaved sister:* We were all too terrified to lighten things up. Mother would have thought that we were being disloyal. I would like to think that we needed to lighten up to stop us all from cracking up.

Counsellor:	*What might have to happen to help you feel less guilty about lightening things up?*
Bereaved sister:	*This conversation in itself has made me think.*
Counsellor:	*So what is one thought you might take away from the conversation?*
Bereaved sister:	*I don't have to keep feeling bad. I can lighten up.*

■ *The mourning process.* Adequate mourning is an essential part of the healing process. The counsellor may validate that some of the bereaved person's feelings of upset, grief or pain are expected, 'normal' and appropriate to her stage in the mourning process. Many people express great relief on hearing this. Positively encouraging mourning activities such as crying, wanting to be alone and thinking of the deceased a lot will allow the bereaved to grieve more freely and openly, and accept the idea of death as a reality. It may also be useful to discuss mourning within certain time-frames, thus giving some structure to what could otherwise seem to be an infinite process. The counsellor may want to see the bereaved person from time to time to assess with her how the mourning process is proceeding. The counsellor can usually reassure the person that her reaction to loss is normal and can help to put the mourning process into a time-frame that is appropriate to the patient:

Bereaved partner:	*I do still get upset. At times I don't know how I will manage from day to day.*
Counsellor:	*I'd be surprised if you didn't feel that way. It's really quite normal at this stage.*
Bereaved partner:	*I know. But it seems to go on and on . . .*
Counsellor:	*How long do you think this will go on? What do you think will have to happen that will tell you it is time to start going out more often with your friends?*
Bereaved partner:	*I'm not sure. Sometimes I really want to go out more, but then I think it's not right. Maybe I'd be being disloyal.*
Counsellor:	*Maybe you can think of one very small thing you could do that might not feel as though you were being disloyal.*

■ *Ending bereavement counselling.* The main aim of bereavement counselling is to help those who are bereaved to reach a point where they are able to look to and plan for the future more comfortably. The ability to do this is an important indication that the period of mourning is drawing to a close. Indications of this are that the bereaved person may talk less about the deceased and start to think about new activities or relationships, or return to previous routines.

Loss and bereavement are not always caused by death. An extreme reaction to the loss of a marital relationship is described below, to illustrate this, and it also highlights how religious, societal and cultural pressures make dealing with loss even more complex, especially when these are added to by integrating into local Western society.

Case Study

Mrs Mazhad, a 34-year-old Pakistani woman, was referred by a psychiatrist for counselling. Her husband had had a psychiatric 'breakdown', and on discharge from hospital said he was not returning to his wife. Mrs Mazhad was inconsolable. She had gone against the wishes of her large Pakistani family in marrying her husband, and had no contact with any of them. She was left with no family support, and she was trying to hold down a job as a solicitor. Her eight-year-old daughter was attending an English private school, but she would not let the headmistress know about their circumstances, nor would she tell the parents of her daughter's friends. No attempts to encourage her to be more open with selected people were able to make her change her mind. She made futile attempts to phone, text and contact her husband. She consulted her GP after the counsellor indicated that she would be able to help with ideas about managing the life she had at present, but was very concerned about her inability to sleep or to eat. On one occasion, Mrs Mazhad had telephoned the counsellor and said she felt suicidal. The counsellor made this known to the GP surgery, and expressed concerned for the eight-year-old daughter. Mrs Mazhad continued to isolate herself and eventually attempted an overdose. This woman had lost 'face' with her family, lost her husband and her family life. Hopes and expectations for the future were shattered, as well as financial security. She was admitted to a private psychiatric hospital. Working with Mrs Mazhad meant paying attention to the micro level (her needs, relationships and wishes); to managing the mezzo level (her religion, culture, societal beliefs and her daughter's needs); and to the macro level (the larger cultural context, Western influences, and private versus NHS care). In this case, it was the counsellor who attempted to work at all three levels. The risk of suicide and concerns for her daughter were ongoing vital concerns. It was Mrs Mazhad's attempted overdose that precipitated a crisis and necessitated a review of future concerns. The key issue was loss against a background of cultural beliefs and isolation.

CONCLUSION

Irrespective of the settings in which they work, all counsellors have some experience of working with people for whom issues about loss are most relevant. There are many different psychological theories about loss and its impact on individuals, couples and families. However, counsellors have to translate these ideas into therapeutic practice. It is sometimes especially difficult to counsel bereaved patients: some may be inconsolable, while others display no overt signs of distress. The ideas and skills described in this chapter offer a framework for practice and some ideas about how to deal with a number of issues that may arise in the course of loss and bereavement counselling.

In certain settings, such as hospitals, it might not be appropriate to offer ongoing bereavement counselling. It may be detrimental to the process of recovery for the bereaved to return to the place where the death occurred. It may be more appropriate for counsellors to refer a bereaved person to a colleague in another setting (a GP practice or specialist bereavement service, for example). In other circumstances, the original counsellor may not be able to take on the specialist work that bereavement counselling entails, for practical or other reasons. Although aspects of bereavement counselling can be carried out by a range of health care professionals, it requires specialized knowledge and skills, and for this reason should be provided only by those with appropriate training and experience. Giving bad news, counselling in terminal care and bereavement counselling are activities that place enormous emotional demands on the counsellor, and it is important that counsellors care for their own well-being as well as that of their patients and make good use of supervision sessions.

Chapter 15

Counselling the 'Worried Well' and Patients with Health Anxieties

INTRODUCTION

Some patients are not reassured when doctors tell them that they do not have an identifiable medical problem. Others do have a medical condition but have become fixated with every aspect of their health and illness to the detriment of getting on with even the most basic aspects of living. They are referred to in the literature as the 'worried well', hypochondriacs and somatizing patients. The problem has a direct effect on the relationship between the doctor, the patient and the patient's family. The sense of impasse and consequent feelings of exasperation and hopelessness often result in negative views developing about such patients, who are perceived to be resistant to change, rigid in their thinking, and a 'drain' on professional and personal resources.

We recognize the difficulties presented by these patients, but also view them as being highly appropriate for referral for counselling. Innovative approaches to counselling are required, as are collaborative working relationships with the patient's professional and family carers. Counsellors

237

can often gain acceptance as a member of the health care team through helping successfully in these cases. Professional colleagues usually recognize that such patients are time-consuming and can leave doctors and nurses feeling exasperated.

THEORETICAL CONCEPTS

Abnormal illness behaviour (such as hypochondriasis) is regarded in psychiatry as a syndrome of mental illness. The diagnosis is made when there is a perceived discrepancy between the patient's reaction to a medical problem and the nature of the medical problem, if indeed there is one (Mayou, 1989). A prerequisite for making this diagnosis is that the patient has been investigated thoroughly for physical illness by a doctor. Furthermore, laboratory tests and diagnostic procedures must have been carried out accurately, and sometimes repeatedly, so that the patient's responses can be considered against objective criteria. Nevertheless, such patients are prone to make subjective interpretations of their condition, which may be at variance with the opinions of health care professionals, who rely on the results of objective diagnostic procedures and laboratory tests. Where patients' conceptualizations of their condition, illness or symptoms differ from those of health care professionals, there is the potential for an impasse to occur in the relationship. This chapter describes how to identify and manage therapeutically those patients with health anxieties, a specialist area for counselling intervention.

These patients use somatic language to describe their difficulties, irrespective of whether these are physical or emotional problems (McDaniel *et al.*, 1992). Bodily aches and pains and specific medical conditions become real for the patient. He may also go to great lengths to convince others that the symptoms are real. The attending doctor may attempt to reassure the patient or offer a psychological explanation (for example, 'These headaches are a sign of stress rather than a brain tumour'). However, reassurance is usually refuted. The 'worried well' may fear that they have contracted a particular illness or they may complain that they already have signs and symptoms of disease, *when in fact there is no medical evidence for this*. The range extends from those who misinterpret physical signs and symptoms and then worry about their health (for example, someone who experiences the symptoms of indigestion and then worries that they have coronary heart disease) to patients with somatic delusions that can even mimic 'real' symptoms, as in the case of pseudo-seizures.

Most people will at some time have transient worries about their health and minor symptoms. However, a small group of patients become fixated by these symptoms and worry about them incessantly. These patients are most likely to be referred to counsellors after doctors have failed to reassure them, in spite of repeated tests, examinations and logical explanations. They may be labelled 'over-anxious', 'hypochondriacal', 'compulsive', 'obsessive' or 'hysterical'. Such labels rarely help to break the cycle of help-seeking behaviour and are not reassuring to the patient. The patient's drive for help and the doctor's response to this are depicted in Figure 15.1.

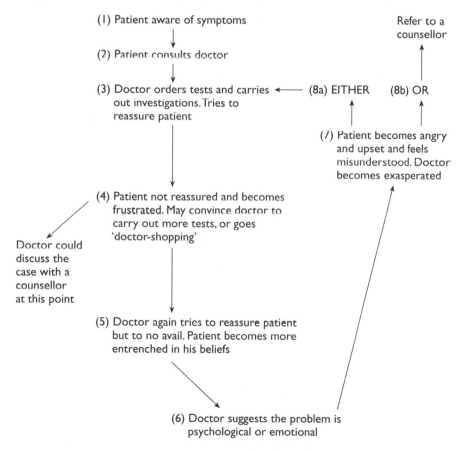

Figure 15.1   Cycle of doctor–patient interaction in 'worried-well' cases

The onset of the patient's worry may coincide with feelings of anxiety, depression or guilt. Counselling sessions frequently focus on uncovering possible 'causes' of the patient's disproportionate and unremitting worry, vigorously exploring the link between emotional problems and their somatic expression. The suggestion to the patient that somatic symptoms may be indicative of emotional problems is, however, often rebuffed. This is because somatic symptoms:

■ Are a more socially acceptable presentation of problems and carry less stigma than psychological problems;
■ Are viewed by the patient as being physical (and consequently amenable to diagnosis and treatment); and
■ This can lead to secondary gains for the patient in the form of attention from increasingly frustrated professional and non-professional care-givers.

Pointing out these processes to the patient rarely alleviates the symptoms. The patient will usually deny consciously misconstruing his symptoms, and this can lead to a more polarized relationship between the patient and the counsellor. There is sometimes an ebb and flow in the patient's experience of these problems, and consequently the certainty with which the conviction, or delusion, is held.

Events and psychological processes in the patient's life may be associated with a tendency to display psychosomatic manifestations of distress. Patients may include the following:

■ *Those with relationship problems.* A fear of illness can indicate difficulties about entering into, remaining in or ending relationships. The worry is a symptom that regulates the social and emotional distance in a relationship. For example, lonely people may find some relief from solitude because care-givers take their somatic complaints seriously. The somatic presentation of a psychological problem may be viewed as a less stigmatizing means of gaining access to treatment, through which there is less risk of rejection for the patient. Thus a person's intractable worry about his health may signal a call for professional help in a troubled relationship.
■ *Those whose social and financial conditions and problems give rise to extensive psychological distress.* These problems can manifest as physical and health symptoms (for example, shortness of breath or migraine) resulting in the patient needing to contact his doctor.

- *Those with past medical or psychological problems, or who have some connection with health care.* There may be an elevated risk for these patients because of their personal experience of health care. Those who have previously been treated for medical problems may be more likely to somatize than those who do not have a past medical history.
- *Misunderstandings of health education messages.* A small 'worried well' group comprises those who may have misunderstood health education messages and believe themselves to be at risk of illness because of life-style, exposure to an infectious agent in foreign countries (for example, avian influenza), or messages about self-diagnosis (as with women and breast cancer). Public health education through mass media campaigns (television, radio, newspapers) convey only limited information. Some people may then need to have a personal interview with an informed counsellor or health professional for their specific questions and anxieties to be addressed.

MANAGING THE 'WORRIED WELL': THE COUNSELLOR'S DILEMMA

It is useful to have an overview of how to respond in a helpful way to the patient's problem through counselling. In the first instance, any worry about a patient's health should be taken seriously and it is essential to defer to medical colleagues to address the problem first.

A problem arises where the patient is not reassured by the doctor. If the counsellor tries to reassure the patient, she will be doing precisely what the doctor has already tried, and failed, to achieve. Although reassurance may alleviate the patient's worries temporarily, it is unlikely to solve the underlying problem. A more effective approach is for the counsellor to present both sides of the dilemma simultaneously. This means, on the one hand, accepting the patient's view of himself as suffering from a physical illness, while at the same time introducing the possibility that these concerns about his health must be anxiety-provoking and stressful for the patient. This opens up the possibility of further discussion with the patient about the impact of illness. Developing these ideas within the counselling relationship helps to broaden the patient's view of his so-called illness without incurring the patient's resistance to being labelled as having a purely psychological problem.

Care must be taken to avoid interpreting the patient's behaviour exclusively in psychological terms at an early stage in the counselling relationship. Interpretation of the problem sometimes has negative connotations and may lead the patient to feel rejected and misunderstood, resulting in more help-seeking behaviour and even ending the counselling relationship. Equally, seeing the patient for counselling in a health care setting, over a prolonged period, could inadvertently reinforce the problem by exposing the patient to a medical context.

GUIDELINES FOR COUNSELLING THE 'WORRIED WELL'

The referral

The importance of the referral process is particularly relevant with somatizing patients. Many of these patients are initially unreceptive to a referral to a counsellor, which is entirely congruent with the nature of how they view their problem:

- The patient believes he has a physical rather than a psychological problem.
- The patient's anger or fear may be increased by the doctor's suggestion of a referral.
- The patient may feel abandoned and misunderstood, relegated to being emotionally disturbed and annoyed at the suggestion that his symptoms are either exaggerated or feigned.
- He may resist a referral by intensifying the pursuit of a medical diagnosis, becoming more demanding of the doctor or seeking second and subsequent opinions from other specialists.
- The patient may even feign cooperation in order to project a receptive openness to any 'medical' investigations and avoid being combative with the doctor, thus confirming suspicions of psychological difficulties (Turk and Salovey, 1996). Even if the patient is not outwardly defensive and 'resistant' to the referral and seems co-operative, the counsellor should assume that he may have difficulty accepting a psychological explanation for the problem.

The first meeting with the patient is more likely to be successful if it includes the referring doctor, even if this is only for a part of the session.

Discussion between the counsellor and doctor before the meeting can also facilitate the referral. Seeing the patient at this first meeting in the doctor's consulting room prevents an abrupt shift in focus from the physical to the psychological. It conveys the counsellor's initial acceptance of the patient's medical definition of the problem. The presence of both the doctor and counsellor can also help to demystify the counselling process for the patient by clarifying what might be achieved through counselling. This can be done by:

- The doctor introducing the counsellor *as a part* of the clinical team, reinforcing the mind–body link;
- Emphasizing the counsellor's expertise in helping people to cope better with illness and medical procedures, including knowledge of specialist skills to help them with their self-esteem, disruption to their life, relationships, distressing emotions and changes in roles and lifestyle;
- Reassuring the patient, at this stage, that medical concerns will continue to be dealt with by the doctor and that the counsellor and doctor will exchange information about the patient's condition and progress.

All these details can enhance the chances of counselling having some positive effect on the patient's condition.

The initial stages of counselling

Counselling should start by getting the patient's view of his problem. Thereafter, acknowledging the adverse effects the patient's symptoms or condition have on his life can be a way of building rapport. This should include some discussion about the impact of the symptoms on the patient's relationships and career and intrusion into leisure activities. The history of the onset, symptoms, significant events and medical investigations should also be addressed. It is important to limit discussion of this gradually from session to session, as otherwise the counsellor may inadvertently reinforce the patient's preoccupation with physical symptoms.

The main emphasis in the initial stages of counselling is to acknowledge the patient's distress and avoid offering psychological interpretations. This is achieved by assuming a collaborative and non-oppositional stance and by using medical language and medically styled interventions in counselling (McDaniel *et al.*, 1992). These may include desensitization interventions, symptom diaries and attention to the patient's sleep, diet and exercise routines. The counsellor should ask affirming questions about how the patient has coped with these symptoms and other unwelcome experiences and events in his life. Where possible, routine problem-defining questions should be asked, which will help the counsellor to construct a wider map of the problem. This may also lead to the counsellor completing a genogram with the patient and eliciting relevant information about the patient's family and illness, and the meanings of transgenerational patterns of illnesses.

Some of the following questions can help the counsellor to explore these issues with the patient:

> 'When did this problem start?'
>
> 'What do you think has caused this problem? What do you think has allowed the problem to continue?'
>
> 'What do you think the symptoms may mean?'
>
> 'What have you done to help alleviate the symptoms? With what effect?'
>
> 'What was happening in other areas of your life (for example, relationships, work) when your worries/symptoms started?'
>
> 'How have these concerns affected you (emotionally)?'
>
> 'Who else has been affected by your symptoms?'
>
> 'How have other health care providers been of help to you with this problem? (Always frame the question positively even if you suspect that the patient will criticize them for not taking him seriously.)'

At the end of the initial stage of counselling, the patient should have had an opportunity to talk about his view of the medical problem, and the impact it has on him, and possibly on those around him. Unlike in some other counselling situations, it may not be possible to discuss and agree on specific treatment goals. The reason for this is that the patient is likely to re-emphasize his somatic concerns, thereby diminishing the place of counselling in treatment.

Main therapeutic interventions

Innovative therapeutic interventions are required to deal with the impasse that may arise between the counsellor and patient in the course of counselling. It mirrors the one that has arisen between the patient and the doctor. An impasse is marked by a 'more-of-the-same' situation (Watzlawick *et al.*, 1974), in which any intervention by the counsellor results in 'no change' and statements beginning 'Yes, but . . .' from the patient. In counselling a worried-well patient, a symmetrical relationship between the counsellor and patient can develop quickly if this process is unchecked, characterized by an increasingly authoritative counsellor trying to convince an equally rigid patient that he is not ill, but with no success (see Figure 15.2).

This can become a 'game without end'. The interaction becomes repetitive and ineffective. Traditional theories about resistance in psychotherapy tend to blame the patient for the impasse. The counsellor may indicate what she perceives as the patient's resistance; or she may vary their interactive behaviour slightly; for example, by the counsellor raising her voice, or adopting a tone of greater authority. Kelly's (1969) work in psychotherapy is helpful for understanding ways to proceed. Kelly suggests that the impasse between the counsellor and patient reflects the 'stuckness' of the counsellor rather than the obduracy of the patient. In other words, the counsellor has not found the right 'key to the door'. To resolve this, the counsellor needs to become creative (and less predictable) in her problem-solving, rather than blaming or labelling the patient.

Cognitive behavioural methods of intervention aimed at changing the patient's beliefs and behaviour, and developing coping skills can also be used (Turk and Salovey, 1996). These interactions assume a fit between the patient's conceptualization of his problem and the rationale for the treatment being offered. As long as the patient is unreceptive to the idea that somatizing is a symptom of a psychological problem, he may resist

Patient — 'These symptoms must indicate that I am ill/infected.' → Counsellor 'The doctor says that all the tests are negative, so you must be well.'

Figure 15.2   Symmetrical relationship between patient and counsellor

cognitive behavioural interventions until such time as his conceptualizations change. For this reason, they may be only partially successful. None the less, cognitive and behavioural interventions can be very useful in the course of a wider treatment approach, especially reinforcement (of more adaptive illness responses), exposure (to feared situations), extinction (of inappropriate illness behaviours) and fostering self-control (over maladaptive thoughts, feelings and behaviours), as well as biofeedback, relaxation training and distraction skills training.

The overall aim is to shift the patient's cognitive and behavioural repertoire away from habitual and rigid automatic thoughts and responses. A key feature is that the patient's physical and psychological symptoms can be translated into identifiable and concrete difficulties, rather than vague and uncontrollable ones. It is especially helpful to gain an understanding of what helps to keep the patient's anxiety going. This might include: the patient seeking reassurance when he becomes preoccupied with certain symptoms; regular self-monitoring and checking of physical symptoms; and spending excessive amounts of time finding out about illness, among other behaviours. Once the maintaining behaviours have been identified, this can form the basis for helping the patient to deal more effectively with his health anxiety. Targeted interventions might include helping the patient to think about other explanations for the symptoms; distraction and thought-blocking techniques; finding ways to stop trying to prove there is a medical cause; learning how not to keep asking for reassurance and checking symptoms, and also to stop behaving as if he were ill. Of course, a thorough assessment of the patient's problem is required as health anxieties might also be a symptom or co-factor of low mood or depression that might also need to be treated.

Cognitive behavioural interventions typically focus upon the *individual's* beliefs and behaviours rather than on the relationship between the individual's beliefs in the context of his family and the impact this has on the therapeutic system of professional carers. Further interventions can be used, which are designed to encourage the individual to view the problem differently. An example may be to place the worry and its impact within the context of family relationships. These can be done with an individual and do not require other family members to be present in the session. This form of intervention is particularly useful when the patient is unable or unwilling to change strongly held beliefs. It is aimed at reducing resistance to change and dismantling these beliefs to allow the patient to move out of his 'stuck' position and to develop a new view of the problem.

Skills for managing an impasse in counselling

A number of approaches can be used to try to move therapy beyond the repetitive cycle of 'Yes, I am ... No, you're not' in counselling. These interventions should be used with great sensitivity and care, and only in the context of an existing therapeutic relationship. This is because, if used too early in a therapeutic relationship, the patient might feel that the counsellor has not fully appreciated and clearly understood the extent of his psychological distress. However, where it becomes necessary and helpful to highlight the apparent impasse in therapy, it can be addressed in one of the following ways:

1   Comment on the apparent stuckness:

   'I feel that each time I try to persuade you that you do not have a tumour, you seem to be quite convinced that you have. If you were the counsellor, what might you say to a patient?'

2   Adopt a one-down, defeated position:

   'Well, you seem to have got me here. I just can't think how I'm going to change your ideas. I just don't seem to be able to throw any new light on this. I'll need to think about this for a while.'

3   Solicit the patient's help:

   'Do you have any ideas about what might help to convince you that you don't have a tumour and that you are not dying?'

4   Discuss the effect of the worry on relationships:

   'How has this worry affected your relationship with your wife?'

5   Ask what might happen if the worry persisted:

   'If this worry never went away, what effect might this have on you, and how might you cope?'

6   Ask what might happen if things got worse:

   'What is the worst thing that could happen to you with this problem?'

7   Ask what might replace this worry:

   'If, for some reason, you stopped worrying about dying, is there anything else you might start to worry about?'

8 Talk hypothetically about the patient actually having the illness:

'You keep trying to convince me that you are terminally ill. You don't believe the doctors when they tell you that all the tests were accurate and reliable. Let's pretend for a few minutes that you are terminally ill. Let's talk about a day in your life as a terminally ill young man. How much of the day would you worry about dying? Who would you talk to about it? What plans would you make? What would you do that was not associated with your illness? How would this be different to what you are doing now?'

9 Discuss some advantages of worrying (reframe):

'Has your worry resulted in anything that might be even slightly good for you?'

10 Indicate that the patient has control:

'You will know when you are ready to stop worrying about your heart and be convinced that the test results were correct.'

The following case example illustrates the application of some of these ideas to working with a patient who had intractable worries about being infected with HIV despite a series of negative test results. The patient self-referred to an HIV counselling service and therefore a link with his doctor was not of primary concern in counselling.

Case Study

Background

David, a 32-year-old warehouse supervisor, telephoned an HIV hotline saying he was concerned that he had become infected with HIV and given it to his wife, Liz (aged 31 years). He had had sexual intercourse with another woman after he got drunk at a party a year before. David reported that, apart from this one episode, he had always been faithful to his wife, and she to him, for the ten years of their marriage. This was his only reported risk of HIV infection.

The couple had moved to London four years previously to find work. David reported that he wanted to move back to Wales because he was mixing with a 'bad' crowd here who encouraged him to drink alcohol, and his wife was opposed to this. He believed his wife wanted him to stay in London because it meant that she could work. He also reported that he had wanted children, but his wife did not.

⏵

It was suspected during the course of his telephone call that this man was excessively and somewhat inappropriately worried about his risk of HIV, and that he required something other than rational explanations and information about HIV. An appointment was offered to him to be seen by a counsellor in a specialist HIV counselling service, which he accepted gratefully. Up to this point, he had had no such offer from other hotline services, despite his making calls to them four times a day on average.

David arrived half an hour early for his appointment and was found pacing around outside the unit waiting eagerly to be seen. On interview, it transpired that David had read extensively about HIV-related symptoms, tests and treatment, in the process of checking out his own risks and his wife's symptoms. He had become so conversant with the topic that he was now able to correct misinformation that the helplines might give him. He was also well aware that his exposure to risk of infection was low, and that his two negative HIV antibody test results, taken three and nine months after the risk encounter, were likely to be accurate. Despite this knowledge, he was still convinced that he had given HIV to his wife. She had recently developed various aches and pains, and he attributed these to her having HIV, although he was aware that these symptoms were atypical of HIV. Furthermore, he was aware of the 'situational' nature of the symptoms, which disappeared when his wife visited her mother in Wales and returned when she came back to London. David had not told his wife of his infidelity.

David reported that his wife had said that she was finding his distress intolerable, but that she could not leave him because she feared he might kill himself. David had confirmed that he had considered suicide as a way of ending his worry, misery and guilt. However, he felt that he could not do this to his wife. He cried bitterly at this point. They were unable to leave each other, yet were also becoming increasingly unable to be together. This position was to some extent reflected by the threat of HIV infection. David and his wife appeared to have little in common other than that they might now share the same virus. However, the virus that might connect them could also separate them, through divorce, suicide or death from HIV.

Counselling interventions

It was clear that HIV had an important place in their relationship. It had organized their beliefs and thinking. Intervention was aimed at enabling David to have a new view of the problem. His compulsion to read about HIV and to telephone hotlines repeatedly was reframed as his now being an expert in the field.

David: I've been phoning HIV hotlines sometimes four times a day because I have been so worried about having HIV.

Counsellor: That's interesting. Tell me, what have you learned from making these calls?

David: That people don't know as much as I do about HIV. They tell me things that are wrong. I know they are wrong because I've read books about it. They don't know what a retrovirus is, or how long it takes to seroconvert.

> Counsellor: So, it seems that you have developed some expertise in HIV hotline services. We don't know which are the better hotlines, so you probably know more about them than we do ...
>
> David: Yes, I could tell you all about them ... (David proceeds enthusiastically to tell the counsellor about HIV hotline services).

David had placed an emphasis on discovering the truth about whether he had HIV. However, he had only attempted to prove he had been infected. The problem was redefined by emphasizing the strength and the consequences of David's belief. It was suggested to him that, irrespective of the evidence against his having HIV, he believed that he was infected and that the difficulty then was how to live with this belief, given that it seemed nothing could be done to change it. David's fear that he had given his wife HIV, because of his infidelity, was reframed as his caring and concern that his wife should have good health.

Reframing the problem was aimed at providing David with a new view of his problem; one that placed it within the context of his relationship with his wife. The task of the counsellor is to provide a context for discussion of problem-solving and the patient's options, as a way of overcoming resistance to change and to move the patient from the stuck position and facilitate new problem-solving.

In David's case, it would seem that the solution he found was for he and his wife to move back to Wales. He phoned the counsellor a month after his visit to say that he had decided not to have another HIV antibody test because he could not stand the stress of it. He had stopped phoning helplines because he realized that they could not tell him any more than he already knew, or might give him wrong information, which annoyed him. When asked why they were returning to Wales, David laughed, saying that if his wife did have AIDS, then this was the best place for her to be. On another level, however, it was also the place where David said that his wife's aches and pains disappeared, as well as the place where he himself would prefer to live.

CONCLUSION

Somatizing and worried-well patients present a unique challenge to health care providers in general and counsellors in particular. Successful treatment requires close collaboration between all the health professionals and innovative therapeutic interventions. Some patients may remain unresponsive to treatment and the possibility of a consultation with, or referral to, other mental health specialists (such as a clinical psychologist or psychiatrist) may then need to be considered. There is also a small group of these patients who, once in counselling, keep producing a worry about symptoms of their health in order to maintain access to, and contact with, the counsellor. This usually occurs when counselling is coming to an end. In such cases, the worry is a ticket of entry to psychological support systems. Unless the counsellor notes this, the patient will revert to the worry at the end of counselling sessions in order to re-engage the counsellor. It can be of some help in these circumstances to say to the patient: 'I will continue to see you for counselling even when you no longer have these worries'. Counsellors need to be sensitive to the different concerns of patients and the indirect ways in which patients may sometimes express these concerns.

Chapter 16

When Progress in Counselling Seems Elusive

INTRODUCTION

Counsellors are trained to be reflective practitioners, learning to identify problems and their possible source, and to work towards their resolution. This can extend to addressing the degree to which the counsellor may inadvertently have caused, maintained or exacerbated a problem. This chapter examines possible sources of 'stuckness' in counselling in health care settings and suggests some ideas and approaches for overcoming these.

WHAT HAPPENS WHEN PROGRESS IS ELUSIVE?

During the counselling process, there may often be episodes in which little or no progress is made with a patient, or indeed there is evidence of some regression in relation to problems or difficulties. Training in counselling includes learning how to recognize when the counselling process has become stuck and to work with the patient in order to free the therapeutic process from the impasse. Progress can be elusive at any stage in counselling from the point of first contact – or even before, if there is some disagreement as to whether counselling should in fact take place – right up to the last moments when a case is being brought to a close. Stuckness is usually characterized by a lack of progress in counselling. Indications of this include:

- Going over familiar issues without evidence of any progress in how the problem is viewed or being resolved;
- Obvious boredom or missed sessions by the patient;
- The counsellor not looking forward to a counselling session;
- The counsellor becoming hostile, argumentative or combative with the patient.

If the feeling or experience of stuckness is not acknowledged or reflected on it can lead to patients dropping out of counselling, the patient's problems being unresolved or becoming intractable, the counsellor acquiring a bad reputation in the hospital or clinic setting and even counsellor 'burnout'. Stuckness, however, need not denote a problem in counselling. Some counsellors may view it as an opportunity to reflect on the process with the patient and move beyond the impasse. Others see it as a time to talk about the idea of 'resistance' in the counselling process, which may manifest as the patient rejecting suggestions and interventions from the counsellor, and be conveyed to the counsellor in terms of 'yes, but . . .'.

CAUSES OF AN IMPASSE

There are numerous possible causes of an impasse in counselling. A common assumption may be that it stems from the patient's reluctance to change, but there are both contextual and personal issues for the counsellor to consider when trying to identify these possible causes.

Patient issues

A number of events or processes may impede the progress of counselling for a patient and these may differ from one situation to another. The following are short examples to illustrate this:

- The patient does not share the counsellor's (or other health care professionals') view of the problem and its possible solution, and therefore does not engage positively with the counselling process.

- The patient does not want to attend counselling meetings and transfers the responsibility for problem-solving onto the counsellor.
- Issues raised in the course of counselling can add to the patient's experience of uncertainty, role confusion and anxiety, in addition to relationship changes brought about by current ill health, either physical or psychological.
- Patients feel unable to make important decisions, either because their current emotional state has drained their capacity to solve problems creatively, or there is little incentive to change. This impasse may be transferred to the relationship between the counsellor and the patient.
- Issues about loss are painful to discuss and not a part of everyday conversations. The patient is unsure of whether or how to talk about her feelings, or afraid of feeling overwhelmed by them or the effect of revealing them to a comparative stranger in counselling sessions.
- Denial of problems can be used as a means of coping with them (either consciously or unconsciously).
- The patient is frustrated by the slow pace of counselling and wants practical solutions, rapid results and evidence of progress, including possibly a 'cure'.
- The patient's needs, wishes, concerns or beliefs are not identified or not met, leaving her feeling frustrated, vulnerable and dissatisfied.

Problems arising within the counselling context

For the counsellor, there may be processes within the work setting that lead directly or indirectly to feelings of stuckness in counselling sessions. These may include some combinations of the following:

- Accepting a referral without first assessing whether it is a suitable case for counselling, and failing to identify or address confounding problems or dynamics between colleagues that may impede progress.
- Insufficient feedback between different members of the health care team resulting in unco-ordinated care, misunderstandings and lack of consensus over approaches to treatment and care.
- Having too much to do in too little time which may lead to a lower standard of care or treatment and the making of unwise decisions. The pressure to practise counselling from an evidence-based perspective

and sometimes according to seemingly rigid guidelines and the requirement to evaluate counselling can also give rise to difficulties during
counselling, especially where these guidelines appear to conflict with
the counsellor's intuition or experience with a particular problem.

■ Inflexibility on the part of the counsellor who is determined to
preserve a traditional model of counselling as practised in an 'ideal'
setting, which is viewed as curative and the antidote to change, pain
and chaos in the patient's life.

■ Not sufficiently noting and responding to changes in the patient's
condition, level and context of social support, mental state or ability
to attend counselling sessions.

■ Not investing sufficient effort into eliciting the patient's engagement in
the process of counselling.

Issues relating to the counsellor

Unresolved personal responses to illness, loss or disability may occur and
these may limit the effectiveness of the counsellor. Other personal issues
may include the following:

■ Inappropriate reactions to a patient's problems, such as giving unrealistic reassurance. This might stem from insufficient therapeutic skills
and training, lack of supervision, stress or fatigue.

■ Over-identification with patients (becoming too close emotionally)
and aspects of their problems, which may lead to breaking professional boundaries, such as giving a patient the counsellor's home telephone number 'so that she can call at any time she needs to talk'.

■ Under-identification with the patient (becoming too distant emotionally), which may lead to inflexibility on the part of the counsellor, a
lack of empathy, or the patient feeling that the counsellor is 'cold' and
'uncaring'.

■ Acting in a way that implies judgement of the patient, her lifestyle or
the strategies she uses to cope with her ill health. This could manifest
as overt criticism of the patient, directing the patient to make different decisions, or implied criticism communicated non-verbally (for
example, frowning, shaking one's head, or a look of exasperation).
This can also present where the counsellor feels that he has to take
sides with the patient, her family or other colleagues.

■ Treating the patient's problem or symptoms without attending to any of her emotional needs. This may arise where the counsellor reduces counselling to the utilization of a series of techniques that exclusively involve problem-solving. It may also occur where the counsellor feels unsure as to how to respond to a patient who cries or says very little.

■ Feeling under pressure to solve every problem, offer definitive answers to questions and create a sense of certainty. The counsellor may also blame himself (erroneously) for failure in counselling. This may be a result of a lack of appreciation of a patient's competencies and lack of expertise in eliciting them.

RECOGNIZING POSSIBLE SIGNS OF STRESS IN THE COUNSELLOR

It is important for counsellors to be able to recognize when they are stressed and how this may interfere with the counselling process. The following questions can help the counsellor to identify the presence and possible source of stress that may lead to an impasse or stuckness when counselling patients:

> Take your 'emotional temperature': are you overly sensitive, or emotionally cold and distant? What has happened to your feelings of empathy?
>
> Are you able to discuss these issues and concerns with your supervisor?
>
> Have you become predictable in how you respond to patients and different problems? Have you lost a feeling of challenge and desire to respond flexibly and creatively?
>
> Are you frequently tired and irritable (for example, from overwork or personal difficulties)?
>
> Are the boundaries between your personal and professional lives sometimes unclear? Do you take too much work home, or go in to work when it is not necessary to do so?
>
> Are there significant changes in your leisure pursuits (for example, too much alcohol and no exercise)?
>
> ⬛➡

Have there been significant changes in your family and personal relationships?

Do you feel a sense of achievement in your work, or does the emotional distress and experience of loss encountered by some of your patients take its toll on you?

Are you affected by stress, ill health, disability or difficulties in your personal relationships?

AN IMPASSE WITHIN THE COUNSELLING RELATIONSHIP

The emphasis up to this point has been on patient, counsellor and contextual factors that affect progress in counselling. This assumes that counselling has started and that the counsellor and patient are both committed to a course of sessions. However, stuckness may also occur at the point of referral and even before there has been agreement to meet for counselling. The risk of this happening in a health care setting is considerable, for a number of reasons:

- The referrer may not have explained clearly the reason for the referral, or gained the patient's cooperation and consent for it.
- The patient may not recognize (or may not *want* to recognize) that there are psychological and relationship issues that might need to be examined in the course of counselling.
- The patient does not understand how the process of counselling may help to resolve her problem.
- The referral may be a gesture by another health care professional, who may be exasperated, frustrated or uninterested, and refers a patient to a colleague merely 'to get the patient off her back'.
- The counsellor may feel that the problem is not of a psychological nature and is therefore inappropriate for that particular counselling service (for example, the patient requires help with housing, income support or sickness benefits).

Failure to address these issues will at some point result in an impasse in counselling. The algorithm shown in Figure 16.1 may help in deciding whether counselling can or should proceed.

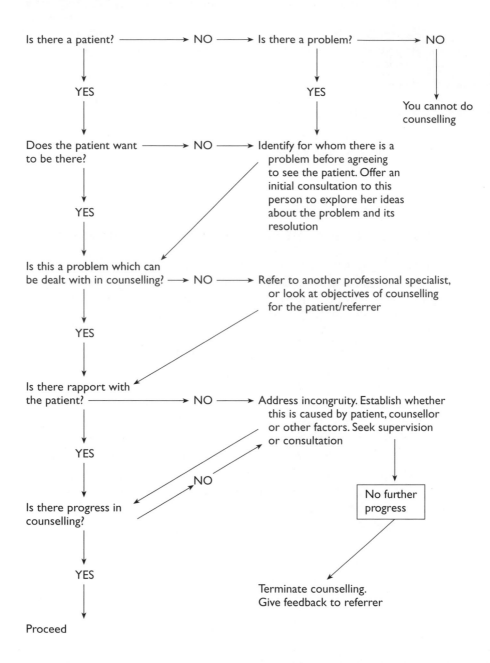

Figure 16.1 Algorithm for deciding whether counselling can proceed

AN IMPASSE ARISING FROM CONFLICTING ROLES AND RELATIONSHIPS BETWEEN PROFESSIONALS

Although all health care professionals may share a common mission of helping to treat and care for their patients and family, they may differ in how they demonstrate their caring for patients and how they relate to them. Doctors and nurses have 'hands on' contact with their patients. In contrast, physical contact between counsellors and their patients is not accepted as part of usual practice. Not only may there be different approaches to care, but complex dynamics such as rivalry between professional carers can also undermine the counselling process. This may result from feelings of envy or misunderstanding over the aims and goals of a particular treatment approach. Two examples in hospital settings illustrate possible problems.

Case Studies

In the first example, it became clear that a counsellor's omission of not explaining to nurses on a ward that counselling sessions might make the patient seem more upset for a short time led to their anxiety that counselling was making the patient more upset. Lack of liaison or feedback to the nurses resulted in them protesting to the referring doctor that the counsellor was upsetting the patient and making it more difficult to care for him. In this case, the patient was being investigated for Crohn's disease and had been admitted for tests by his doctor. One consequence of the patient's anxiety about being in hospital was that he developed abdominal pains and diarrhoea, possibly relating to symptoms of anxiety and distress. The nurses believed that these symptoms were exacerbated by counselling sessions, in which the patient spoke about his extreme worry about being diagnosed with the condition and the effect it could have on his family life and career. Figure 16.2 overleaf illustrates the effects of the problem between the nurses and counsellor.

This misunderstanding could have been avoided if the counsellor had explained to the nurses and to the patient that psychological problems sometimes get worse initially, especially if the patient remains anxious about the outcome of the tests and investigations. Instead, in this case, poor liaison resulted in the patient becoming more distressed, his being prescribed sedative medication, and possibly to a deterioration in the relationship between the professional groups most directly involved.

The second example shows that it is possible that two professional groups, each with a remit for psychological care (in this case, a health adviser in a genito-urinary medicine clinic, and a hospital-based counsellor) could have conflicting approaches to patient care. The patient had recently been diagnosed with hepatitis B, which he

||||➤

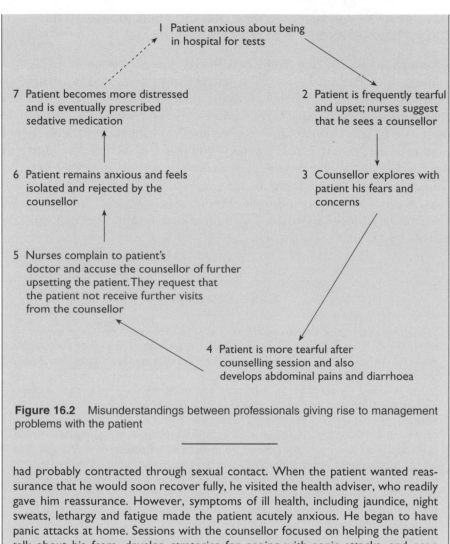

Figure 16.2 Misunderstandings between professionals giving rise to management problems with the patient

had probably contracted through sexual contact. When the patient wanted reassurance that he would soon recover fully, he visited the health adviser, who readily gave him reassurance. However, symptoms of ill health, including jaundice, night sweats, lethargy and fatigue made the patient acutely anxious. He began to have panic attacks at home. Sessions with the counsellor focused on helping the patient talk about his fears, develop strategies for coping with panic attacks, and cope better with his illness. As soon as the patient felt better and the panic attacks abated, he would seek out the health adviser for further reassurance sessions until the cycle was repeated.

The second case example indicates a split in the health care team between the 'good' and 'bad' care professionals, and consequently the dilution of focus and intensity in counselling. Collaborative work, or an agreement that only one of the professionals would work directly with the patient, could help to avoid such splits and their consequences. It could be argued that in the latter case the split was not unduly harmful to the patient, because reassurance did not necessarily exacerbate the patient's symptoms. Indeed, reassurance may have been containing for the patient and helped to strengthen his ability to cope. None the less, it could also be reasoned that a deterioration in the patient's condition could have led to a breakdown in the relationship with the health adviser, in whom the patient would no longer have confidence.

Although different mental health professionals may be involved in any one case, it is preferable to limit direct patient contact to only one counsellor, or for others to be invited in on an ad hoc basis similar to the role of a consultation-liaison psychiatrist in a general hospital.

Case Study

In this case example, the counsellor had worked closely with the consultant haematologist to develop a comprehensive care and treatment service for patients with sickle cell disease. The team comprised nurses, a medical social worker, a physiotherapist and a junior doctor on rotation. All new patients were seen initially by the consultant haematologist and then by the counsellor. This arrangement changed soon after the appointment of a specialist registrar in haematology. He felt that patients only needed to be referred to the counsellor when they displayed obvious signs of psychopathology. In practice, no new patients were seen by the counsellor in the first two months of the specialist registrar's appointment. The counsellor first discussed this with the specialist registrar who remained adamant that he would not routinely refer new cases to the counsellor. Feeling frustrated, the counsellor then discussed the problem with the consultant haematologist. Although the consultant was sympathetic to the counsellor, he did not want to interfere with the practice of the specialist registrar, whom he relied on to reduce his workload. The problematic triangular relationship remained unchanged until a patient committed suicide eight months later. The specialist registrar then asked the counsellor for help with counselling the bereaved relatives, one of whom was also being treated for sickle cell disease. This tragic event coincidentally resulted in a closer working relationship between the specialist registrar and the counsellor. It provided an opportunity for the two professionals to discuss how the counselling service could best be introduced to patients in the future, and led to fortnightly case meetings attended by all members of the unit, where patients' psychological and social problems were discussed. By virtue of the professional hierarchy, only the consultant haematologist could have insisted on his specialist registrar referring all new patients to the counsellor. Even so, the specialist registrar might have

⏭

remained sceptical, and referrals to the counsellor might not have been well made. Experience has taught us to be patient and use every opportunity to define and redefine the position, role and tasks of the counsellor. Impatience leads to resistance and ill-feeling between colleagues.

AVOIDING, UNDERSTANDING AND MANAGING AN IMPASSE

Having some strategies and procedures for dealing with an impasse or 'stuckness' in counselling can help to avoid these situations, understand them better and manage them when they occur. Highlighting possible sources or causes of 'stuckness' is a first step towards its resolution. An initial task for the counsellor is to reflect on the situation confronting him by answering a series of self-reflective questions about the case or problem. Some suggestions for questions are:

Is this a problem I can solve by myself or does it require the help or intervention of others? Can supervision or consultation help?

Why does this problem occur at this point in time?

What is the worst possible consequence of this problem? What might happen if the problem is not addressed?

What is expected of me (by the patient, referrer, colleagues, line manager) in relation to this problem?

If other colleagues were in a similar position, what might they be inclined to do?

It is also helpful to consider other ways of resolving an impasse in counselling. This can be achieved in a number of ways:

■ *Arrange for consultation or supervision.* Another counsellor or consultant may view the problem differently, or at least be able to advise on alternative options for solving the problem. The act of describing the problem to another professional familiar with complex interpersonal and organizational dynamics may in itself prove helpful. A consultant or supervisor can provide useful feedback about what you may be doing to cause, maintain or exacerbate problems. It does not necessarily imply that the counsellor has failed to discern his role in a problem; it is difficult to observe and be objective about a process of which one is a part.

- *Discuss the problem with a line manager.* Although one's supervisor may also be a line manager, these functions are often separated in health care settings. Indeed, counsellors working in some health care settings may not have the support of a team or a whole department of counsellors or related mental health professionals. This in itself may present a problem for the counsellor (and managers), who may be unclear about tasks, expectations and accountability associated with this work. None the less, someone within the management structure is likely to have been designated the line manager with whom counsellors can discuss professional or organizational problems. In a GP practice, this could be the senior partner or practice manager. In a hospital, this may be the head of therapy services, a consultant psychologist, psychiatrist or psychotherapist, or a senior member of nursing or medical staff. Although preferable, it is not uncommon for a counsellor's line manager to come from another professional background. Consultation with a line manager could prove an efficient way of facilitating the progression of counselling.

- *Arrange a team meeting.* Given the importance of interprofessional collaboration and the potential problems that arise when this does not work well, other colleagues may be affected directly or indirectly by the slow progress, or complete lack of it, in counselling. Most medical specialities have regular patient case discussions or ward rounds. Although professional colleagues welcome counsellors' attendance at these meetings, being accepted as a permanent and loyal member of the multi-disciplinary team may take years to achieve. This process is slower and more difficult if the counsellor is not attached to any particular speciality and is required to work with teams across the spectrum of specialities. None the less, ad hoc meetings with key personnel or with a team with which one has loose links are an additional way to explore and resolve problems. It also provides a further opportunity to clarify the role of the counsellor and strengthen professional relationships.

- *Arrange for personal therapy.* If there are personal problems that interfere with counselling, especially those relating to loss, health concerns or disability, personal therapy can help to address and resolve some of them so that they do not affect either the patient's treatment or the counsellor's well-being.

CONCLUSION

An impasse can arise in counselling for a number of reasons. It may be caused by difficulties in the counsellor–patient relationship, between the counsellor and the referrer or other professionals, as a consequence of organizational dynamics and pressures and because the counsellor is inexperienced in a particular area of work, or stressed at work. A self-reflecting counsellor should be able to identify the source of the impasse and recognize the 'stuckness' that may follow in counselling sessions. Counsellors have long recognized that the complex interpersonal dynamics in counselling sessions and the practice of counselling make it inevitable that an impasse will occur. Solutions are to be found in (i) recognition of and reflection on these dynamics; (ii) understanding the relevant influence of contextual and organizational issues in counselling; (iii) more effective team collaboration; (iv) supervision or consultation; and (v) the counsellor's own course of personal therapy.

From the perspective of working in partnership with the patient, and in line with the understanding of the nature of the counselling relationship in this book, open and reflective discussion with the patient about an impasse in the counselling process can contribute greatly to its early identification and resolution. Eliciting the patient's interest and cooperation in solving the problem of an impasse in counselling can be seen as an opportunity for collaborative work with the patient. The first step in addressing an impasse might usefully be to invite the patient's experience, explanation and expertise in how to resolve it. In so doing, an impasse in the counselling process may be viewed as a shared problem between counsellor and patient, both of whom must work collaboratively to try to overcome it, just as with any other problem that presents during the course of counselling.

Chapter 17

Counselling for the Prevention of Ill Health

INTRODUCTION

The physical and mental health implications of being diagnosed with an illness, particularly if it is chronic, degenerative, associated with disability, terminal, or transmissible to others (through infection or genetic conditions), mean that prevention should be uppermost in the minds of health care professionals. This includes the prevention of disease and disease progression, somatic manifestations of stress, mental health and social or family problems.

Diagnosis of a physical illness can affect individuals and their families in a number of ways. One important effect is the potential for anxiety about the diagnosis, investigations, treatment or prognosis. The patient may not have any signs or symptoms of disease; just 'knowing' he *has* the disease is sufficient to stimulate fearful thoughts. These thoughts, in turn, can affect the individual's behaviour and the concomitant physiological 'fight or flight' response of the sympathetic nervous system may be triggered. Initially, the individual engages in the *alarm* phase of the stress response, preparing to attack or defend against the perceived threat (Selye, 1956). The individual is able to maintain this response in the *resistance* phase for a considerable time before submitting to the *exhaustion* phase following prolonged exposure to stress. Cardiovascular and immune function changes may occur to make the individual more vulnerable to illness.

Psychologically, an exhausted individual may lose motivation, feel helpless, lack confidence, withdraw from others and become depressed. This compounds the illness process, as well as the person's motivation and approach to treatment and healthy living.

Case Study

Mrs Davis had been diagnosed with multiple sclerosis, but was told 'not to worry' by her doctor until serious symptoms occurred. Mrs Davis found this very difficult to do, and became increasingly anxious. Two years later she was referred for psychological treatment of anxiety when she said she was having difficulty coping. Had she been referred early, post-diagnostically, for preventive counselling, she could have been taught anxiety management strategies as well as having the opportunity to discuss her fears and feelings about her diagnosis, and consider the implications for her and her family. By increasing her sense of control and ability to cope with different scenarios, she might not have needed crisis intervention. Her adaptation to diagnosis and disease progression could also have been improved with preventive intervention.

As has been stated in Chapter 11, many of the above mental and physical health complications arise from the individual's cognitions and fears, rather than from the disease process itself. How can illness, stress, anxiety and depression be prevented?

THEORETICAL BACKGROUND

Current psychological models of health-risk behaviours and precaution adoption include the Health Belief Model (Becker, 1974), Theory of Reasoned Action (Fishbein and Ajzen, 1975) and the Precaution Adoption Process (Weinstein, 1988). They are cognitive, individualistic models focusing on the individual's thoughts and beliefs.

The Health Belief Model

The Health Belief Model indicates that a person's perceived vulnerability to a health threat, their perceived severity of the threat and the cost–benefit of adopting a preventive action are central to whether an individual adopts a more healthy lifestyle. However, the limitations of this model include the assumption that humans are able to make rational and logical decisions about their behaviour and that their individual beliefs are robust and not easily influenced by the beliefs of significant others.

This model suggests that, for preventive counselling work, the counsellor needs to understand the individual's perceived vulnerability to health risk, his beliefs about the severity of that threat, and the costs–benefits of changing health-risk behaviour or adopting preventive behaviour. Hypothetical future-orientated questions can be used to elicit the individual's beliefs, and as such bring this cognitive process to conscious awareness for discussion with the counsellor and significant others. It may be that, in doing so, the individual will be able to make a more reasoned decision based on the available evidence, rather than an irrational one fuelled by emotion and confusion.

Theory of Reasoned Action

The Theory of Reasoned Action is, as the name suggests, a model that relies on logical and rational thought processes that influence human behaviour. In particular, this model proposes that health-risk behaviour and precaution adoption are related to the individual's intentions. These, in turn, are linked to the private attitudes the individual holds about a particular behaviour, and to that person's beliefs about subjective norms and how other people might view this particular behaviour. The model encompasses a social comparison component and places greater value on shared belief systems. This model has similar limitations to the Health Belief Model, but it can account for seemingly irrational health behaviours when these behaviours are considered in the context of the patient's peers, family or culture. An example would be smoking or drug use, which may be a peer-led, socially sanctioned activity. Although the individual may know logically that such behaviour is a health risk, he is able to continue engaging in it by rationalizing his use of tobacco or drugs, or denying their adverse consequences. For some individuals the need to be accepted socially or to fit into the family, for example, is seemingly greater than their need to remain physically healthy. Indeed, working clinically with patients who are having difficulty in changing their health-risk behaviour, we have often found that the individual has to reconstrue their whole existence, and not just one simple aspect of behaviour, in order to be able to adapt and change. Frequently, it includes involving significant others, who are integral to the maintenance and change of health-risk behaviour and precaution adoption.

The Precaution Adoption Process

This model similarly focuses on individual thought processes, but in addition it describes the adoption of healthy behaviour in accordance with five stages of development. These are:

1   Knowledge;
2   Risk acknowledgement;
3   Personal risk acknowledgement;
4   Intention to act;
5   Action.

The model proposes that individuals have to know about the extent of a health risk as the first stage towards adopting a preventive measure. In this respect, education is fundamental to behaviour change but, unlike many health education programmes, this model suggests that education alone is not sufficient for behaviour change. The second stage of this model indicates the need for individuals to understand the risk attached to certain behaviour. This is different from stage 3, when individuals are required to acknowledge their own personal risk. Many people who are trying to change their health-risk behaviour find that moving from stage 2 to stage 3 is a frequent stumbling block. They may well know about a health-risk behaviour and accept that it is risky, but not feel that they are personally vulnerable. Life-style studies indicate that people overestimate their ability to avoid health hazards, and underestimate their risk of becoming personally vulnerable. This is a somewhat 'rose-tinted' view of one's health actions.

Stage 4 is similar to Fishbein and Ajzen's (1975) model in that it identifies intentions to act as key predictors of subsequent action. Again, many individuals find that moving from stage 4 to stage 5, the action stage, is difficult. They may well intend to do all sorts of things (for example, stop smoking, reduce alcohol consumption, use condoms) but when the time comes they are not able to follow through their intentions. Again, one key factor that may influence people's intentions to engage in a particular behaviour may be the views and beliefs of significant others. In a study

looking at condom use by college students to prevent HIV and other sexually transmitted diseases, it was observed that while students may have
had condoms with them at the time of intercourse with a new partner (and
intended to use them), there were many students who in fact did not use
them. It would appear that communication between the couple, and the
use of alcohol and drugs, were major influences on whether or not a
couple used a condom, even though they may have intended to do so.

The implication of the above models for preventive counselling is that the
counsellor needs to understand the individual's beliefs in the context of
their relationships with others. In particular, it may be useful to include
partners, parents or children when considering the obstacles to behaviour
change, and determining what would have to happen to enable a person to
adopt a healthier life-style. A family consultation can have the added
advantage of disseminating the health education message to other members
of the family, as well as activating the patient's natural support network to
ensure change and the subsequent maintenance of behaviour change.

DEVELOPING A SYSTEMIC APPROACH TO THE PREVENTION OF HEALTH PROBLEMS

A systemic approach to preventive counselling and the use of 'motivational interviewing' strategies (Miller and Rollnick, 1991) may be particularly useful for helping individuals to understand their individual beliefs
in a social context (partner, family, peers, colleagues at work, culture). By
using hypothetical and relationship-based questions, individuals can start
to develop a different view of how their beliefs and behaviour fit into the
wider context of their relationships with significant others. The reciprocity of the relationship becomes apparent as the person understands that
the 'ping-pong' of ideas between himself and others generates a new belief
system, one that has synergy and a dynamic that is greater than any one
person's individual contribution. The patient can develop an understanding not only of how others influence his beliefs and behaviour, but also of
how the individual's thoughts and actions affect other people's. It may
become clearer to the patient and his family, or work context, what would
have to happen in order for the individual to develop a healthy lifestyle.
By developing the 'group mind', individuals are better able to understand
and develop their role in order to assist the adaptation process. Rather
than the individual changing while the context remains the same, the

patient and context are both influenced as new behaviours are established.

Two main advantages of a systemic approach are that they include significant others who influence the patient's thoughts and actions, and that behaviour change remains the responsibility of the patient and his family. The counsellor provides a context in which change can occur. It is a non-directive approach and, ultimately, choice remains the prerogative of the individual. This approach is different from other person-centred therapies, however, in that in asking hypothetical and relationship-based questions, new material and ideas can be brought into the conversation, rather than reflecting back old material and old ideas – which might maintain the 'stuckness' of the patient. Past, present and future questions can also be useful to change the emphasis from looking at what went wrong to looking at what would have to happen for things to be right, and developing a more solution-focused approach.

THE ROLE OF THE COUNSELLOR IN PREVENTION

Early intervention

The main aim of a preventive approach to counselling is to pre-empt problems and assist the patient to be proactive in his coping responses. Rather than react to a crisis, the patient can discuss the implications of investigations, treatment and the prognosis in a hypothetical way with the counsellor, to prepare himself psychologically for difficult situations or bad news and mobilize his coping resources and natural support network. Ultimately, preventive counselling aims to assist the patient and his family in their adaptation to illness. If preventive counselling is successful, then therapy as such is not required. Preventive counselling offers the opportunity for the early detection of problems, circumnavigating crisis situations and encouraging a relatively stable path for the patient through this adaptation process. Reducing stresses at source will in turn have an impact on the individual and his family, to reduce anxiety, stress-related symptoms and depression.

Instigating the counselling or consultation process pre-diagnostically, or as soon as practicable thereafter, is vital if one is to work preventatively with patients. The counsellor needs to introduce herself to the patient to promote personal contact and accessibility. An initial meeting is a prime opportunity to develop a link upon which a therapeutic relationship can be based in the future and to inform the patient of possible areas in which the counsellor may be helpful. Information-giving is also part of preventive counselling – for example, about genetic diseases, the effects of smoking, or about contraception – and is integral to the counselling process in health care contexts. Myths about therapy and counsellors can be dispelled and patients' questions answered. Below are some of the questions the counsellor might ask at the initial meeting:

'I understand that you have recently been told by your GP that you have MS. What do you understand about this illness?'

'How has it affected your thoughts and feelings?'

'What has helped you to cope these last few weeks?'

'Who have you talked to about it?'

'What worries you most about this illness?'

Stress management

Stress management techniques can be taught to patients and their families in group presentations, through information sheets, audio tapes, online therapy packages and DVDs that can be used in everyday life and without supervision. These techniques are an important component of the cognitive behavioural approach. The individual is taught to recognize the interaction between their thoughts, feelings and behaviour, especially the connection between worrying and fearful thoughts, sympathetic nervous system arousal and stress behaviour. Relaxation training is an important part of any stress management approach, as it teaches the individual ways to counteract the effects of sympathetic nervous system arousal. Other important components in stress management include problem-solving, decision-making, coping, effectiveness training and other individual-based methods of reducing stress at source, or the impact of stress on the individual.

Less common are systemic approaches to stress management that include family and organizational interventions. This may reflect the difficulty of trying to identify sources and consequences of stress within the family or workplace. However, for some patients, it may be particularly helpful to address how their stress is affected by, and in turn affects, the family or their work setting. Stress and anxiety are context bound, and in this respect can be modified by changing the context in which they arise. The following example illustrates the importance of looking at the context:

Case Study

A counsellor was asked to offer staff support to ward nurses who, according to their manager, were stressed by 'their workload and the emotionally charged nature of patient problems'. The manager wanted them to 'offload' to the counsellor. The counsellor could have offered one-to-one counselling or group counselling, but instead decided to look at the context in which stress was arising for these nurses. It transpired that the nurses most affected were night duty nurses, who tended to work in isolation, without support and supervision. These were also the nurses least likely to be able to attend a support group. The counsellor decided to have a meeting with the manager to look at what the manager could do to improve the supervision and support of these nurses, reduce isolation, and improve time management and work delegation practices. The impact on the ward nurses was favourable. Morale increased and reports of stress decreased. The nurses no longer felt they needed a counsellor, but rather looked to each other for support and guidance. The manager was also pleased with her improved management skills and decided to apply for an in-house nurse management training course.

Social support

Research has shown repeatedly (Leiter, 1990) that social support is a major influence on reducing anxiety, stress and depression. Preventive counselling in health should always involve promoting access for patients to their natural support network, including family, friends and voluntary agencies. Empowering the individual to look to their own natural resources is preferable to encouraging a dependent relationship with the patient. If the patient feels that the only person he can confide in is the counsellor, then the counsellor's absence may make the patient feel impotent. The counsellor is also at risk of occupational stress and burnout if she feels unable to share a patient's care with other individuals and promote patient responsibility for adaptation to illness.

Promoting social support may include talking to the patient to establish who it is best to talk to in the family, how the patient can do this, when he can do it, and what the possible responses might be. Preventive counselling may include role-playing situations of disclosure, or reacting to negative or upsetting responses. Using hypothetical questions and role-play, the patient is encouraged to consider a variety of possible outcomes so that he feels better able to cope. The following are examples of such hypothetical questions:

> 'Who else knows that you have been told to stop smoking?'
>
> 'If your seven-year-old son had heard and understood our conversation, what would he say about the risks to your health about your continuing to smoke?'

Role-play and rehearsing difficult or feared situations play an important part in prevention. They can facilitate problem-solving and communication, helping to prevent illness (for example, familial or sexually transmitted diseases), and reduce worry, stress, isolation and depression.

Social support for some individuals, especially if they are isolated or unable to access their natural support network, may involve voluntary and statutory agencies. Having a daily purpose and being with others can help to inoculate the individual against isolation, being consumed by negative or worrying thoughts and depression.

Some individuals will enjoy the opportunity of meeting other people who have similar health problems or risk behaviour (for example, alcohol misuse, smoking, binge eating), but may be unaware of how to do this. Other patients fear meeting others with the same disease or condition and would prefer to develop a non-illness-related social network. It may be helpful for some patients to think about courses they might enjoy, or voluntary work with which they could become involved, particularly for those who find paid employment difficult, in order to increase their social network. This might also have the advantage of increasing the patient's sense of achievement and distract him from worrying or negative thoughts.

Lifestyles

Promoting healthy lifestyles is an important part of preventive intervention. Most people know what constitutes a healthy lifestyle, but feel that for one reason or another it is difficult to change the habits of a lifetime. In particular, some people would like to reduce their smoking behaviour or alcohol consumption, increase exercise and relaxation, or adopt a healthier diet or safer sex. Preventive counselling can include looking at the individual and family beliefs that prevent the individual from making lifestyle changes. The individualistic cognitive models described earlier in this chapter are particularly useful for considering underlying beliefs that inspire behaviour and obstacles to change. Understanding 'what went wrong', however, is limited in its intervention, and sometimes a more useful and solution-focused question to ask is 'What would have to happen in order for things to change?', or 'If Peter were to give up smoking, what would help him not to start again?', or even 'What would help you to use condoms with your partner?'

A major benefit of considering lifestyle changes with the patient is the increased sense of control and the options it can give patients. With patients for whom medical treatments are limited or unavailable, complementary therapies and self-help programmes can be encouraged. Patients in such situations can feel that they are actively helping themselves – albeit in a small way – and promoting optimum health in the face of illness, disability and their own mortality.

Children, families and prevention

Healthy and unhealthy lifestyles are frequently learnt in families and handed down through generations. Cultural, political, medical and religious influences may affect the family's beliefs about health and illness; other important influences for children, other than parents and siblings, include their peers and the school environment. Drug and alcohol use and smoking, for example, are often tried out during the adolescent years in some cultures. Some children role-model their behaviour on that of their parents or an older sibling or significant other, learning both healthy and unhealthy ways of living. The peer group is also very influential – peer pressure encourages peer unity and peer-led behaviour, such as substance abuse in a worst-case scenario. Prevention, then, needs to involve a consideration of the context in which health behaviour is learnt or unhealthy behaviour is changed. Including other family members as part of the consultation process is important if children and other family members are to understand the context in which health beliefs and lifestyles develop and change. Similarly, prevention programmes and interventions need to generalize across settings to include home, school and work environments and not simply health care settings.

CONCLUSION

Many counsellors who work in health care settings are inundated with referrals when patients have problems or reach crisis level. Rarely is there an opportunity to work preventatively with patients unless contact is made at an early stage prior to investigations or after diagnosis. Where it is known that patients with particular diagnoses are likely to develop anxiety, depression or other psychological or relationship problems, it would seem to make good sense to offer early intervention, whether it be individual, family or group-based. The counsellor is then in the optimum position for pre-empting problems, developing patient coping skills and resources, thus averting a crisis and, in some instances, assisting in the prevention of distressing circumstances. The patient and his family can be better prepared and supported to deal with difficult and distressing situations, unpredictability, uncertainty, fear, confusion and despair. Patients are less likely to feel stress, anxiety or depression if they can be helped to feel more in control and better able to resolve stressful situations, learn techniques to reduce signs of stress and anxiety, develop a repertoire of coping responses, access social support and develop health-promoting behaviour.

Chapter 18

Work Stress and Staff Support

INTRODUCTION

The many ongoing and varied challenges faced by the different professional groups employed in health care settings is well known. In addition to the 'normal' demands of the busy and demanding health care context, a survey of NHS staff conducted by the Commission for Healthcare Audit and Inspection (2006) revealed that a high proportion of staff have been bullied, harassed and abused by both patients and colleagues, and have witnessed untoward events at work. In addition, health care workers are recipients and absorbers of human distress, and consequently they are likely to be secondarily 'distressed'. The topic of staff stress is a specialist one in its own right, and the subject of many books and papers (for example, McLeod, 2001; Mitchie and Williams, 2003; Borkowski, 2005). Stress for counsellors may have many causes, including the counsellors themselves perhaps being affected by health problems in their own personal lives. Regular clinical supervision and personal therapy at appropriate times are imperative, in order to recognize and address the personal issues that might affect one's counselling practice.

Burnout has been defined as the end stage of prolonged exposure to stress at work (Chernis, 1980). It can also be viewed as the individual's solution to unsupportable levels of stress. The health worker, however, has largely been viewed in isolation from his context and many stress management interventions are employee-focused, treating the worker rather than the context in which the stress arises. This runs counter to research evidence, which suggests that organizational stress-prevention programmes are more effective than individual coping initiatives (Cooper and Cartwright, 1994). An organizational approach takes into account the context in which stress arises, the reciprocity and dynamic nature of work relationships (both with patients and with colleagues) and how change in one part of the team effects change in another. Stress in this chapter will be considered as being organizationally mediated rather than as a clinical problem requiring individual clinical intervention. It will not, however, ignore the individual's own ability to be effective in reducing his own stress levels, as he develops a 'revised' understanding of his role in relation to the patient, and to the specific organizational context in which he operates.

AN INPUT–OUTPUT MODEL OF HEALTH WORKER STRESS

An overview of the stress and burnout literature in health care reflects an input–output model of the sources and consequences of stress and burnout (Schaufeli *et al.*, 1993). The *input* includes stressors such as working with distressed patients, large caseloads and occupational risk or hazard. A further example might be having to cope with the aftermath in a medical setting of receiving and treating traumatized people, such as those affected by the London bombings of 7 July 2005. The apparently continuous reorganization of the NHS workplace is another example of work-related stress. The *output* includes cognitive, emotional, behavioural and physiological manifestations of stress, such as loss of concentration, memory problems, angry outbursts and frequent illness, such as chronic back pain, anxiety and depression.

The stressors are thought to emanate primarily from patient contact and organizational mechanisms (Schaufeli *et al.*, 1993). Pervasive in the 'caring professions' are frequent encounters with emotionally charged and stressful situations. This chronic exposure may take its toll on the health worker, particularly if the employee is not adequately trained and supported to deal with these situations.

A transactional model of occupational stress (Cox and Mackay, 1981) considers how the external stressors become internalized physiologically, and the impact this has on health and behaviour. The mediating mechanisms of interest in this model are the individual's perceptions of stress and his access to coping resources.

Some health workers may be particularly vulnerable to stress and burnout, having come into this type of work because of certain personality attributes or personal agendas and histories. Burnout is more likely in empathic, sensitive and dedicated workers, but it also occurs in those who are over-enthusiastic, idealistic and prone to over-identification with patients. Even the most resilient and skilled of professionals can succumb to work stress and experience psychological trauma (NICE, 2005), as a direct consequence of their work.

The effects of occupational stress may include worker irritability, anxiety, low morale, increased use of alcohol, increased illness and accidents, decreased performance, depression, suicide, interpersonal relationship difficulties and burnout (Schaufeli *et al.*, 1993; Cooper and Cartwright, 1994). In human, economic and legal terms, occupational stress is costly. In addition, patient care and relationships with colleagues at work and with family at home are likely to be compromised by worker stress.

SOURCES OF STRESS IN A HEALTH CARE CONTEXT

Cooper (1983) has identified six major sources of stress in the workplace. These are: job-specific stressors such as physical risk from infection; the role within the organization, including role ambiguity, conflict and territoriality; career structures and processes; interpersonal relationships at work; organizational structures; and the effects of work pressures on family life. Most jobs have an element of health-risk factors, role ambiguity, interrelationship problems and career limitations, which may impinge on family life and so on. Are there specific and unique factors for counsellors working in a health care setting?

Traditionally, stress and burnout research in health care has focused on job-specific stressors, including the emotionally challenging nature of the work, the fear of contagion, and heavy workload (Cooper, 1983). Counsellors are frequently exposed to emotionally charged situations and the distress of patients and their significant others. They are also often approached by health care workers for support and understanding in the absence of other staff support mechanisms.

The organizational structure is an important source of stress. The NHS in the UK, for example, continues to undergo substantial organizational change. The advent of time-limited and managed care, as well as payment by results and demands to following specific guidelines and protocols in practice, coupled with the reorganization of departments and the impact on working practices and staffing levels, have generated a potential source of stress for employees. All health care professionals have had to adapt and develop new identities, roles and tasks at work and deal with the loss of colleagues, teams, career plans and, in some cases, even their jobs. Funding of services may mean that one service is favoured over another, and this may manifest as interpersonal and interdepartmental conflict. Counselling is a recent addition to the mainstream structure and many counsellors work in isolation, even if they are seen as part of a multi-disciplinary team. They are often managed by non-counselling professionals and may have no counselling peers as part of the service in which they work. There is still a measure of discord about counselling structure and counselling pay scales within the NHS structure, yet the number of posts for counsellors is increasing. This situation can lead to ambiguity, conflict and confusion – yet another source of stress for counsellors.

In addition, an inherent pressure on the counsellor working in any busy health care setting is that their theoretical framework has more often than not been developed to work with the individual patient alone, often in the context of private practice. Counsellors' training frequently falls short of developing the skills and expertise necessary to be able to respond effectively and efficiently to large numbers of patients, where the service is free of charge and the patient has not actively chosen them to be their counsellor, and where there is a lack of clarity about lines of accountability and role definition in the context of the multi-disciplinary team. In addition, counsellors often find themselves in the position of being compelled to work with patients with diverse needs, for compulsory treatment.

Career structures and processes are affected by organizational change and provide a context for worker stress. Some health workers may be more vulnerable to stress because of the increasingly limited nature of their posts. They may be time-limited (on a short-term contract), cost-limited (vulnerable to reduced funding and cost-improvement initiatives), or career-limited (have limited career progression and development opportunities). Counsellors may be affected by stress because their posts lack security, planning, decision-making, development opportunities, career enhancement, personal development, or a sense of achievement or satisfaction. This may result in decreased morale, boredom and burnout.

The psychological, medical and social implications of illness necessitate multi-disciplinary and multi-agency collaboration. A lack of clarity with regard to leadership structures, objectives or ascribed roles and tasks can produce role ambiguity and conflict, a precursor of occupational stress and burnout. Change and uncertainty within the UK NHS provide ample scope for interpersonal relationship ambiguity, confusion, personal insecurity and conflict. Poor management, supervision and collegial relationships may contribute to stress and burnout, while good work-based relationships may buffer the individual against stress (Leiter, 1991).

THE DEVELOPMENT OF BURNOUT

Burnout is a transactional process between external work stressors, internal worker strain and mediating psychological mechanisms (Chernis, 1980). In this respect, it is similar to a transactional model of stress and occurs in three stages, as follows:

- Stage 1 is where work demands are perceived to exceed personal resources
- Stage 2 is characterized by an emotional and physiological response to this discrepancy, resulting in anxiety, tension, fatigue and exhaustion
- Stage 3 involves changes in attitude and behaviour, such as adopting a detached stance towards patients and a more self-absorbed, self-protective approach to work.

Burnout can be construed as a disengagement from stressors associated with working in human services. This process could be a coping mechanism or a defence on the part of the worker, to reduce exposure to stressful encounters with patients or clients. Burnout can be characterized by emotional exhaustion, depersonalization and reduced personal accomplishment associated with working in social or caring professions such as teaching, the health services and police work (Maslach and Jackson, 1986). Emotional exhaustion is a state of feeling overstretched or taxed by the demands of providing human services. Depersonalization refers to an attitude of uncaringness or callousness towards recipients. Reduced personal accomplishment is the sense of decline in competence or achievement in working with the public.

THE EFFECTS OF STRESS ON THE HEALTH WORKER AND WORK ENVIRONMENT

Health worker stress has an impact on collegial relationships, team and organizational functioning, and patient care. These effects will in turn have repercussions for the individual employee and so on in a circular fashion. The consequences of stress are also the sources of stress. Cause–effect analysis in stress and burnout research provides a linear view or narrative of occupational stress. The interpersonal context of stress, however, is obscured. This is particularly relevant when considering the dynamic nature of workplace relationships and how the stressor and buffering effects of the same relationship can fluctuate over time and across situations. It is not simply a matter of people; stress is context-bound.

ORGANIZATIONAL APPROACHES TO STRESS

Current initiatives in health care settings to reduce stress at work include stress management workshops, training in relaxation and coping skills, individual counselling, and staff support groups (Cooper and Cartwright, 1994). Employee assistance, stress management, team building, conflict resolution skills and counselling initiatives may increase individual coping. Many health organizations have trained staff support counsellors to help staff to cope better with the stress of their work (Gale, 2007).

Research evidence indicates that organizational interventions are sometimes more effective than individual programmes. It may be that organization-based initiatives enhance the buffering effect of positive collegial relationships (Leiter, 1991). Some interventions, such as team building or management development, however, can also improve inter-personal relationships, staff morale and communication at work, and thus reduce stress at source. How organizational interventions are planned and delivered is vital to their appropriateness and success. It can be helpful to view a request for intervention systemically and metaphorically rather than simply as a literal request. What does the intervention mean to the managers, to the employees and to the organization as a whole (including the person being asked to intervene)? What effect is it likely to have? Who is likely to benefit, and who will not?

Work group, team and organizational interventions require organizational analysis and interpretation. Organization-trained facilitation is required to promote worker understanding of work relationships, ensure a constructive atmosphere and prevent staff from becoming negative and destructive, targeting scapegoated individuals.

GUIDELINES FOR REDUCING STRESS AT WORK FOR COUNSELLORS

The following guidelines outline ways in which the counsellor can develop optimum work conditions to reduce the occupational sources of stress. These principles are derived from theoretical and research observations and can also be applied to other health care workers.

- Revise the view of the patient to one who is competent and able to be engaged in the maintenance of his own well-being; do not take on the burden of the patient as if it were one's own.
- Try to avoid working in isolation. Establish links with other health care professionals as well as counselling peers.
- Define team confidentiality parameters and access consultation and support with colleagues.
- Have a clearly defined job description and negotiate your role within the wider team (and encourage colleagues to do likewise). This is always context specific.
- Have a clear accountability and management structure and seek to clarify ambiguous links with your manager.
- Negotiate caseloads with your manager and referrers to clarify acceptable numbers and appropriateness of referral requests and service provision.
- Be prepared to adapt your working style to accommodate changes in patient numbers, patient needs and referrer or management needs.
- Be prepared to adapt your practice to the specific context.
- Have regular supervision and access staff support and development initiatives. If these are not available, look to create them in consultation with your manager and peers.
- Have regular appraisal sessions with your manager to review your work and set achievable objectives.

CONCLUSION

Counsellors can facilitate or provide a context for change and staff support, while maintaining team responsibility for the problem and its resolution. A good understanding of the specifics of the context in which stress manifests itself and is mediated at work is needed among health care professionals, especially counsellors. This includes the stress-inducing and stress-reducing roles that workplace relationships play in moderating occupational stress and burnout. Collegial relationships, power dynamics, team functioning and communication will be important areas in the future for organizational stress research and prevention in health care teams. The development of stress interventions for counsellors and other health care professionals needs to take into account work-based relationships in the broadest sense and include relationships with colleagues and patients, as well as the recursive nature of the sources and effects of stress. Organizational stress-prevention programmes may offer more appropriate and effective staff support and development initiatives if they take into account the context in which stress is mediated rather than pathologizing the health care worker.

The principles that underlie this book, which encourage health care professionals to view and engage with patients in a different way, in terms of encouraging patients to be actively engaged in contributing to the maintenance of their own well being, can reduce high levels of stress among health care professionals. While this book does not set out to be the panacea of all ills related to stress among health professionals, if the main theme is fully taken on board, it can contribute to eliciting high levels of creativity in the individual health care professional that may lead to increased freshness and hopefulness with each patient engagement.

Bibliography

APA (American Psychiatric Association) (1994) *Diagnostic and Statistical Manual of Mental Disorders* (4th edn), Washington, DC: American Psychiatric Association.

Anderson, H. and Goolishian, H. (1988) 'Human Systems as Linguistic Systems: Preliminary and Evolving Ideas about the Implications for Clinical Theory', *Family Process,* 27, pp. 371–93.

Baile, W., Buckman, R. and Lenzi, R. (2000) 'SPIKES – a Six Step Protocol for Delivering Bad News: Application to the Patient with Cancer', *The Oncologist,* 5, pp. 302–11.

Bateson, G. (1979) *Mind and Nature*, New York: Dutton.

Beck, A. (1967) *Depression: Clinical, Experimental and Theoretical Aspects*, New York: Harper & Row.

Beck, A. T., Rush, A. J., Shaw, B. F. and Emery, G. (1979) *Cognitive Therapy of Depression*, New York: Guilford Press.

Becker, M. (ed.) (1974) 'The Health Belief Model and Personal Health Behaviour', *Health Education Monographs,* 2, 324–508.

Bor, R. and McCann, D. (eds) (1999) *The Practice of Counselling in Primary Care*, London: Sage.

Bor, R., Gill, S., Miller, R. and Parrott, C. (2004) *Doing Therapy Briefly*, Basingstoke: Palgrave.

Borkowski, N. (2005) *Organizational Behaviour in Health Care*, Sudbury, MA.: Jones & Bartlett.

Bowlby, J. (1975) *The Making and Breaking of Affectional Bonds*, London: Tavistock.

Brewin, T. (1996) *Relating to the Relatives: Breaking Bad News, Communication and Support*, New York: Radcliffe Medical Press.

Bricker, D. and Young, J. (1993) *A Client's Guide to Schema Focused Therapy*, New York: The Cognitive Therapy Centre.

British Association for Counselling and Psychotherapy (2002) *Ethical Framework for Good Practice in Counselling and Psychotherapy*, Rugby: BAC.

BMA (British Medical Association) (2001) *Consent, Rights and Choices in Health Care for Children and Young People*, London: BMJ Books.

Buckman, R. (1984) 'Breaking Bad News: Why Is It Still So Difficult?', *British Medical Journal*, 288, pp. 1597–9.

Burns, D. (1990) *The Feeling Good Handbook*, New York: Penguin.

Byng-Hall, J. (1995) *Rewriting Family Scripts*, New York: Guilford Press.

Campbell, D. and Draper, R. (1985) *Applications of Systemic Family Therapy: The Milan Approach*, London: Grune & Stratton.

Campbell, D., Coldicott, T. and Kinsella, K. (1994) *Systemic Work with Organizations*, London: Karnac.

Carter, B. and McGoldrick, M. (1981) *The Family Life Cycle*, New York: Gardiner Press.

Cecchin, G. (1987) 'Hypothesizing, Circularity, Neutrality Revisited: An Invitation to Curiosity', *Family Process*, 26, pp. 405–13.

Chernis, C. (1980) *Staff Burnout: Job Stress in the Human Services*, Beverly Hills, CA.: Sage.

Commission for Healthcare Audit and Inspection (2006) *National Survey of NHS Staff 2005. Summary of Key Findings*, London: Healthcare Commission.

Cooper, C. (1983) 'Identifying Stresses at Work: Recent Research Developments', *Journal of Psychosomatic Research*, 2, pp. 369–76.

Cooper, C. and Cartwright, S. (1994) 'Stress Management Interventions in the Workplace: Stress Counselling and Stress Audits', *British Journal of Guidance and Counselling*, 22, pp. 65–73.

Cox, T. and Mackay, C. (1981) 'A Transactional Approach to Occupational Stress', in E. Corlett and J. Richardson (eds), *Stress, Work Design and Productivity*, Chichester: John Wiley.

Curwen, B., Ruddel, P. and Palmer, S. (2000) *Brief Cognitive Behaviour Therapy*, London: Sage.

de Shazer, S. (1985) *Keys to Solutions in Brief Therapy*, New York: W. W. Norton.

Doherty, W. and Baird, M. (1983) *Family Therapy and Family Medicine*, New York: Guilford Press.

Dosanjh, S., Barnes, J. and Bhandari, M. (2001) 'Barriers to Breaking Bad News Among Medical and Surgical Residents', *Medical Education*, 35, pp. 197–205.

du Plessis, P. and Hirst, F. (2006) 'Written Communication and Counselling', in R. Bor and M. Watts (eds), *The Trainee Handbook* (2nd edn), London: Sage.

Edwards, M. and Davis, H. (1998) *Counselling Children with Chronic Medical Conditions*, Leicester: BPS Books.

Edwards, A., Elwyn, G., Matthews, E. and Pill, R. (2001) 'Presenting Risk Information – A Review of the Effects Of "Framing" and Other Manipulations on Patient Outcomes', *Journal of Health Communication*, 6, pp. 61–2.

Engel, G. (1977) 'The Need for a New Medical Model: A Challenge for Biomedicine', *Science*, 196, pp. 129–36.

Evans, A. and Bor, R. (2005) 'Working in a Healthcare Setting: Professional and Ethical Challenges', in R. Tribe and J. Morrisey (eds), *Handbook of Professional Practice for Psychologists, Counsellors and Psychotherapists*, Hove: Brunner Routledge.

Fennell, M. (1999) 'Depression', in K. Hawton, P. Salkovskis, J. Kirk and D. Clark (eds), *Cognitive Behaviour Therapy for Psychiatric Problems: A Practical Guide*, Oxford: Oxford Medical Publications.

Fishbein, M. and Ajzen, I. (1975) *Belief Attitude, Intention and Behavior: An Introduction to Theory and Research*, Reading, MA.: Addison-Wesley.

Foster, J. and Murphy, A. (2005) *Psychological Therapies in Primary Care: Setting Up a Managed Service*, London: Karnac.

Fruggeri, L. (2001) 'The Constructivist-Systemic Approach and Context Analysis', in L. Fruggeri, U. Telfner, A. Castellucci, M. Marzari and M. Matteini (eds), *New Systemic Ideas from the Italian Mental Health Movement*, London: Karnac.

Gale, N. (2007) 'The Life of a Counselling Psychologist Supporting NHS Staff to Care for Patients', *Counselling Psychology Review*, 22, pp. 27–31.

Griffith, J. and Griffith, M. (1994) *The Body Speaks: Therapeutic Dialogues for Mind–Body Problems*, New York: Basic Books.

Harrington, J., Noble, L. and Newman, S. (2004) 'Improving Patients' Communication with Doctors: A Systematic Review of Intervention Studies', *Patient Education and Counselling*, 52, pp. 7–16.

Hawton, K. Salkovskis, P. Kirk, J. and Clark, D. (1999) *Cognitive Behaviour Therapy for Psychiatric Problems: A Practical Guide*, Oxford: Oxford Medical Publications.

Hillier, D. (2006) *Communicating Health Risks to the Public*, Oxford: Gower.

Hoyt, M. (1995) *Brief Therapy and Managed Care*, San Francisco: Jossey-Bass.

Josse, J. (1993) 'Use of Family Trees in General Practice', *Postgraduate Update*, May, 1, pp. 775–80.

Kadera, S., Lambert, M. and Andrews, A. (1996) 'How Much Therapy Is Really Enough? A Session-by-session Analysis of the Psychotherapy Dose-effect Relationship', *Journal of Psychotherapy Practice and Research*, 5, pp. 132–51.

Kelly, G. (1969) 'Man's Construction of His Alternatives', in B. Maher (ed.), *Clinical Psychology and Personality: The Selected Papers of George Kelly*, New York: John Wiley.

Kübler-Ross, E. (1969) *On Death and Dying*, New York: W. W. Norton.

Layard, R., Chairman, Centre for Economic Performance (2006) *The Depression Report: A New Deal for Depression and Anxiety Disorders*, London: London School of Economics and Political Science and the Economic and Social Research Council. Available at: http://cep.lse.ac.uk/research/mentalhealth

Leahy, R. (2003) *Cognitive Therapy Techniques: A Practitioner's Guide*, New York: Guilford Press.

Leiter, M. (1990) 'The Impact of Family Resources, Control Coping, and Skill Utilisation on the Development of Burnout: A Longitudinal Study', *Human Relations,* 43, pp. 1167–83.

Leiter, M. (1991) 'The Dream Denied: Professional Burnout and the Constraints of Human Service Organisations', *Canadian Psychology,* 32, pp. 547–55.

Lloyd, M. and Bor, R. (2009) *Communication Skills for Medicine,* Edinburgh: Churchill Livingstone.

Maslach, C. and Jackson, S. (1986) *Maslach Burnout Inventory Manual* (2nd edn), Palo Alto, CA.: Consulting Psychologists Press.

Mayou, R. (1989) 'Illness Behaviour and Psychiatry', *General Hospital Psychiatry,* 11, pp. 307–12.

McDaniel, S. and Campbell, T. (1986) 'Physicians and Family Therapists: The Risk of Collaboration', *Family Systems Medicine,* 4, pp. 4–10.

McDaniel, S., Hepworth, J. and Doherty, W. (1992) *Medical Family Therapy,* New York: Basic Books.

McGoldrick, M. and Gerson, R. (1985) *Genograms in Family Assessment,* New York: W. W. Norton.

McLaughlan, C. (1990) 'Handling Distressed Relatives and Breaking Bad News', *British Medical Journal,* 301, pp. 1145–9.

McLeod, J. (2001) *Counselling in the Workplace: The Facts. A Systematic Study of the Research Evidence,* Rugby: British Association for Counselling and Psychotherapy.

Mears, A. (2007) 'The Criminalization of HIV Transmission in England and Wales: A Brief Review of the Issues Arising', *Current Opinion in Infectious Diseases,* 20, pp. 47–53.

Mitchie, S. and Williams, S. (2003) 'Reducing Work Related Psychological Ill Health and Sickness Absence: A Systematic Literature Review', *Occupational and Environmental Medicine,* 30, pp. 3–9.

Middleton, H., Shaw, I., Hull, S. and Feder, G. (2005) 'NICE Guidelines for the Management of Depression', Editorial, *British Medical Journal,* 330, pp. 267–8.

Miller, R. and Telfer, P. (1996) 'HCV Counselling in Haemophilia Care', *Haemophilia,* 2, pp. 1–4.

Miller, S., Duncan, B. and Hubble, M. (1997) *Escape from Babel: Towards a Unifying Language for Psychotherapy Practice,* New York: W. W. Norton.

Miller, W. and Rollnick, S. (1991) *Motivational Interviewing: Preparing People to Change Addictive Behavior,* New York: Guilford Press.

Mooney, K. and Padesky, C. (2000) 'Applying Client Creativity to Recurrent Problems: Constructing Possibilities and Tolerating Doubts', *Journal of Cognitive Psychotherapy,* 14, pp. 149–61.

NICE (National Institute for Clinical Excellence) (2004) *Depression: Management of Depression in Primary and Secondary Care,* London: NICE.

NICE (National Institute for Clinical Excellence) (2005) *Post Traumatic Stress Disorder (PTSD): The Management of PTSD in Adults and Children in Primary and Secondary Care*, London: NICE.

Padesky, C. (1993) 'Socratic Questioning: Changing Minds or Guiding Discovery?', Paper delivered at the European Congress of Behavioural Therapies, London, September.

Padesky, C. (1994) 'Schema Change Processes in Cognitive Therapy', *Clinical Psychology and Psychotherapy*, 1, pp. 267–8.

Padesky, C. A. and Greenberger, D. (1995) *Mind Over Mood*, New York: Guilford Press.

Paling, J. (2003) 'Strategies to Help Patients Understand Risks', *British Medical Journal*, 327, pp. 745–8.

Papazian, R. (1994) 'Trace Your Family Tree: Charting Your Relatives' Medical History Can Save Your Life', *American Health*, 13, pp. 80–5.

Powell, T. (2000) *The Mental Health Handbook*, Bicester: Speechmark.

Ptacek, J. and Eberhardt, T. (1996) 'Breaking Bad News: A Review of the Literature', *Journal of the American Medical Association*, 276, pp. 496–502.

Quick, E. (1996) *Doing What Works in Brief Therapy*, San Diego: Academic Press.

Rogers, C. (1951) *Patient-Centered Therapy*, Boston: Houghton Mifflin.

Rolland, J. (1984) 'Toward a Psychosocial Typology of Chronic and Life Threatening Illness', *Family Systems Medicine*, 2, pp. 245–62.

Rolland, J. (1994a) *Families, Illness and Disability*, New York: Basic Books.

Rolland, J. (1994b) 'In Sickness and in Health: The Impact of Illness on Couples' Relationships', *Journal of Marital and Family Therapy*, 20, pp. 327–47.

Roth, A. and Fonagy, P. (2004) *What Works for Whom? A Critical Review of Psychotherapy Research* (2nd edn), New York: Guilford Press.

Schaufeli, W., Maslach, C. and Marek, T. (1993) *Professional Burnout: Recent Developments in Theory and Research*, Washington, DC: Taylor & Francis.

Seaburn, D., Lorenz, A., Gunn, W., Gawinski, B. and Mauksch, L. (1996) *Models of Collaboration: A Guide for Mental Health Professionals Working with Health Care Practitioners*, New York: Basic Books.

Selvini Palazzoli, M., Boscolo, L., Cecchin, G. and Prata, G. (1980a) 'Hypothesizing, Circularity, Neutrality: Three Guidelines for the Conductor of the Session', *Family Process*, 19, pp. 3–12.

Selvini Palazzoli, M., Boscolo, L., Cecchin, G. and Prata, G. (1980b) 'The Problem of the Referring Person', *Journal of Marital and Family Therapy*, 6, pp. 3–9.

Selye, H. (1956) *The Stress of Life*, New York: McGraw-Hill.

Sharp, K. (1994) 'All in the Family? Your Medical History', *Current Health*, 20, pp. 29–33.

Simpson, R. and Bor, R. (2001) '"I'm Not Picking Up a Heart-Beat". Experience of Sonographers Giving Bad News to Women During Ultrasound', *British Journal of Medical Psychology*, 74, pp. 255–72.

Stroebe, M., Schut, H. and Stroebe, W. (2007) 'Health Outcomes of Bereavement', *Lancet*, 370, pp. 1960–73.

Talmon, M. (1990) *Single-Session Therapy*, San Francisco: Jossey-Bass.

Tomm, K. (1987a) 'Interventive Interviewing. Part 1: Strategizing as a Fourth Guideline for the Therapist', *Family Process*, 26, pp. 3–13.

Tomm, K. (1987b) 'Interventive Interviewing. Part 2: Reflexive Questioning as a Means to Enable Self-Healing', *Family Process*, 26, pp. 167–84.

Turk, D. and Salovey, P. (1996) 'Cognitive Behavioural Treatment of Illness Behaviour', in P. Nicassio and T. Smith (eds), *Managing Chronic Illness: A Biopsychosocial Perspective*, Washington, DC: APA Press, pp. 245–84.

Utsün, T., Ayuso-Mateos, J., Chatterji, S., Mathers, C. and Murray, C. (2004) 'Global Burden of Depressive Disorders in the Year 2000', *British Journal of Psychiatry*, 184, pp. 386–92.

Watzlawick, P., Weakland, J. and Fisch, R. (1974) *Change: Principles of Problem Formation and Problem Resolution*, New York: W. W. Norton.

Weinstein, N. (1988) 'The Precaution Adoption Process', *Health Psychology*, 7, pp. 355–86.

Wells, A. (1997) *Cognitive Therapy of Anxiety Disorders. A Practice Manual and Conceptual Guide*, Chichester: Wiley.

White, C. (2001) *Cognitive Behavioural Therapy for Chronic Medical Problems*, Chichester: Wiley.

Wright, L., Watson, W. and Bell, J. (1996) *Beliefs: The Heart of Healing in Families and Illness*, New York: Basic Books.

Young, J., Klosko, J. and Weishaar, M. (2003) *Schema Therapy: A Practitioner's Guide*, New York: Guilford Press.

Index